W9-BYO-231

Billy Graham
Evangelistic Association

DEAR FRIEND,

I am pleased to send you this copy of *Answers to Life's Problems* by my father, Billy Graham.

This book comprises my father's response to thousands of letters over the years from people who have asked for advice. Throughout the book, he shows how God's Word provides guidance on such issues as love, prayer, guilt, anger, and more.

If you would like to know more about the Billy Graham Evangelistic Association, please contact us. We would appreciate knowing how this book or our ministry has touched your life.

May God bless you.

Sincerely,

Franklin Graham
President

ANSWERS
TO LIFE'S PROBLEMS

GUIDANCE, INSPIRATION, and HOPE
for THE CHALLENGES of TODAY

BILLY GRAHAM

This **Billy Graham Library Selection** special edition
is published with permission from W Publishing Group,
a division of Thomas Nelson, Inc.

W PUBLISHING GROUP™

A Division of Thomas Nelson, Inc.

ANSWERS TO LIFE'S PROBLEMS
© 1960, 1988, 2003 by Billy Graham

© 1960, 1987, 1988 by Chicago Tribune-N.Y. News Syndicate, Inc.

The material appearing in this book is a collection drawn from
Dr. Graham's newspaper columns syndicated under the title "My Answer"
by the Chicago Tribune-New York News Syndicate Company, Inc.

All rights reserved. No portion of this book may be reproduced in any form
whatsoever, except for brief quotation in reviews, without the written
permission of the publisher.

Unless otherwise indicated, Scripture quotations are from the New
International Version of the Bible, published by the Zondervan
Corporation, © 1973, 1978, 1984 by the International Bible Society. Used
by permission.

Those marked NASB are from the New American Standard Bible, © 1960,
1962, 1963, 1968, 1971, 1972, 1973, 1975, 1977, 1995 by the Lockman
Foundation.

Those marked KJV are from the King James Version.

Those marked TLB are from The Living Bible, © 1971 Tyndale House
Publishers, used by permission.

Those marked Phillips are from The New Testament in Modern English by
J. B. Phillips, published by The Macmillan Company, © 1958, 1960, 1972 by
J. B. Phillips.

Those marked AMP are from The Amplified Bible, © 1954, 1958, 1962, 1964,
1965, 1987 by the Lockman Foundation.

Library of Congress Cataloging-in-Publication Data

Graham, Billy, 1918–
     Answers to life's problems
          p.   cm.
     Includes index
     ISBN 1-59328-013-0
     Previous ISBN 0-8499-0642-3
                    0-8499-3564-4 (tp)
     1.   Christian life-Miscellanea.   I.   Title

Printed in the United States of America

The whole Bible was given to us
by inspiration from God
and is useful to teach us
what is true
and to make us realize
what is wrong with our lives;
it straightens us out
and helps us do what is right.
2 Timothy 3:1 TLB

Contents

Part V. Biblical Questions

Introduction

If talk is cheap, advice is free.

Advice columnists, astrologers and books offering tips on how to make money, how to avoid disease, and how to get in physical shape are as plentiful as cars during rush hour in our major cities. But not all advice is good. Much of this advice is based on human wisdom or false hopes or the wrong motives—and many who take such advice are disappointed and disillusioned.

Those who grew up in the troubled 1960s in America were told by the media, the rock music culture, their professors at college, and their friends that the values held by their parents and grandparents were old-fashioned. They threw off what they regarded as encumbrances in favor of "alternate lifestyles" and "doing your own thing." There was widespread cultural support for their ideas and behavior. "Doing your own thing" became the "in" thing to do.

Tragically, a survey published in *Rolling Stone* magazine revealed that those who bought into the '60s counterculture mentality and believed the lies they were told are now having trouble communicating to their own children the necessity of the values they rejected. The survey reveals that having overdosed on drugs and "free" love (which turned out not to be free at all) the flower children of the '60s now "embrace psychiatry as something to be relied on."

Is there a standard which can be depended on to give good advice and accurate information and answers to questions about ourselves and our lives?

There is. For many years I have been writing a newspaper column called "My Answer." Actually, the column has been more than *my* answer to every imaginable question people have sent me. My answers are based on what the Bible says. Though cultures differ and times change, the Word of our

God stands forever as an unchanging source of answers to all of life's problems.

Former President Reagan once stated that the answer to all of life's problems can be found in the Bible, if people would only read it. He was right, because every problem known to humanity has a spiritual origin.

Chances are that you will find the answer to one or more of your questions about God, the Bible, interpersonal relationships, job frustrations, the universe, and a host of other subjects in this book. I am convinced that the major reason many of us seem to have so many unresolved problems is that we are ignorant of what God has to say about our problems or we reject His answer out of hand without ever giving it a try.

In more than fifty years as an evangelist I have read many books, consulted many psychologists and other experts in many fields, but I have yet to discover a source of information, practical advice and hope that compares to the wisdom found in the Bible.

My prayer is that you will discover in this book that source of information and, more important, God's plan for your redemption through Jesus Christ.

Billy Graham

Part 1

Relationships

1 Is There Such a Thing As True Love?

I am in my early twenties and I have always had very high moral standards. I date a lot, but frankly I'm very disillusioned about men because all they seem to be interested in is sex. I want someone to love me for myself, but now I'm beginning to wonder if there is such a thing as true love.

There was a popular song a few years ago which contained the lyric, "I was looking for love in all the wrong places." There is a lot of so-called love in our world today which is not really love but is instead based on selfishness and even lust. In fact, I get many letters every day from people who got married because they wanted their own selfish needs satisfied, and have only later come to realize that this does not work.

But there is such a thing as love—honest, selfless love. This is the kind of love the Bible talks about when it speaks of God's love for us. It is also the kind of love that the Bible describes briefly but profoundly in 1 Corinthians 13:4–7: "Love is patient, love is kind. It does not envy, it does not boast, it is not proud. It is not rude, it is not self-seeking, it is not easily angered, it keeps no record of wrongs. Love does not delight in evil but rejoices with the truth. It always protects, always trusts, always hopes, always perseveres."

My prayer is that you will stick to your standards—you will be glad you did in the years ahead. But more than that, I pray that you will commit this whole area of your life—and in fact every area of your life—to Jesus Christ. God wants to teach you what true love is, as you come to experience and understand His love for you. He also has His perfect will for your life—including your future husband, if it is His will for you to be married. Don't be satisfied with anyone less than the one who is God's will for your life's mate, no matter what the pressures might be.

We live in a time when God's standards are often dismissed or scorned as old-fashioned and useless. But God's standards have not changed, and neither have His promises to those who follow Christ. There are many young men who are seeking to honor God in their lives, and you should trust God that He will lead you in the way that is best for your life.

My boyfriend is not perfect and sometimes I wonder if he would make a very thoughtful or sensitive husband, but I am afraid of letting go of him because I wonder if I will ever find another husband. What should I do about him?

I suspect there are many women reading this who would like to write you and say, "Don't feel you have to take the first eligible man who comes along! If he is insensitive and selfish now, he will be insensitive and selfish as a husband. This is what I did, and I have regretted it ever since!"

No husband or wife is going to be perfect, of course; after all, you probably have your faults as well! But seriously, my concern for you is this: more than anything else, you need to learn to trust your future to God and obey Him. This is true for everything in your life, including your marriage.

One of the greatest truths of the Bible is that God loves us. And because He loves us, He wants to give us what is best for us. I firmly believe that if it is God's will for you to be married, then He has already chosen a man who should be your husband. Seek God's will and trust Him, because His will is best. "Which of you," said Jesus, "if his son asks for bread, will give him a stone? . . . If you, then, though you are evil, know how to give good gifts to your children, how much more will your Father in heaven give good gifts to those who ask him!" (Matthew 7:9, 11).

Look for a husband who honors Christ in his life and wants His will. That man will be loving and sensitive, and it will be your joy to be loving and sensitive to his needs in return.

Some time ago I found out that my boyfriend is involved in selling drugs. I guess I ought to stop going with him, but I think I love him and I hope somehow I can reform him. Do you think there is any hope of this?

I know you are concerned for your boyfriend and want to help him, but I seriously doubt if you will be able to make him reform. In addition, marriage is not a reform school. I have met many women who believe that their mothering instincts extend to the men they marry. There is a high probability that instead of you reforming him, he will instead influence you and cause you to become involved in things that are wrong. It may be that breaking off your relationship will be the one thing that will shake him into realizing the seriousness of what he is doing.

What he is doing *is* serious—not only in the eyes of the law but in the eyes of God. The reason is that he is causing others to get involved in drugs, and is therefore affecting countless lives in terrible ways. You need to talk frankly with him about this. You also need to realize that there is probably very little future in this kind of relationship. What if you were to get married some day? What kind of husband and father would he make?

Your boyfriend and you have a deeper need, however—even deeper than the need to stop what he is doing and live a responsible life. You both need to come to Jesus Christ and turn your lives over to Him. Right now you are living for yourselves. But God created you, and He loves you. He wants you to do what is right and to follow Him because He knows that is the only way to true peace and happiness in life. Jesus said, "I have come that they may have life, and have it to the full" (John 10:10).

God has a perfect plan for your life—including His will for your marriage with a man who loves Christ. The road you and your boyfriend are on is wrong and will only lead to disaster. Follow God's way before it is too late.

I feel like I am really in love with a man who works in the same office I do. He doesn't really know my feelings, however, as we have never dated. Should I express them to him? The problem is that he has a wife and family.

Turn the question around. What if you were married to this man and another woman was writing to me asking for a divorce because she was in love with your husband? As strongly as I can, I urge you to put this relationship out of your mind—even if it means changing jobs. Unless you do, there is only pain and heartache ahead. If somehow you were to win him and cause him to leave his family, you would be wrecking the lives of many people. And you would never have a secure marriage for yourself either, because what assurance would you have that he would not turn around and leave you, just as he left his wife? No, the only right thing for you to do is put this idea behind you.

Your letter tells me that you are searching for love. There is nothing wrong in that as long as you pursue your search in the right direction. After all, God made us so we would love others and experience love ourselves. But you need to realize that love—lasting, true love—will elude you if you go about it selfishly and without regard to the consequences for others.

I am concerned, therefore, about your present situation. But even more I am concerned about the whole direction of your life. Your greatest need right now is not just a human companion or love. Your greatest need is to realize that you are God's creature. God loves you and He has a perfect plan for your life. He knows what your true needs are, and if it is His will for you to be married (as it probably is), then He has someone who will be the right husband for you if you will trust Him and let Him lead you. Trust God to lead you to the man He has for your husband—a man who will be a committed Christian and who will love you unselfishly.

I grew up in a one-parent family. I am old enough that it should no longer trouble me, but my problem is that right now I am in love with a young woman who is also from a broken home. Do you think this would in any way influence our happiness in marriage?

All things being equal, it would seem to me that your chances for a happy married life would be very good. Having felt the pain of a broken home, you have probably learned the importance of laying a solid foundation for a home that will remain

united and happy. The mistakes of your parents in both instances will serve as warnings for you not to fail in the same
way.

In making your plans, I would urge you to be utterly frank
and open with each other in all areas so that no misunderstandings arise. Do not base your love on a mutual sympathy
because of your unfortunate experiences, but on genuine respect and admiration. Then you should include Christ in your
planning. Even though many homes have some degree of marital happiness without Him, there is much that is lacking in any
home when Christ is not received and honored.

Have your time of worship together, confessing your faults
and praying for each other. This will cement your lives to each
other and the happiness you seek will be the result of God's
blessing and presence. The Living Bible says: "The man who
finds a wife finds a good thing; she is a blessing to him from
the Lord" (Proverbs 18:22).

*The man who wants to marry me claims to be a Christian. So I
could on that basis marry him. But every now and then he lies to
me, and it troubles me, for I cannot endure deception. Am I safe in
marrying him, seeing that he is a Christian?*

Just because a person claims to be a Christian does not necessarily mean that he is one. In fact, when you say this young
man uses deception now and then, has it never occurred to you
that he may be deceiving you when he makes the claim to a
Christian faith?

Truthfulness and honesty are basic in the Christian walk.
Jesus once said: "I am the way, the truth and the life" (John 14:6).
In another place He said, "I came to bear witness to the truth"
(John 1:7). Truth is consistency. If this young man will deceive
you in one matter, he may deceive you in many for he lacks
respect for the truth.

David once confessed to God in his repentance: "Thou de-
sirest truth in the inward parts" (Psalm 51:6 KJV). You can live
with many other faults more easily than with dishonesty. By all
means avoid it.

I am in love with a fine young man, but my parents do not approve of him. To what extent is one obligated to parents?

The Bible teaches everywhere that we are to honor our parents, but it does not teach that they have the right to control their adult children. "Honor your father and your mother, that your days may be long in the land which the Lord your God gives you" (Exodus 10:12 RSV). The New Testament says: "Children, obey your parents in all things: for this is well-pleasing to the Lord." There was a period in life when you were directly responsible to them. You were to be obedient in all things. What they have forgotten is that such a relationship does not continue in adulthood. You should still honor them as your parents, but you are not obligated to forego the joy of married life and your own family for them.

But there is another aspect to this problem. We sometimes discover the will of God through giving heed to the counsel of others if they are definitely committed Christians. I am sure you want God's will in the choice of a life partner. Consider carefully their point of view, but then make your decision, seeking the Lord's leading as you do so.

At times I think I am going to die of a broken heart. I had been living with my boyfriend for three years, always hoping we would get married, but last week he told me to get out because he didn't want anything more to do with me. Why has God done this to me, when I really love this man?

Suppose you had an accident and were injured because you decided you would ignore the speed limit and instead travel twice as fast as you should. Who would be to blame for your accident? The person who set the speed limit, or you? I think you know the answer: You would be to blame. Your accident came about because you refused to obey the speed limit.

In the same way, we must never blame God for things which are a result of our own actions—especially when those actions are in direct violation of God's clear law. The Bible warns, "Do not be deceived: God cannot be mocked. A man reaps what he sows" (Galatians 6:7). It was wrong in God's eyes for you to live with this man outside the commitment of marriage, for His Word is clear on this point. You therefore cannot blame Him for the result.

But where do you go from here? In the past you have sought your security in this relationship—a relationship where there was never any lasting commitment. Will you make the same mistake again? I pray not. God loves you, and He does not want you to drift through life with no anchor. Make Christ your anchor, and He will change you and give you a whole new reason for living.

I am an eighteen-year-old girl, a freshman in college. I have fallen in love with a senior who wants me to marry him now although he has not yet made up his mind what his life's work shall be. Should I give up my college career for him?

The very fact that you are weighing your own career against the uncertainties of marriage makes me feel that you are not yet ready to make this momentous decision. Obviously you have known this young man for only a few months. Also, his own future plans are so indefinite that they give you pause. This all adds up to a strong indication that you should wait. Waiting has two advantages. It will enable you to know your heart and to decide whether it is love or other considerations which have attracted you to each other. Also, it will give both of you time to mature in your thinking and planning. Finally, a Christian has the right and privilege of asking God's guidance in everything. The Bible says, "Seek ye first the kingdom of God; and all these things will be added unto you" (Luke 12:31 KJV).

My boyfriend and I want to be engaged very soon but both of our parents object. Though we are quite young, we are serious but don't intend to get married for at least three years. Should we insist on doing it our way?

Perhaps your parents are objecting on the basis of your age alone. They perhaps think you aren't mature enough to make this all-important decision. There seems to be only one reason why you insist on an engagement: Because you are afraid that one or the other might feel too free otherwise. I would warn you that if you cannot trust each other under the present conditions you are perhaps not genuinely in love.

Then you must always take into account your mutual relationship in Christ. You must not hope for a completely successful marriage if it is done merely on your own. I would suggest, therefore, that you follow the suggestion of your parents. All they object to is the formality of engagement, and that is not the most important part of it. Your mutual commitment of your lives to Christ is all you need. This in addition to your love for each other will make your present friendship become even more meaningful in years to come.

I have been living with my boyfriend for over a year. I know this is wrong, but I get scared whenever I think of leaving him because I'm afraid to be alone. Pray that I'll have wisdom to know what is right.

Yes, I will pray that you will know what is right—but more than that I will be praying that you will *do* what is right. I think you have come to realize that what you are doing is wrong in God's eyes, since you admit that you know it is wrong. But the problem for you is not so much knowing what is wrong, but acting upon that knowledge.

God's Word, the Bible, makes it clear that sex outside of the commitment of marriage is wrong. One of the Ten Commandments declares simply, "You shall not commit adultery" (Exodus 20:14). The reason is because God has given marriage to us for our good, and the sexual relationship is to be confined to marriage. Ultimately if sexual relationships are treated casually, marriage itself—and therefore the family—is endangered. I stress this because I want you to realize that what you are doing is wrong in the eyes of God.

There is no shortcut to doing the right thing. God's will—which is perfect and best for you in the long run—is for you to break off this relationship. It will not be easy, I know, but I pray that you will have the courage to do what is right.

But beyond that, my prayer for you is that you will not only do what is right in this situation, but that you will come to see your own need of God and yield your life totally and without reserve to Jesus Christ. You need God's forgiveness, and you need His guidance in your life every day. You need strength to do what is right, and you need to discover God's perfect will for your life.

Turn to Christ. You are never alone when Christ is with you, and you can experience the joy that comes from knowing that you are a child of God and He is with you every day.

I am living with my boyfriend, who is the father of my baby. I know this is wrong, but I love my boyfriend deeply and just can't imagine life without him. The problem is he seems to be growing more and more distant toward me and now I am afraid he is going to leave me all alone. I just don't know what to do.

There may be someone reading this question right now who is being tempted to do the same thing you have done. My prayer is that your experience will be a warning to them and that they will have the courage to turn their backs on this temptation. The problem—as you have sadly discovered—is that the kind of relationship you have had may have seemed ideal for a time. But when there is no commitment (unlike marriage, which involves a vow of commitment), things eventually become unraveled.

It will not be easy for you to do the right thing, I suspect. But doing the wrong thing will only lead to a deadend of heartache and grief. What is the right thing? The right thing is for you to end this relationship, especially if (as you indicate) your boyfriend shows little evidence of being in love with you and wanting to make a commitment of marriage to you. What you are now doing is morally wrong in God's eyes and continuing in this relationship only increases the problem. Your child needs the example and security of a stable home life.

But I want to point out a very important fact to you. You are fearful about the future and concerned about being alone. But you are not alone—God is with you. You need to turn to

Him and find in Him the forgiveness and security you need. And He wants you to come to Him because He loves you.

What you have done is wrong and your life will not necessarily be easy as a single parent. But God cares for you. "The Lord is compassionate and gracious, slow to anger, abounding in love . . . as high as the heavens are above the earth, so great is his love for those who fear him" (Psalm 103:8, 11).

2 Isn't Sex an Expression of Love?

My boyfriend and I have talked about sex a lot. We have decided that if two people really love each other sex before marriage is all right. Don't you think sex is supposed to be an expression of love?

Yes, sex is an expression of love—but it also should be combined with deep commitment. That is one reason why the Bible tells us that the sexual relationship is to be confined to marriage. God has been very clear on this, and I strongly urge you to reconsider your position and do what He wants you to do. Let me warn you honestly that it is easy to talk yourself into doing something that is wrong, and which you will later regret.

God tells us, "Among you there must not be even a hint of sexual immorality, or of any kind of impurity" (Ephesians 5:3). The more I study the Bible and the more I see the results in the lives of those who disobey God's law, the more I see that God has actually given this commandment for our own good—physically, emotionally, socially, and spiritually.

We are seeing, for instance, an alarming rise in sexually transmitted diseases because of widespread sexual immorality in our country. The specter of AIDS hovers over us like a plague. God also knows that we need and want the security of true commitment in love—a commitment that can only come when two people pledge themselves to each other alone in the bond of marriage. God has also told us, "You shall not commit adultery" (Exodus 20:14) to preserve the family, which is the basic essential unit of any society. History does not give us a single example of a civilization that survived once its families broke up.

My prayer is that you and your friend will give your lives to Christ and discover the joy of having Him lead you every day.

I have a friend who says sex before marriage is okay, because the Bible only talks about adultery, which is having sexual relations with someone once you are married. Is this true? I need to know because my boyfriend is putting pressure on me about having sex with him.

The Bible makes it clear that sexual relations outside the bond of marriage are wrong in the eyes of God—and you should not take this lightly.

This is true when the marriage bond is broken through adultery. Jesus summed up the Ten Commandments when He said, "Do not murder, do not commit adultery . . ." (Matthew 19:18). But it is equally true for every kind of sexual relationship outside marriage. The Bible commands, "Flee from sexual immorality. All other sins a man commits are outside his body, but he who sins sexually sins against his own body" (1 Corinthians 6:18). The word translated as "sexual immorality" in this verse is actually a general term in the language in which the New Testament was originally written, and it includes not only fornication but adultery, lust, and incest. (Interestingly enough we also get our word "pornography" from this word.)

Although this sin has become common in our society, I urge you to keep yourself pure. God has given sex to us, and His purposes for it can only be fulfilled within the commitment of marriage. You need God's guidance for the future, and you need His strength also to live as you should—particularly in our time, when there are so many pressures on you to turn your back on God's way.

My boyfriend and I are deeply in love and have talked a great deal about marriage. We are compatible in every way, except he has no interest in God or the church. These are very important to me, however. Do you think this will be a problem when we get married?

Yes, I must frankly warn you that this can become a serious problem later on. It is far better for you to face it and deal with it now rather than to wait until even greater harm may be done.

I have met many women who, after years of marriage and attempts to reform their husbands wish that they had listened to the Bible's advice about a life partner and had married a man who was a committed Christian. How will it be a problem if you marry him? This can happen in several ways. The most obvious is what you will do with your children and their spiritual upbringing. Even if your husband were to agree that they could be active in Sunday school and church (which is not always the case), by his example he is teaching them that he thinks God is unimportant—and that can be a powerful influence on them. Why should they take Christ seriously when He means nothing to someone they respect and love?

But it can affect your marriage in other ways as well. Inevitably a person who is uninterested in God and His will is going to have different priorities, and this will cause tension. Or you have to face the possibility that over the years he will influence you and slowly but surely draw you away from your own commitment to Christ.

The Bible's message is clear: "Do not be yoked together with unbelievers" (2 Corinthians 6:14). Have you definitely made your own commitment to Jesus Christ? Share your convictions honestly with your boyfriend, and pray that God will help him realize his own need of Christ. However, if he continues to have no interest in Christ, trust God to lead you to another He has chosen for you so your family will be united in Christ.

I am a student in a university and was reared in a Christian home. I was shocked to find out that many students live for sex and seem to have no moral restraints. I feel completely out of place here. Should I try to make an adjustment to this way of life?

Some young people still believe that they must "sow their wild oats." What they forget is that "Whatsoever a man soweth, that shall he also reap" (Galatians 6:7 KJV).

By all means, don't conform to those who have been overwhelmed by the tide of immorality sweeping our country!

Professor Sorokin of Harvard once said that America is a vic-
tim of a sex revolution that could ruin our nation. What will
our future be if young people like you, with ideals and convictions, yield to the pressures to be immoral?

Many marital breakdowns can be traced to loose morals
of college years. "Wild oats" have a way of hounding people
throughout the years, and springing up at the most embarrassing moments.

While there are some who laugh at a person with standards and ideals, most people will admire you. Our nation grew
strong in an era when moral standards were emphasized, and
it will grow weak when we condone that which we once condemned. Help stem the tide of adultery, divorce, and obscenity
in America by standing true to your convictions. You are the
kind of young person our world needs.

*My fiancée is of another faith. Now that we are making definite
plans for the wedding we are for the first time meeting with innu-
merable objections. Should we proceed according to plan in spite of
these objections?*

You had better settle religious questions before the wedding
even if it means postponement. Your families no doubt waited
until the last minute, thinking that you would not go ahead with
your plans. You do see that there's a conflict and that there is no
ground where you can stand in agreement. Some would advise
that you simply agree to disagree, but that is not practical when
two people will live as intimately as husband and wife. To have a
happy life together, you must have confidence and respect, and
you must have substantial agreement in your faith. The Christian
loves Christ as well as believes in Him. It is much more than
intellectual assent, it is commitment. Therefore, unless you reach
a complete agreement, you will be wiser to cancel your plans.
Amos 3:3 asks: "Can two walk together except they be agreed?"
This question must always be answered with a firm *no*.

*Is it necessary to confess all of the details of a sinful life to one's
mate after marriage? If so, should this confession include the names
of anyone in sex sins?*

It is unfortunate in a marriage if there is an array of sordid memories of past sins on the part of either partner If young people could only realize that a happy marriage depends not only on the present, but also upon the past, they would be more reluctant to enter into loose, intimate relations with anyone and everyone. Many a marriage has been imperiled by the backlash of past sins which were not confessed, but "found out."

As to the necessity of confessing past sins to one's mate, I don't think this is always advisable or necessary. I have known of homes that were wrecked by such confessions. The main thing is to confess any past wrongs to God, resolve to be true to your marriage vows, and absolve the black past by a spotless present. The Bible says: "He who conceals his sins does not prosper, but whoever confesses them and renounces them finds mercy" (Proverbs 28:13).

When I was very young I married, but our marriage ended after less than two years. With my second husband I have had two lovely children, but I am troubled all the time about something I heard concerning divorce and remarriage. Am I living in sin because I had a husband and separated from him?

Until we come to Christ, all our lives are sinful and wrong. That is why God has provided a salvation that covers and removes all our sins and makes a new creature out of a sinful and sinning one. Because you have trusted Christ, He has forgiven all your past sins. The Bible speaks of the sin of the people of God, putting away a husband or wife for the express purpose of taking another (Matthew 19:1–10). God's ideal is for permanence in the marriage bond, but the key is your attitude now. Jesus said to the woman at the well, "Go and sin no more." Christ's blood cleanses from *all* sin. "If we confess our sins, he is faithful and just to forgive us our sins, and to cleanse us from *all* unrighteousness" (1 John 1:9 KJV).

My counsel to you is to simply thank God for forgiving your past, and then purpose to live entirely for Him. Be the kind of devoted wife and mother you should be in the light of your present Christian faith. If God has forgiven your sins, why should you continue to refuse to forgive yourself? You are not glorifying God as you should unless you take His forgiveness and the freedom He secures for us (Galatians 5:1).

I grew up thinking that sex was something dirty and shameful, and now that I am married that attitude is still with me and is causing me a problem. How can I change?

Sex is a gift of God which—like any of His other gifts—can become something destructive and twisted when we misuse it or use it selfishly. And when we do misuse it, it can become something dirty and shameful. But when we understand why God gave us this awesome gift of sex, and when we use it in accordance with His will, then it can be a source of great happiness and joy.

Why did God give us sex? The most obvious reason is to continue the human race from one generation to another. God told Adam and Eve, "Be fruitful and increase in number; fill the earth and subdue it" (Genesis 1:28). God also gave us the sexual relationship for our pleasure There is nothing wrong with this—as long as our passions do not control or dominate us—and God delights in giving us good things. Sex is also an expression of love and unity between husband and wife. It is a sign of their commitment to each other in the bonds of marriage.

This, incidentally, is why the Bible tells us that sex is to be practiced only within marriage. The sexual relationship should be a sign of commitment and love—the kind of commitment that is part of the marriage vow of two people to each other. "Marriage should be honored by all, and the marriage bed kept pure, for God will judge the adulterer and all the sexually immoral" (Hebrews 13:4).

Realize that God did not intend for sex to be dirty but beautiful—when it is used in accordance with His standards. If you need the help of an experienced Christian counselor who can help you work through your attitudes, don't hesitate to seek it. But most of all let the truth of God's Word help you overcome the misconceptions you may have, and pray that God will help you be the best wife you can be to your husband in every way possible.

*I know it is supposed to be wrong to have sex before marriage, but I
just can't seem to say no to the boys I date. I'm afraid no one will
like me if I refuse to give in. Please help me get out of this rut.*

You are being treated by your boyfriends like those disposable
cans and bottles which, once the contents have been consumed,
are tossed in the trash. Sex is not a shortcut to love because it
lacks the commitment necessary for genuine love to grow.

Has it ever occurred to you that rather than having people
really like you because of what you are doing, they instead
probably only lose their respect for you? In addition, you are
only hurting yourself because as long as you try to buy friendship in this way, you will never learn what it means to have a
lasting, fulfilling, and loving relationship with others.

God did not make a mistake when He commanded, "You
shall not commit adultery" (Exodus 20:14). Why did He give us
this command? (The command, incidentally, covers all types
of sexual immorality.) He gave us this command not because
He wanted to restrict us and make us unhappy, but because He
loves us. And because He loves us and created us, He knows
what is best for us. God has restricted the exercise of His gift
of sex to marriage, because it is only within the commitment of
marriage that true love can be fully expressed between a man
and a woman.

There is no shortcut for your problem. You need to turn
away from what you are doing, and you need to turn to God.
God loves you—you don't need to buy His love for you. All
you need to do is accept it.

*I have been keeping company with a man for fifteen years. We
have broken the Seventh Commandment many times. I could have
married him long ago, but did not want to leave my home. Now we
are planning to marry. What chance of happiness do we have?*

Yours is not an ideal setting for married happiness, but I
sincerely hope you can get your lives straightened out. To begin with, your relationship with this man seems to have been
on a purely biological level, and sex is certainly not the only
ingredient of marital bliss. In fact, marriages that are based on

this alone are doomed to failure. The divorce courts are full of disillusioned people who mistakenly thought that animal magnetism was true love.

Do you love this man, and are you both willing to take God into your marriage partnership? The Bible says: "What God hath joined together let not man put asunder" (Matthew 19:6 KJV). The only really sound marriages are those based on mutual respect. In the light of your continuously breaking the Seventh Commandment, do you two have respect, admiration, and love for each other?

Marriage may ease your conscience a bit, but if I were you two, I would bow before God together and ask Him to forgive you for deliberately breaking His law, and jeopardizing your reputations and your influence in the community. He has said: "Though your sins be as scarlet, they shall be as wool." With God you can be happy.

3 We No Longer Love Each Other

My husband and I no longer love each other, and there just doesn't seem to be much point in keeping our marriage together any longer. Do you think we are wrong to think like this?

Genuine love is not (or should not be) based on feelings. God doesn't always feel good about what we are doing, but He always loves us. The question is not how you feel about your husband at the moment. The question is, are you *willing* to love him? If you are, then feelings of love will follow. If you are not willing to love him, then you will experience no feelings at all. Our culture puts feelings first, but true love isn't based on feelings. That is why there are so many divorces today. When the early romantic feelings in a marriage do not remain constant as they do during dating, many people believe divorce is the answer. They try to find someone else who can rekindle those good feelings. Some marry many times, in constant search of a 'high" that can never be maintained.

My prayer is that you and your husband will do everything possible to restore the joy and happiness that once were central to your marriage. I hope you will do this first of all because marriage is a sacred vow or commitment you both made before God, and it is a very serious matter to break that vow. I also hope you will do it because God gave marriage to us for our happiness, and I believe with His help you can discover what it means to build your lives together on Christ's foundation.

As you look back on your marriage, it would be good for you to think about what has gone wrong. Has there been a slow drifting apart, a slackening in communication and trust? Have other things—a job, money, personal ambitions—come between you and your husband? Have there been little things—a sharp tongue, an unforgiving spirit—that have eaten away at your relationship? One of the hardest things you both may have to do is to face these and say "I'm sorry." And yet it could be the first step in restoring a wonderful relationship.

But I also want to challenge you to add a new element to your marriage that your letter suggests has been lacking. That missing ingredient is God. Elsewhere in your letter (in a part I have not quoted) you acknowledge that God has played almost no part in your lives. But God gave marriage to us, and a solid marriage actually involves three—you, your husband, and God. Let God heal your marriage. It is worth it, and He wants to help you if you will but turn to Him.

I have been married for several years, and I am beginning to worry about our marriage. At first we were deeply in love, but now those feelings of love seem to be fading. How can we get them back?

Some years ago there was a popular song which included the phrase, "I'm hooked on a feeling." And, "If it feels good, do it," was a popular slogan in the 1960s. I have observed, however, that there is a distinction between romance (feelings) and true love. They are often related to each other very closely, but there is a difference. Let me explain.

Romantic love is often very emotional. Two people are attracted to each other, and strong feelings develop between them. This is often what people mean when they say they are in love—they have strong romantic feelings toward another person. There is nothing wrong with this, of course—there is definitely an emotional side to true love.

But the problem with merely romantic love is that it gradually fades as time goes on. Unfortunately, when this happens a couple may decide that there is no longer any hope for love in their relationship and decide to end the marriage.

I hope, however, that this will not be the case with you. It need not be if you will work at establishing your relationship on true love. True love includes romantic love, but it is more than that. True love involves a commitment to each other, and a settled determination to be kind and considerate to the other person instead of selfish.

Love, you see, is more than a feeling—it also is an action. Look at the characteristics of true love that the Bible lists: "Love is patient, love is kind. It does not envy, it does not boast, it is not proud. It is not rude, it is not self-seeking, it is not easily angered, it keeps no record of wrongs. Love does not delight in evil but rejoices with the truth. It always protects, always trusts, always hopes, always perseveres" (1 Corinthians 13:4–7).

This is the kind of love God has for us, and my prayer is that you and your wife will discover His love by giving yourselves to Christ and basing your marriage on Him. Then work on expressing true love to each other. When you do, you will find that the feelings of romance you once had will grow again, and your love will be far deeper and richer than you could ever imagine.

I can't believe this is happening to me. My husband is in his late middle age, and he says he has fallen in love with a girl who is in her early twenties. He says he just can't help it. Please pray for me.

Yes, I will pray for you, and I also will pray for your husband. What he is doing is wrong, and (as you know personally) it is hurting a lot of people. What he may not realize (or at least admit) is that he also is hurting himself.

I have often asked myself why this kind of thing happens. It is, unfortunately, not that uncommon for a man who is middle-aged or older to start acting like a giddy teenager in love and leave his family for a much younger woman. Perhaps one reason is a secret fear of growing older, or at least a refusal to face the fact that he is getting older. Perhaps it is very flattering to his ego to find that he is "not as old as he thought he was," and is attractive to a younger woman. It makes him "feel young again" and diverts his attention from the fact that he is getting older.

Whatever the reason, your husband must come to grips with the fact that he is responsible for his actions. His statement that "he just can't help it" is not true—he is just unwilling to do what is right, break off this relationship, and concentrate on being a good husband and father. The truth is that he is getting older, and rather than try to escape from that inevitable fact he instead needs to come to grips with it and discover that it can be a wonderful time of life.

Your husband needs to repent of this action of his, and there is no shortcut to that. It not only is something which hurts you, but it is wrong in God's eyes as well. Marriage was given to us by God, and when you both took your marriage vows you were making them before God as well as other people. "Therefore what God has joined together, let man not separate" (Matthew 19:6). In the meantime, concentrate on being the best wife you possibly can, letting your husband know that you love him and will forgive him for what he has done.

My husband is breaking my heart because he is involved with another woman. He says he knows it is wrong, but he says God will forgive him anyway so it doesn't really matter. Is this true, or is he just deceiving himself?

The Bible asks, "Shall we go on sinning that grace may increase?" (Romans 6:1). I believe your husband is in a very dangerous position for several reasons, and my prayer is that he will realize the foolishness of what he is doing and turn from it.

God's forgiveness in the Bible is always—without exception—related closely to repentance. Repentance involves a recognition on our part that what we are doing is wrong, and it also involves a deliberate turning from sin as well. It is not enough to know that what we are doing is wrong in God's eyes. We also are commanded to turn from it. Jesus declared, "I have not come to call the righteous, but sinners to repentance" (Luke 5:32). Paul stated that God "now . . . commands all people everywhere to repent" (Acts 17:30). Many other verses could be quoted. We make a mockery of God's forgiveness when we deliberately engage in sin because we think He will forgive it later.

Your husband also is deceiving himself in thinking that he will find true happiness in rejecting God's way for his life and instead is embracing a life of sin. Yes, for a time he may think he has found happiness but it is only an illusion. He will never find lasting happiness or security in this way. The Bible warns, "But the wicked are like the tossing sea, which cannot rest, whose waves cast up mire and mud. 'There is no peace,' says my God, 'for the wicked'" (Isaiah 57:20–21).

Pray for your husband, that God will convict him of the seriousness of his sin and his responsibility to fulfill the vow he took before God when you were married. And pray that God will make you the best wife you possibly can be, so that he will realize that your home can be a place of joy and security.

I feel like I am in a hole that I have dug for myself. I have had several extramarital affairs to get back at my husband, who often treats me unkindly. However, I realize that I have only hurt myself. Can God forgive me and help me, or is it too late to do anything about the mess I have made of things?

I am sorry that for so long you have been deceived into thinking that kind of life would solve anything. As you have discovered, however, there is not only no future in living that way, but it also is destructive. It has not solved your marriage problems nor has it brought you real happiness and security. I mention this because it may be there is someone reading this who is tempted to do what you have done, and your experience will be a warning to that person.

You need God's forgiveness—not only for the sins you have mentioned, but for every other sin you have committed as well. The greatest sin is that you have turned your back on God and tried to live your life without Him. But I want you to know a very important truth. God loves you, in spite of what you have done. He is willing to forgive you and He has done every·thing possible to make your forgiveness possible by sending His Son into the world to die on the cross for your sins. In Christ "we have redemption through his blood, the forgiveness of sins, in accordance with the riches of God's grace that he lavished on us" (Ephesians 1:7–8).

You need His wisdom and help—and He can help you begin to rebuild your marriage and your life if you will let Him rule in your life.

I need your prayers for my marriage. My husband never shows any love for me, and just gets upset whenever I try to get him to be a better husband.

I am sorry that your marriage has not been happy and filled with love. God's plan for marriage is perfect, and He wants marriage to be a source of great joy and strength.

I don't know the details of your situation, of course, but let me first suggest that you be very careful about slipping into a resentful, complaining, nagging attitude which will only cause your husband to become even more withdrawn and even hostile. The Bible says, "Better to live in a desert than with a quarrelsome and ill-tempered wife" (Proverbs 21:19). Your husband needs to know your feelings and you need to learn to communicate with him—but without angering him or cutting off your communication if at all possible. Will your husband go with you to consult a trained Christian counselor?

This leads me to a second suggestion: I would encourage you to do everything you can to express your love to your husband. The little acts of kindness, the care you take with your appearance around the house, the effort you make to turn your house into a warm, secure home—all these will signal your husband that you care for him. They also will show him that you want your home to be a place of happiness and peace. In time you may find that he will respond. But whether he responds at first or not, your calling as a wife is to be the best wife he could ever ask for.

Your letter, however, suggests to me that neither you nor your husband have ever considered seriously your relationship to God. God created you, and God brought you together as husband and wife when you took a vow together before Him pledging your commitment to each other "till death do us part." Why don't you take your marriage back to the One who made it and let Him fix it? Make Christ the center and foundation of your lives and your marriage. Seek to live each day as He would have you live. Then pray for your husband, that he too will not only realize his responsibilities as a husband, but will come to see his own need of Christ and seek to do God's will also.

My husband and I have had troubles for years, but finally he has packed his bags and left to go live with another woman. I am angry and depressed, and just don't know what to do. Can you offer me any hope?

I do not know whether or not your husband will ever return to you, although I pray that your marriage will somehow get on the right track and you and your husband will discover the joy that God intended marriage to be. But I can offer you hope of another type—and it may be that God will work in ways you could never imagine to bring healing to your marriage.

God wants to help you in this situation. He wants to help you overcome the bitterness and anger that you feel, and He wants to encourage you. He loves you, and He knows that anger and depression will never help you deal with your problems—they only make them worse. Listen to what the Bible says: "Cast your cares on the Lord and he will sustain you" (Psalm 55:22). Or again, "Cast all your anxiety on him because he cares for you" (1 Peter 5:7). God wants you to take this problem and put it into His hands. He wants you to learn to trust Him and look to Him for strength. The first step you need to take, therefore, is to admit to God that you are angry and depressed, but that you want to commit this whole situation to Him and seek His will and strength.

I would be less than honest with you if I did not tell you of the possibility that your marriage may never be restored. While God's will is that every marriage will endure, man's sin has poisoned many relationships. You should pray for your husband, but you should also move forward with your own life and with what God might do in and through you.

Then get involved in a church where Christ is preached and you can meet other Christians. You may well find some of them who have a similar background to you, and they can help you deal with the problems and adjustment you face.

What do you think is the biggest problem in marriages? I have heard people say it is finances, but in my experience the biggest problem is in-laws who try to interfere.

There are many practical concerns that can cause serious problems in a marriage, and I think you have mentioned two of them. I get many letters from couples who have allowed money problems to drive a wedge between them, and I also get many letters from people who have some other problem (including in-laws who interfere or try to dominate the lives of a young couple). The real question is not what the biggest problem is in marriages generally—the real question is what is wrong specifically in each marriage that is in difficulty.

But I also believe that there is usually a deeper problem involved in many marriages, whatever the immediate practical problems may seem to be. This is the spiritual problem. Marriage was designed by God. And He meant for it actually to involve three people—the man, the woman, and God. When God is left out of a marriage, that marriage will always be less than God intended it to be, even if it is seemingly a happy one. When God is left out of a marriage, it means you have two individuals who will often be competing with each other instead of loving each other and forgiving each other. But when each partner is seeking God's will, and when each partner is allowing God to take away the natural selfishness of his or her heart and replace it with sacrificial love, then there will be joy and peace.

That is why the Bible stresses that a marriage ideally should be a picture or a reflection of Christ's love for His people. "Husbands, love your wives, just as Christ loved the church and gave himself up for her" (Ephesians 5:25).

As to your experience with interfering in-laws, they need to understand that breaking into a marriage can be like a burglar breaking into a home. It can be a violation of one's privacy and sow seeds of discontent that may actually contribute more to marital stress than to the resolution of problems. You should gently tell them that while you appreciate their concern, you would rather have their prayers, and that if you need more than their prayers you will let them know.

I always had very romantic ideas about marriage, but they have surely been shattered. We had a child in our first year of marriage, and my husband not only works full time, but goes to school full time. It just seems like a rat race and sometimes I feel like just throwing up my hands and walking away. What's so great about marriage anyway?

Yes, I'm afraid many young people today have very romantic ideas about marriage—ideas that do not necessarily reflect the truth. That is not to say that romance is wrong, not at all. But romantic feelings alone are not enough when the problems and strains come—as they inevitably do.

Let me first of all encourage you by telling you that your situation will probably not last forever. I would hope that you and your husband have talked honestly (and not bitterly) about this, and that the time will come when his schooling will be over and the pressures can ease. The only danger, however, is that you both allow this period of time to become a permanent pattern, so that once school is over your husband allows something else to take its place and you both drift farther and farther apart.

But don't wait until some distant time to deal with this problem. You and your husband need to face honestly the pressures upon each of you. He needs to understand the pressures you face and you need to see the ones he faces. You both made a vow to each other—a vow not only before other people but before God. You vowed that you would be faithful and loving to each other, even when circumstances were difficult. Marriage is a big responsibility, and you need to pray that God will give you strength and wisdom to fulfill your responsibilities right now.

God did not intend for marriage to be a rat race. That is why my prayer for you and your husband is that you will both yield your lives to Christ and let Him be Lord of your lives and your marriage. You would gain nothing by running away, and you would hurt deeply the lives of many others. Ask Christ to help you and to show you how you both can discover the joy of marriage, and then take practical steps to make the most use of the time you and your husband have together.

A few weeks ago my husband confessed to me that he had had an affair with a girl who works in his office. He says it is all over, and I believe him, but down inside I wonder if I should really forgive him.

Forgiveness does not come easily to us, especially when someone we have trusted betrays our trust. And yet if we do not learn to forgive, we will discover that we can never really rebuild trust. The fact that your husband confessed his action to you probably indicates his sorrow over what he has done, and his yearning for your forgiveness.

The Bible tells us that we are to forgive others—even when they repeatedly offend us. On one occasion Peter asked Jesus, "Lord, how many times shall I forgive my brother when he sins against me? Up to seven times?" Jesus' reply was that our forgiveness should be limitless: "I tell you, not seven times, but seventy-seven times" (Matthew 18:21–22).

But how is it possible for us to forgive others who have hurt us? I believe it is only possible when we concentrate not on what others have done to us, but on what we have done to God—and how He has forgiven us anyway. Do you realize just how much you have sinned against God? That does not mean you have been a terrible person, as far as human standards go. But God created you, and yet you have left Him out of your life. You have turned your back on Him, and sinned against Him in thought, word, and deed. You do not deserve anything from Him except His judgment—and neither does any one of us.

God, however, loves you and has made it possible for you to be forgiven through Jesus Christ, His Son. That is how we are to forgive others—as God has forgiven us in Christ. "Be kind and compassionate to one another, forgiving each other, just as in Christ God forgave you" (Ephesians 4:32). Then I pray that you and your husband will learn to walk with Christ each day and rebuild your marriage on the solid foundation of Christ.

I guess I am just a very mixed-up person. I separated from my husband a few months ago, then got pregnant by another man. Now my husband wants me back again, and is pressuring me to have an abortion. I just don't know how to sort out my life.

You have two problems, actually—an immediate problem concerning the child growing inside you, and a long-range problem concerning the direction of your life. In a few short paragraphs I can't say everything I would like to say, but I hope you will find someone you can trust (like a pastor) who can help you through these difficulties.

First of all, I hope you will not give in to the pressure to have an abortion. I realize that in some ways that would seem to solve a problem rather easily—but do not add still another wrong to the wrongs you have already done. That little life within you is a child, made in the image of God, and it would be tragic to take that life. It may be that the best choice will be for you to allow the child to be adopted—but that decision should be made only after you have looked carefully at all your options and talked with a counselor who can help you think them through.

Second, I am also very concerned about your future—not just in the next few months, but years from now. So far you have been drifting in life, searching for happiness and yet never really finding it. As long as you keep drifting with no real purpose in life, you will always be subject to tangled problems like you are facing now.

So far in your life God has played no part. You have lived apart from Him, as if He didn't even exist. But God not only exists—He loves you and wants you to become His child. He wants you to learn the joy of walking with Him every day, seeking His will for your life and obeying His guidelines and moral laws.

You may not understand everything about God right now, but He loves you and wants you to turn to Him for forgiveness and new life.

The biggest problem in our marriage can be summed up in one word: Money. It seems like we are fighting more and more, and it almost always boils down to differences about money. I feel we are sliding down a hill out of control and will wreck our marriage, but I don't know what to do.

Not long ago I was talking with a psychologist who deals with many people who have marriage problems. He said that arguments over money were a major part of the problem for most of the people he counseled.

There are at least two levels or dimensions to your problem. The first—and more important—is the whole question of what place money (and all that it represents) has in your life. Right now it seems that money and material things concern you most and dominate you. But the Bible warns us against putting money in first place in our lives. That is a place only God should occupy, and money must never take His rightful place. Money has become your master, but Jesus declared, "No one can serve two masters. Either he will hate the one and love the other, or he will be devoted to the one and despise the other. You cannot serve both God and Money" (Matthew 6:24). We become like the God we worship.

The other dimension of your question is the practical one. If you are heavily in debt or do not know how to make a realistic budget for your finances, get advice from someone who can help you. If you seemingly can't control your use of credit, get rid of the credit cards or the charge accounts. Credit can be like a drug. Many people get "hooked" and can't seem to break away and control their finances. Instead, they are controlled by them. God wants to control your life and if you determine to submit your life (and finances) to Him, He will help you. Find an honest financial adviser who will help you get out of debt and establish a budget for you to live within.

My husband is a slave to things, I have decided. He works all the time, and when I try to get him to slow down and spend time just enjoying life he says he can't afford to do it because he wants to provide us with lots of financial security. I worry about him, particularly since a friend of ours about the same age dropped dead of a heart attack a week ago and the same thing could happen to my husband. What can I do to help him?

It is surprisingly easy for some men (and women) to fall into your husband's trap, without ever really thinking about it or realizing how illogical it is. For example, if you were to ask most of them why they work so diligently to give their families financial security, they would say it is because they love them. But they fail to see that never spending time with their children and spouse (as well as working themselves into an early death) is the most unloving thing they can do.

Your husband needs to readjust his priorities. Yes, he has a responsibility to provide financially for his family. But he also has a God-given responsibility to provide for the emotional and spiritual welfare of his family—and he cannot do that if he is totally preoccupied with money and things. Jesus declared, "Therefore I tell you, do not worry about your life, what you will eat or drink; or about your body, what you will wear. Is not life more important than food, and the body more important than clothes? . . . But seek first his kingdom and his righteousness, and all these things will be given to you as well" (Matthew 6:25, 33).

Pray for your husband—and pray for yourself also—that God will help you make your home a warm and happy place where your husband will discover a new joy in family life together.

I am married to a very wonderful person. In spite of the fact that I respect him very highly, I have fallen in love with another man who shows me the attention I crave, while my husband seems to take me for granted. I feel I can't break off with the one I love, but don't know how to bring the news to my husband. What is the right thing to do?

There should be no question concerning what is right. If you want God's answer, it would be that you forget the passing infatuation and settle down. It is easy for another to show you attention when it only involves periodic favors and demonstrations without all the responsibility of being married. If you still consider your husband a wonderful person and if you respect him, you are playing the part of a foolish child to entertain thoughts of infatuation which belong to high-school-age people.

Often if we will demonstrate our love to our mates, the love we are searching for will be reciprocated. But if we first demand love and affection before showing it ourselves, the other partner in the marriage frequently plays the same game and a high wall is erected between the two. Follow the biblical admonition to be obedient and submissive to your husband, and you may find him much more affectionate than you think. Secondly, this infatuation is a sin in God's sight. Confess it and allow this experience to bring you to a true relationship with Christ and your husband.

I have a fine husband but I have been unfaithful to him. Now I realize how very wrong I have been. What should I do?

The Bible tells us that when David realized he was guilty of a similar sin he cried out to God for forgiveness and he was forgiven. Read Psalm 51 after reading 2 Samuel chapters 11 and 12. Here you will see that conviction of sin, sorrow for sin, and turning to God for forgiveness are the steps to cleansing and pardon. David's sin had been known to many and the prophet Nathan told him he had caused "The enemies of the Lord to blaspheme." In your case public confession of your sin could do more harm than good. You should refuse to again associate with the other guilty parties. Having confessed your sin to God and asked Christ for forgiveness, ask Him also for the strength to live a life for His glory. Show your husband how dearly you love him. Try to be the best wife, homemaker, mother, neighbor, and friend possible. Remember you can never do this in your own strength. Ask God daily for the necessary power to overcome sin and live for Him. Spend time in Bible study and prayer. If you do these things you will find the sordid past will become only an unhappy memory.

I have absolute proof that my husband is being unfaithful to me. We have been married ten years and have three children. What shall I do?

There are three areas you must consider and in all three you must ask God's guidance and help. *First,* your husband's soul is at stake and he needs to recognize his sin and ask God's forgiveness. Ask God to give you the grace and wisdom to face your husband with this sin and let him see that you love him and are concerned over his soul's welfare. It may be that God will use you to resolve this problem and win your husband at the same time.

Second, look at yourself: your heart is heavy and your pride is hurt and you are carrying a great burden. Again you must pray for the love and grace to do the right thing.

You can leave your husband but the problem is still unsolved. If he can be won back, it will be far better. Your husband also needs to know that he cannot continue to behave as he is without serious repercussions. Marriage is a contract, not only between the two people involved, but also with God Himself. In human affairs, when a contract is violated, a person can sue in a court of law. Sometimes a smart lawyer can win an acquittal for his client from the judge. But God is just. Your husband will ultimately pay a severe penalty unless he repents.

Third, you must consider your children. If you separate from your husband your children immediately face the problems of a broken home. This can have serious consequences for them. They need a father, just as you need a husband. Also, despite what he has done, he needs his wife and children. Let me urge you to pray earnestly about this and then act in the wisdom and strength God will give you.

My husband became seriously involved with another woman. He has become a Christian and is thoroughly repentant but we decided to move to another town. Now this woman has followed us to this town. What shall we do?

Not knowing the status of the other woman, I can only advise you in a general way. I feel that you and your husband are to be congratulated on your mutual love and trust for one another. You both have passed through deep waters and God has evidently provided the forgiveness and grace needed. Let me urge you both to stick together as never before and to make all your plans accordingly. I would completely ignore this other woman. If she makes advances, as well she may, be sure that she is given to understand that this affair is finished and her presence is unwelcome. In all this, let me urge you two to pray each day for guidance to meet the problems which may arise. Ask God to give you the wisdom and love and good common sense which will ensure that this difficulty is met in His way. If the woman is a schemer, be particularly careful that she does not maneuver you or your husband into a compromising situation. I appreciate the difficulty and embarrassment of your situation, but you have a source of help and blessing in the Lord Jesus Christ which will certainly see you through. Finally, pray for this woman: ask God to convict her of her sin, as He did your husband. She has an eternal soul for which Christ also died.

When we married my husband was not working, and he said it was because of a temporary layoff in his factory. But it has been five years now and he hasn't held a steady job since then. He always has an excuse of some sort, but I have had to face the fact that he is just lazy and is content to let me support us. Can I do anything about this or should I leave him?

What can you do? First, it may be that your husband's apparent laziness is a symptom of a deeper problem which needs to be dealt with. For example, some people have very little confidence in their abilities and become easily discouraged when things do not go exactly right. They are very fearful of failure, and that fear makes them avoid any challenges in life—including a job. Encourage your husband to seek some vocational counseling; your pastor may be able to point you to an agency in your community that can help him face his problems—even if his real problem is only laziness. Pray for your husband also, that he will realize God commands him to be more responsible, and will give his life to Christ, who can take away his selfish attitude. Talk frankly but lovingly with him about your concerns.

Do everything you can to keep your marriage intact. When you married you took a solemn vow before God that you would be faithful to each other "for better or for worse." Your situation may not be ideal, but with God's help it can change.

My husband has had a lot of problems with depression and other things, and frankly it has been a great strain on me having to take care of him all the time. Now I find myself attracted to a man in my office, and I think a lot about how happy my life would be if I could be married to him. I know this is a fantasy, but is there anything wrong with dreaming like that?

Yes there is, and I urge you to face this and seek God's help to overcome this so you can have the attitude God wants you to have.

Why are these fantasies wrong? For one thing, as long as you allow these fantasies to build you will be more and more resentful of your husband and his situation—instead of realizing that God wants to bless you and make you a blessing right where you are. For another thing, fantasies like this easily lead to action. Every day I get letters from people who have wrecked their lives because they have allowed fantasies to get out of hand and ended up breaking their marriage vows. They never started out intending to do so, and often excused their thoughts as innocent and unimportant—but their thoughts led eventually to action. Jesus said, "For out of the heart come evil thoughts, murder, adultery, sexual immorality" (Matthew 15:19).

I urge you to repent of your sins—not just your fantasies, but every sin you have committed—and ask Christ to forgive you. Then turn your life over to Him, and ask Him to give you strength to avoid temptation and to be an encouragement and help to your husband. Pray for him also, that he too will come to Christ and discover the joy of knowing Christ is with him every hour of the day. "But those who hope in the Lord will renew their strength" (Isaiah 40:31).

On account of my husband's business, I am left alone much of the time. A woman becomes weary just being with other women at times, and I wonder if any harm would be done by having an occasional meal with a man friend who frequently invites me to dine with him.

Try to have a frank talk with your husband at the next opportunity. Perhaps some solution can be reached. Make it a spiritual matter, in which together you take your problem to the Lord in prayer. Someone has rightly said, "More things are wrought by prayer than this world dreams of." Finally, you had better face the blunt fact that your desire for male friendship in your husband's absence could well lead to intimacy that you now cannot foresee, but which happens in many cases.

Perhaps you should consider whether you have too much time on your hands. Call your pastor, local hospital or community service agency and ask whether you might be able to volunteer to help others who are in need. You will discover the truth of the Scripture that it really *is* more blessed to give than to receive. You also will learn that it is in giving to others that we receive back many times what we have invested.

My wife is expecting her first baby and her disposition has changed so much that I hardly know her. Sometimes I feel that she hates me and it is breaking my heart. What can I do?

Your question seems to indicate that you do not feel a part of this baby when, in fact, you are. You speak of the child as "her" instead of "our" baby. Creating a child involves more than biology. It involves a spiritual and psychological sharing of both parents.

I believe your physician can explain the problem to you and give you sound advice which will clear things up for both you and your wife. I am told that such personality changes may occur at times like this and that they usually clear up spontaneously after the baby comes. Your wife needs your love now more than ever and although it may be hard for her to reciprocate she will know that you are trying to be loving and considerate and it will help. I presume that you are a Christian, but in any case let me urge you to take Christ fully into your heart. Thank Him for this new life which is being entrusted to you two and pray daily that you may be given the wisdom and strength to raise this little one for Him.

Let me also suggest that there is no married couple who have not encountered problems of adjustment and clashes in personality. These things can all be met and resolved by exercising the mutual love and consideration which all Christians should have for one another. Nothing helps more in a home than the family altar, a time when you and your wife join together in reading a portion from the Bible and praying together. Also, do not neglect worship together: "And all Judah stood before the Lord, with their little ones, their wives and their children" (2 Chronicles 20:13).

My husband and I have been married a little more than a year. Until I became a Christian we got along very well, but since I received Christ we seem to argue all the time. I am at the point of leaving him but want your counsel.

The apostle Peter had something to say about this. He said: "Wives, fit in with your husband's plans; for then if they refuse to listen when you talk to them about the Lord, they will be won by your respectful, pure behavior. Your godly lives will speak to them better than any words" (1 Peter 3:1 AMP).

This is no easy assignment, but the responsibility is upon you, not on your husband, to live a life that will challenge him to make his own decision. This cannot be done by nagging and lecturing, but by the manifestation of a spirit of meekness and submission that he has not discovered in you before.

The pattern is Jesus Christ who, though He was God, emptied Himself and took on the form of a servant. Christ submitted His human will to His Heavenly Father and that is what I am asking you to do with your husband. While you should never submit to anything that is against the will of God (like staying home from church or Bible study), you will learn that there are many ways in which you can submit to him. God knows your motives and as you pray for your husband, God will deal with him through the power of His Spirit. As you submit to your husband, let your countenance be joyful. This should not be a burden, but a delight, because you are, in fact, submitting to the will of God and your husband will be won over as much by your joy as by your submission.

My husband and I have been married for over twenty years, but we have lost all feeling for each other. We just live in the same house together. Can anything be done about this?

God meant for marriage to be a joyous and supportive relationship, and that is true for *your* marriage as well. I know it is often very difficult to heal a marriage that has almost fallen apart—but God can help you do it, and I pray you will have the courage and patience to rebuild your relationship. In the short term it may seem much easier to just let things continue to drift, but now is the time to decide you will do whatever is necessary to strengthen your marriage. It will be worth it.

What can you do? First, I hope you and your husband can face honestly together your need to strengthen your marriage. It is not easy to restore communication when it has been lacking for so long, but make it your goal to be honest with each other—not in anger, but in a spirit of sincere seeking. But even if your husband is reluctant to face the problem, determine in your heart that you will do your best, no matter what his initial reaction may be.

A good marriage takes three persons: you, your husband, and God. Let Christ be the foundation of your life and your marriage. Christ can give you a new understanding of what it means to love another person. As you begin to understand from the Bible how much He loves you, you will begin to see how we are to love others—selflessly and consistently.

There is much more I could write, but let me close with this simple suggestion: take time for the practical little acts that tell a person you care. Learn to praise instead of criticize. You both need to learn to communicate and do the fun things you used to do. Put forth a special effort to make your house a home. Show him you are willing to make his needs and desires come first, and I believe you will find him responding as time goes along.

My husband has become almost impossible to live with. I don't know whether he's getting senile or what. We are both in our seventies, and life is hard enough without him complaining all the time. Sometimes I think it's more than I can bear.

Your husband may have some medical problems. Be sure that he has a thorough medical examination by your doctor. You should not put this off any longer, and many problems can be treated very successfully. This would help not only your husband but you as well.

But let me also suggest that regardless of what your husband's exact problem may be, God calls you to be the best wife you can possibly be. God is able to help you and give you strength and wisdom whenever you face particularly difficult situations.

God loves you, and He wants you to come to know Him personally. He wants to help you, and He wants you to put Him first in your lives. God has blessed you both by giving you long lives—but some day you both will die and go into eternity. How tragic it would be for you to miss the joy and peace of God's Heaven because you never took time to think about your need of Christ and invite Him into your lives. I urge you to turn to Christ right now. The reason for your husband's attitude may be that he is reassessing life and wondering whether it has been productive or what he might have done differently.

Then, when you do, God Himself comes to dwell within you by His Holy Spirit. No, you may not feel that you can bear the burdens you are facing—but the Spirit can help you as you seek God's help every day. The fruit of the Spirit, the Bible says, is "love, joy, peace, patience, kindness, goodness, faithfulness, gentleness and self-control" (Galatians 5:22–23). You need those qualities, and Christ can give them to you as you turn to Him.

I am into my second marriage, and although we have only been married a year, it seems like my love is beginning to fade already. My husband is a good man, but I find myself thinking about other men. Now I am wondering if I'll ever have a stable marriage.

I cannot help but feel that you have probably confused romantic feelings with true love. There is nothing wrong with romantic feelings, of course, but it is easy for these to fade after a period of time if there is not something deeper. When these romantic feelings begin to fade they can even deceive us into thinking that true love has gone forever.

It is very possible that there is a missing ingredient in your marriage. What is it? It is commitment—a determination on your part that you will remain committed to your husband for the rest of your life, no matter what the future may hold for you. True love, you see, is more than feelings of romance. True love involves a steadfast commitment of two people to each other. When you married this is actually what you vowed, both before those who witnessed your marriage and before God. God is the One who gave marriage to us, and He intended it to be a lifetime commitment. Jesus declared, "Therefore what God has joined together, let man not separate" (Matthew 19:6).

It would, therefore, be very wrong for you to be misled by your feelings and become interested in another man. You can have a stable marriage, however, if you determine in your heart that you are committed to your husband, and that you will do everything possible to make your relationship grow and become stronger.

4 How Should We Raise Our Children?

My wife and I do not agree on the matter of disciplining our children. I maintain that a child needs a firm hand and a spanking now and then. My wife says that all they need is love and understanding. Who is right?

Discipline and love are related. They are two sides of the same coin. Correct discipline is an act of love. "The Lord disciplines those he loves," says the Bible (Hebrews 12:6). The purpose of discipline is not only correction. It is to help a child conform to God's standard so that the child will be able to lead a happy and productive life.

But there must be the right kind of discipline and parents must agree on it. A child will sometimes exploit different approaches to discipline by his parents and that could be damaging to your child and to each of you.

One of our children rarely needed to be disciplined. Even if I spoke to her reprovingly, her heart would be broken. Another of our children only responded to punitive discipline, and paid little attention to the "soft reproof." I think it is hard to lay down any hard and fast rules because children vary so much. The Bible teaches that discipline should be used when required. But it suggests that discipline and love must go hand in hand. It says: "For whom the Lord loveth he correcteth; even as a father the son in whom he delighteth" (Proverbs 3:12 KJV).

It is much easier on the nerves to just let children go, than to plan and execute the kind of discipline they need. But greater than discipline is the power of a good example. Children are more impressed by conduct they can see than by lectures and spankings. If parents would live the Christian life before them, it would have a tremendous influence upon their children.

My husband and I have been Christians for many years. We have a daughter who is past thirty years of age and is still at home with us. She helps around the house but has no plans for the future. What is our responsibility?

Part of our job as parents in rearing our children is to teach them to take responsibility for their own lives. Your daughter appears to have reached a certain level of maturity and then stopped. Perhaps she lacks self-confidence or has grown so dependent on you that she is afraid of failure if she steps out on her own. An easy transition would be to secure employment while living at home for a time and then be completely on her own. She also may be concerned about what you will do without her. Assure her that you can manage. In addition, encourage her to become a part of a group of working single adults at your church. They will serve as role models and can probably help her come out of her shell and, then, out of your house.

I am a Christian widow and mother of seven children. My daughter has married a man who is not religious and has been married three times before. I feel that she walked into sin with her eyes open. Can I allow him to come to my house, and should I accept him into my home and heart? How can I do this?

The Bible says that even while we were yet sinners, God sent Christ to die for us, so that we might be acceptable in His sight and be welcomed back into His family from which sin had separated us. Since God, who was the offended party, willingly offered to take us back when we disobeyed Him and went our own ways, can you do any less?

In reaching out to your new son-in-law, you are demonstrating God's love toward him. Your goal ought to be at least twofold: You ought to want to win him to Christ (and your daughter, too, if she has never made that commitment), and you should do all you can to make sure that this marriage works. If you are cold and have an attitude of rejection, your daughter might blame you if the marriage does not work, causing severe damage to your relationship. Submit your anger, disappointment, and pride to God and ask Him to work His marvelous love and power in the lives of your daughter, your son-in-law, and yourself.

Sometimes our little boy refuses to say his prayers. What should we do?

Don't try to force your child to pray. Every night set aside fifteen minutes or half an hour before his bedtime for reading and conversation. Show your child pictures of Jesus, and tell him stories of the Savior. Talk to him of the heavenly Father. Explain to him that God sends the sun and the rain. Tell him it is God who makes the flowers grow, and gives us food.

Let your child hear you pray, using simple words he can understand. Say: "Thank You, God, for the good things You've given me." Do this for a few days. Then some evening when you've finished praying, ask, "Isn't there something you would like to thank God for?" If your child says only a few words, be content.

There is no better way to encourage a boy or girl to pray. Later you'll want to teach your child to ask God to forgive the mistakes he's made, and to pray for strength to do what is right. But don't be impatient, or try to force your little one. Let him hear you pray. Surround him with love. Tell him of Jesus and the heavenly Father. And soon he'll want to express his thoughts in prayer.

I have two grown-up sons. One of my daughters-in-law has a terribly jealous and possessive nature. She resents our son coming to visit us and scarcely ever allows us to see their child. This is a great grief to my husband and myself. What can we do?

You say that your daughter-in-law is jealous when your son visits you and that she does not want their child in your home. You don't say whether your daughter-in-law is invited on these visits. Make every effort to include your daughter-in-law in family gatherings. Invite her to lunch by herself and without your son. Ask her advice about things. Offer to come to their house to babysit so that they might enjoy a night out together. Look for ways to demonstrate unconditional love for your daughter-in-law and when she sees that it is genuine, her attitude toward you and the entire relationship is most likely to change.

I'd like to know what guidelines you would give for raising children. We are about to have our first child, and I think about it a lot when I see some of the problems other families seem to have.

I have honestly hesitated to answer your question in this brief column because there is so much that could be said about this complex topic! I am sure you will spend many years to come trying to find out more about being a parent—particularly because each child is different, and what works for one is not necessarily useful for another. But I am thankful you are concerned about this. God has given parents a great responsibility, and it demands our best with God's help.

But let me suggest three general guidelines that may help you to get started in your thinking. First, surround your child with love. I know that sounds simple, but it is easy to forget sometimes. For example, some parents in their zeal to have their child behave better will constantly criticize their child. A child who constantly is hammered with criticism grows up feeling he is not loved and also that he is not worth very much. Love your child—and don't be afraid to express that love, even when it is difficult or when he has done something that is wrong. Be quick to praise.

Then have clear guidelines about behavior and discipline. The other day I heard a leading psychiatrist say on national television that we need more discipline today, and I agree. We discipline not out of anger (or at least we shouldn't), but out of love, knowing that a child needs to learn he is responsible for his actions. Don't change the rules all the time either, or threaten punishment and then not carry it out.

Most of all, make it your priority to help your child spiritually. Pray with him, and pray for him consistently. Let him see that Christ matters in your life, and teach him about Christ in a way He can understand. We do all we can to protect our children from physical harm. In the same way, do all you can to help him spiritually so that some day he will come to his own commitment to Christ.

My husband left me and my small daughter several years ago. It is very hard being a single parent. Do you have any suggestions to help me?

There is no magic formula that will take away all the problems of being a single parent; in the best of situations, I am sure it is still often a difficult task. But think of it as a challenge you can meet with God's help, and I am thankful you have a desire to be the best parent you can be for your daughter.

First, realize that you can never do this job completely by yourself—you need God's help. He can give you wisdom as you look to Him and seek to do His will. But more than that, God wants you to make Him the foundation of your life. Does God have His rightful place in your life? His rightful place, because He created us and redeemed us in Christ, is at the center of our lives. So I pray that you will give your life to Christ, and that you will seek to teach your young daughter about God's love for her as well.

Let your life also be an example to your young daughter. Surround her with love, and do all you can to minimize the insecurity she may feel because of the lack of a father. A child must have a male role model. It may be a brother, an uncle, a grandfather, or a pastor who can help fill the vacuum left by an absent father.

Although I know you may be faced with heavy financial pressures, I hope you won't let those pressures preoccupy you and keep you from spending as much time as possible with your daughter. Christ can give you the joy and peace that will mean so much to her—as well as to you. Don't be overly protective, but establish reasonable rules and discipline in your home.

Then don't be afraid to ask for help from other people. If you are not active in a church I hope you will find one where Christ is preached, and one which has an active program. You

may be surprised to find others there who have a similar background, and they can help you as you learn to live as a single
parent.

*Maybe there isn't any answer to this, because I know they didn't
have television in Bible times, but do you think we ought to control what our children watch on television? My husband says we
shouldn't bother because they need to know what the world is like
anyway, but I am concerned about what the violence and immorality they see on TV might do to them.*

Not long ago I read about some wells in our part of the country
that were contaminated because of a nearby chemical waste
dump, and you have probably read similar stories. Now let me
ask you a question: Would you allow your children to drink
water from such a well? Of course not, because you know it
could seriously harm them physically.

The same thing is true with our children's moral and spiritual health. Just as they are affected physically by the things
they eat, so they are affected morally and spiritually by the
things they see and hear—whether on television or elsewhere.
Yes, they need to learn what the world is like—but they will
learn that soon enough anyway. I would strongly encourage
you, therefore, to control what your children watch and set
forth some clearcut guidelines for their viewing habits. That is
not to say all television is a bad influence, any more than all
wells are poisoned, but you need to exercise discernment. The
Bible says, "Listen, my son. . . . Hold on to instruction, do not
let it go; guard it well, for it is your life. Do not set foot on the
path of the wicked or walk in the way of evil men" (Proverbs
4:10, 13–14).

Beyond that, however, ask God to help you make your
home a place where Christ is honored. Your example of love and
purity and commitment to Christ will be the greatest influence
on your children.

*I am worried about some of the attitudes and ideas my two grade
school children are picking up at school. For example, my daughter*

has one teacher who is quite open about saying he has no religious beliefs, and that there is no such thing as right and wrong. I don't want to get my children in trouble, but is there anything I can do?

This is a problem millions of parents face today, since public education in many parts of our country has become secular and is sometimes even prejudiced against those who have strong religious convictions. Even teachers who have strong moral and spiritual convictions are often discouraged from voicing them, and this is a tragedy which is doing incalculable harm to our nation.

What can you do? First, discuss your problem with other parents who would share your concern. (Parents in your church would be a good place to begin.) You may find out, for example, that parents in your area have already discovered ways of letting their voices be heard. Do not be afraid of speaking to the principal of the school, either, particularly if this teacher is making fun of your children's beliefs and the values they have been taught to respect. Don't be hostile or angry—that seldom does anything but get others angry—but ask God to help you and give you wisdom.

You may also wish to consider a Christian school or even home schooling, if possible. Both movements have grown rapidly in recent years and are producing the attitudes and values in children that the public schools often ignore or reject.

Then do all you can to teach your children what you know is right—both by your words and by your example to them. "These commandments that I give you today are to be upon your hearts. Impress them on your children. Talk about them when you sit at home and when you walk along the road, when you lie down and when you get up" (Deuteronomy 6:6–7). You also may need to tell them candidly that while they should respect their teacher, they also should realize he has ideas which are in conflict with God's Word.

I guess this isn't a spiritual problem or anything, but we are in turmoil because our daughter is marrying a man we honestly do not approve of. Their backgrounds are so different, and he seems to have little direction in life. My husband even thinks we ought to tell her

*we won't go to the wedding. I know we can't forbid her to marry him,
but we don't know what to do.*

I assume you have voiced your concerns to your daughter, and
if she has chosen to ignore your advice, it is her responsibility
and you can do little more. I would urge you, however, not to
cut yourself off from her—which is what you would be doing
if you refuse to go to the wedding. This would not only be
embarrassing for her, but would almost certainly cause a deep
split between you. It also is very unlikely that you would
change her mind about her marriage by threatening to boycott
the wedding. Five or ten or twenty years from now you will
deeply regret the hurt you will have caused. The Bible says,
"Live in harmony with one another. . . . If it is possible, as far
as it depends on you, live at peace with everyone" (Romans
12:16, 18).

God is able to bring good out of what we think is wrong.
Right now you see no hope for this marriage—but God can help
them make it a successful marriage, if they will commit their
lives to Christ and seek to follow Him. Let your daughter know
that you are praying she will make the right decision and that
she will seek God's will for her marriage.

*I work in a home for elderly people, and it makes me angry to see the
way the families of some of these people treat them. Some of these
people never have anyone visit them or write them a letter. Don't
you think this is wrong?*

Yes, I certainly do. I sometimes wonder how people who neglect their parents will feel when they too are old, and find that
their own children are following their example and have abandoned them.

The Bible gives special emphasis to the responsibilities of
parents to children, and children to their parents. In fact, one
of the Ten Commandments stressed this: "Honor your father
and your mother, so that you may live long in the land the Lord
your God is giving you" (Exodus 20:12). This implies that God
will bless us when we honor our parents, and that when we fail
to honor them His blessing will not be upon us. If we love our

parents we will want to do what is best for them—and abandoning them to lives of intense loneliness is not an expression of love or honor.

I hope that your question will make many people stop and think about ways they can honor their parents right now, no matter how old they may be or how far removed they may be in distance. It is far too easy in our busy lives to plan to do something for our parents—even write them a letter or make a phone call—and then never get around to it. They probably did not treat us with such neglect when we were children, and now we should make it one of our priorities to help them and encourage them and express our love to them.

Also, I would like to point out that God has given you a unique opportunity. All around you each day are people who are lonely and discouraged. Encourage them and show them that you care. But more than that, if you know Christ you also have an opportunity to share His message of salvation with them. Let this be a challenge to you, to grow in your own spiritual commitment to Christ and then to share His love and grace with those you see every day.

We were shocked when our son came home from college for a brief visit and said that he had become religious. We have never been very religious but now I'm afraid he might have gotten involved in a cult or something. How can I find out if this is the case?

Don't automatically assume that your son has become involved in a cult (although that is always a possibility). I say that because there are many, many college students today who are turning to Jesus Christ and finding a genuine and living faith in Him. If your son has found Christ, you should rejoice in that because it is the most important decision he will ever make.

Since I do not know the details of your son's religious beliefs it is impossible for me to say if he has sincerely become a follower of Christ or if he has instead become involved in some cult. A pastor who is knowledgeable about such groups can help you.

Your son's experience—whatever its nature—understandably is a matter of concern to you. But I hope that it will also cause you to be concerned about something else which is also extremely important, and that is your own spiritual condition. So far God has meant little to you and your husband—but have you ever asked yourselves if God is real and if He should have a significant place in your lives?

Inside each of us there is a hunger for God. We may not recognize it, but each of us senses emptiness and a hunger for something. I suspect that your son has been looking for something to fill that spiritual void in his life, and if he has found Christ his spiritual emptiness has been met. Now it is your turn, and the greatest thing that could happen to your family would be for all of you to be united together in Christ as you turn in faith to Him.

I don't know what to do about my mother. She only lives a few miles from us, and she is constantly criticizing the way we are raising our children. She even does it in front of them. We don't want to hurt her but how can we handle this?

There is no easy solution to this, but for the sake of your family you probably will have to confront her directly with this and ask her to quit. If you do not, but instead let her continue, it will have a harmful effect on your children and your ability to guide them wisely as parents. Also, I suspect, it will keep you and your husband angry or anxious every time she comes to your house, and that is not good.

I know that you run the risk of hurting her, and you should do everything possible to let her know that you love her and respect her opinions. You should explain to her why you are concerned about this—not because you are stubborn and resent anyone telling you how to handle your family, but because it is causing unnecessary strain and also undermines your authority over your children.

It may be your mother has not adjusted to the fact that you are no longer "her little daughter," but are an adult who has her own family now. You need to be sensitive to her needs. But at the same time you also must be sensitive to the needs of your family. Let her know that you honor her as your parent, but that you are the parents of your children, not she. Also, let her know that if she has ideas that are helpful you want to listen to her and gain from her wisdom.

Pray for your mother. It may be that this is a difficult period of her life, and she needs your encouragement. More than that, show her by your example that Christ's love means much to you and you in turn have learned to love others for His sake.

We have a young child, and my mother-in-law is urging us to do something to teach our child about religion. I have always felt that we would just wait and let the child make his own decisions about religion when he grows up. Should we follow her advice?

Yes, you should. The Bible says, "Train a child in the way he should go, and when he is old he will not turn from it" (Proverbs 22:6). It also commands us to do all we can to help our children understand God's truth.

It is true, of course, that the time must come when a child makes his own decision for Christ. But that does not mean we should neglect to guide and instruct him. After all, you seek to protect your child from physical dangers, and you help him to understand (for example) why it is important to be careful when he crosses the street. You also feed him a balanced diet so he will grow physically. He does not know what is best for him at this age, and part of your responsibility is to help him and keep him from harm.

It is important to guard your child physically—but it also is very important to guard him spiritually as well. He is not just a physical or mental being—God has given him a spiritual nature as well. In fact, the most important decision he will ever make in his life will be whether or not he will trust Christ for his salvation and follow Him in his life. Now is the time to help nim understand that God loves him and wants him to be His child.

Your question, however, suggests to me that you and your husband do not give much attention to God in your lives. What will you teach your child—not only by your words, but by your actions? If Christ means little to you, your child will probably grow up thinking Christ doesn't need to be very important in his life. But you need Christ. You need to make Him the foundation of your marriage and your family.

Will you please pray for our son? He burned himself out years ago on the drug LSD, and he still has flashbacks and is unable to work. What can we do for him?

First of all, I am deeply sorry for what has happened to your son, and I pray that some who read this will be alerted to the dangers of drug usage. Some people contend that taking drugs—such as marijuana, cocaine/crack, LSD, or any of the other well-known drugs—is a harmless habit that brings inner happiness. But that is not true.

What can you do for your son? (I assume you have done as much as possible to get him whatever medical help he needs.) The most important thing you can do is to pray for him. At first that may not sound like very much to you—but I put it first because it could be the most significant thing possible to bring encouragement and healing to your son. That does not mean that your son will be automatically restored to complete health once you pray. But God wants to help him and strengthen him, and you should pray that God will work in his life—not only to help him overcome the effects of his drug-taking, but to help him come to a personal faith and trust in Jesus Christ. Often a person becomes involved in drugs because he or she is searching for meaning and purpose in life. But God is the only One who can give us true meaning and inner peace.

Then do all you can to encourage your son and assure him of your love. I also hope you will be able to direct him to other Christian young people (perhaps in your church) who can encourage him. You may be surprised how many young people today have been involved in drugs and then have renounced them and turned to Jesus Christ. They can be a source of real strength to your son. They also can help him gain confidence in himself—something that needs to happen before he will feel able to handle a job. God loves your son, and you can take hope from that fact.

My husband and I just don't know what to do about our son, who is our only child. Since he got married and moved away he and his wife have almost nothing to do with us. They make it clear they

don't want us to visit, and never write or call. We even have a new
grandson we have never seen. I guess there isn't any answer, but
what do you suggest we do?

Whatever his reasons, your son is wrong in cutting himself off
so completely from you. Some day when his own children are
grown and then follow his example of paying no attention to
parents, he may realize just how wrong he has been.

For the present, do what you can—even if it seems useless
or of little immediate value—to keep some contact with him.
Even if he never writes, write to let him know of happenings in
the family, and even call occasionally. Remember occasions like
birthdays or other special times with cards or gifts, both for your
son and for his wife and son. Don't use your letters or calls,
however, as opportunities to complain about their treatment of
you; this will only make the gap larger. If you need to apologize
for things you have said or done in the past that may have aggravated the problem, don't hesitate to do so. The Bible says,
"Do not repay anyone evil for evil . . . . If it is possible, *so
far as it depends on you,* live at peace with everyone" (Romans
12:17–18, emphasis added).

Then pray for your son and his family. His desire to be independent of you may be a sign of his spiritual struggle—a struggle to be independent of God. But God can work in his heart to
show him his need of Christ, and if he turns to Christ he also
will realize his responsibility to show more love toward you.

Don't give up, although it may take time for things to
change. As your grandson grows older he will realize that other
children have a different and happy relationship with their
grandparents and he may persuade his parents to establish
closer contact with you.

My husband and I have just become parents of a baby girl. Until
now we have never thought of religion, and we would appreciate
your help on how to begin.

The first realization of responsibility often makes us realize
how much we need divine assistance and guidance. Becoming

parents makes you sense your responsibility to another soul. You must give her direction and instruction until she can make her own decisions. I would suggest that you first secure a Bible and begin systematic, thoughtful reading together. Begin with the Gospel of John. As you come to any particular Scripture that calls for a decision or action, accept it and act upon it. Questions of a critical nature can wait. As an example, when you read John 1:12, it says that "As many as received him, to them gave he the right to become children of God." Ask yourselves: "Have we received Christ, and do we have the right to become children of God?" Continue that way of life through a personal faith.

Above all, obey God's Word and always settle each question as you come to it. Problems you can't understand will soon have their solution as you progress in your prayerful search for the truth.

In the school where my children attend, there has been much dishonesty and even some immorality. I don't like to have my children associate with such people, but cannot afford to send them to a private school. Are there any steps I can take to protect my children?

There is a danger of protecting our children too much. That is, we can withdraw them from society as it is until they come to have a Pharisaic attitude. We must face the real situation. These dishonest and immoral children are a normal cross-section of humanity and your children will always have to live in contact with them. The wise course of action is to give your children the spiritual and moral training and example at home that will equip them for working and doing business with such people. They will be more likely to develop strong spiritual powers through opposition than through living in a situation where they never need to make decisions. The important thing is to give them the grounding they need in the Scriptures, let them see sin in its real light, and show them that with Christ as Savior and as their guide, they can face opposition and win. Their small victories will prepare them for the larger battles ahead.

Many modern child psychologists disapprove of spanking a child. What do you think?

You must begin by asking yourself a question. Why would you consider spanking your child? Some people spank only when they are angry and that is the wrong motivation. The purpose of any punishment is to produce in the child a willingness to behave properly the next time he or she is tempted to misbehave. The child must grow to realize that there is more to fear than physical punishment from incorrect behavior. What you want your child to learn is that all of life consists of rules and regulations. Those who learn to submit to those rules will prosper in business, in home life and family relationships, and in their relationship with God. If that becomes your motivation for spanking (and no other punishment works), then when your child is an adult, the chances are good that your child will not depart from the way in which you have trained him or her.

I worry about the impact TV is having on our family. The children leave the table before they've finished eating. My husband cares more about the programs than about me. What can I do?

Sit down as a family and discuss not only the use of the TV, but rules you must follow to maintain an orderly, happy home. Let the children know what is expected of them. Don't indulge them today and then scold tomorrow. However, sometimes it may be wise to change the dinner hour to let the children see a good program. Talk this over as a family. Decide, with God's help, what is best for all. Then stick to it.

This will be easier if you begin the day with God. Family devotions are as important as breakfast. Read the Bible and pray together. Ask God for guidance, and He will show you how to use all the good things He has given you. TV, like the family car, can be a disrupting force; or it can bring the members of your family together as you share the best it has to offer.

My ten-year-old son wants to spend all of his spare time playing ball. How can I keep him from wasting his time?

It is possible that he is not wasting his time as much as you think. Young people need the recreation and stimulation to be found in wholesome games. They have much excess energy and playing ball is a good way to channel it into a wholesome activity. This does not mean that he should be permitted to neglect home duties. These should be assigned to him and he should be required to carry them out. But do not make his work a punishment—make it a share of the responsibilities in which all participate. Then let him understand that you want him to have a good time, and I know of no better way than playing ball. It might be a good thing for you to go along some afternoon and watch the game. It means much to our children if they find we are interested in their sports and in their friends. Learn about the game so you can appreciate the plays. This will give him a feeling of your interest and that in turn will make him happy to tell you about his other experiences and friendships. Above all else let your boy know that you love him and are interested in what he is doing. His spiritual welfare must come first and if you prove to him your understanding of his boyish interests you have a stronger bond to help him in spiritual matters.

I hear you speak of family devotions. Is a family altar really practical in this fast-paced age?

Family devotions are not only practical, they are essential in the well-adjusted home. I list below seven reasons why I consider family worship important:
1. It unifies the homelife, and puts faith in the place of friction.
2. It brings to the family group a sense of God's presence.
3. It shows the children that God is relevant to everyday living, and not just a Being to be worshiped on Sunday.

4. It gives members of the family an opportunity for self-examination and confession of sin.
5. It strengthens the members of the household for the tasks and responsibilities they are to face during the day.
6. It insulates us against the hurts and misunderstandings which come our way.
7. It supplements the work of the church, and makes our home a sanctuary where Christ is honored.

The Bible says: "And thou shalt teach them diligently unto thy children, and shalt talk of them when thou sittest in thine house . . ." (Deuteronomy 6:7 KJV). I cannot tell you *how* or *what* your family worship should be, I can only urge you to have a regular time together when you honor God.

My sister and her husband are wonderful Christians. They are kind and loving in the home, and yet one of their daughters completely rebels against the Bible, the church, etc. Why is this?

This is not at all unusual. In the Christian ethic, no one is forced to follow Christ. The Bible says: "Whosoever will, may come." Christianity is an involvement of the will, and no one can be coerced into becoming a Christian.

I have observed a number of rebellious children from Christian homes, but this is usually just a stage in the child's development. It is often a sign of strong character in the child. Some children take things for granted, and others will not accept truth until they have examined it carefully. In the end, these types often make outstanding Christians.

We don't want our children to be rubber stamps of what we believe just to please us. We want their faith to be deep-rooted and strong. Don't be discouraged if there is a temporary revolt against Christ and His claims upon life. Some of the strongest Christians I know (including my wife) are people who were slow to accept the truth of Christ in their late teens.

I have been raised in an atmosphere where social drinking has been taken as a matter of course. My daughter is showing signs of becoming addicted to liquor. What is the Christian solution?

Your problem is being reflected in thousands of American homes today. The scourge of alcoholism and the hurt it causes to relatives, friends, and colleagues is growing. It is now being considered as a disease and the emphasis seems to be on teaching people how to drink in moderation. As I see it, under present conditions, there is but one safe and Christian solution—total abstinence. Liquor is not necessary either for health or for so-called gracious living. On the other hand, it is the cause of untold sorrow, suffering, and material loss, not to mention the spiritual implications of drinking.

In the Bible, in the Book of Proverbs, we read these words: "Wine is a mocker, strong drink is raging: and whosoever is deceived thereby is not wise" (20:1 KJV). These words were written nearly three thousand years ago but they describe the situation today. In America it seems to be a peculiar problem—Americans seem unusually lacking in judgment or restraint about liquor. One of our leading officials told me that the gravest danger to America centered in the cocktail lounges in Washington. Liquor loosens tongues and removes inhibitions and can do infinite harm. As to your daughter, ask God to help her and set out on a program immediately whereby you set an example. If you have alcohol in the home, get rid of it. Your pastor or doctor will know of effective treatment programs (such as Alcoholics Anonymous) in your community. Above all, point her to Christ who will give her victory over her desire.

I am only a young person, but my faith in Jesus is very real. Neither my father nor mother are Christians, and they won't let me go to the church I like. They would rather have me stay home than go there. Sometimes I sneak out, but then it bothers me. Should I sneak out anyhow to hear God's Word preached?

Talk with the pastor of the church you have been attending and explain your problem to him. He will probably have heard it before. Yours is a common problem. Ask him to speak with your parents, who probably feel threatened by your new faith in Christ. Your parents may be under conviction because of their own sin, but the best witness you can be to them during this time of your life is to be loving, thoughtful, respectful, and Christlike in your relationship with them. In doing so, you will be showing them (as well as telling them) about the value of a relationship with Christ. You should not neglect your Bible reading and prayer time. You ought to go to church, but you should not be 'sneaky" about it. This is where your pastor comes in. He may be able to work out a compromise and, in the process, minister to your parents.

Our sixteen-year-old is rebellious and we are afraid he will become a problem to us. My husband and I both work. Can you recommend some place where we can send him so he will be properly managed?

There is no substitute for a home for a sixteen-year-old boy. Many of our finest young people are presently rebelling against neglect more than anything else. They need the sense of security that comes from a home where they are loved and wanted. They need the discipline of a well-ordered home to prepare them for social obligations as adults. It would be far better for you to adjust your scale of living to a smaller budget, and have the necessary time to give to your young son. In a short time he will be leaving home. Then you will forever re-gret that you did not give him the home training for which there is no good substitute. Teach him the basic principles of good character. Teach him eternal values. Help him to find his way to God as he observes your life and your walk with God. You have the solution to your problem within reach. Do not neglect it while you have opportunity. And remember there is no substitute for love.

I am concerned about some of the books my son is having to read in high school. I don't like the language or the philosophy they convey. Do you think I have a right to be concerned about this?

I know this is a common problem facing millions of parents to-day, and it also is an area of some controversy in the courts. However, if your children are in public schools they probably will confront this issue, and the first thing you should do is be able to talk candidly with your children about this—and listen to them as well.

Yes, you should be concerned about this, and perhaps there are ways in your community that you and other parents can express your concern to the school administration or school board. It especially concerns me that children today often can come away from school with a thorough knowledge of various secular and even anti-religious points of view—and yet cannot pray or read the Bible in the classroom or be taught in any measure the basic beliefs of Christians.

This means that you need to make a special effort to train your son so that he realizes the difference between the truth of God's Word, the Bible, and various philosophies that are being presented through his reading assignments. I am convinced we need to do more to instruct our children in God's standards of right and wrong. When the Law was given to the people of God in the Old Testament, they were commanded, "Love the Lord your God . . . these commandments that I give you today are to be upon your hearts. Impress them on your children. Talk about them when you sit at home and when you walk along the road, when you lie down and when you get up" (Deuteronomy 6:5–7).

Then realize too that God can use the experiences your son is facing to help him understand the way many people today think. If he is a Christian, he should be praying not only that he will not be affected in a wrong way, but that God will help him to reach out to his classmates who are searching for meaning in life.

I'm sure you must get many letters from people like us, but we don't know what to do. Our son has totally rebelled against everything he was taught, and is living a life that is not only wrong but will eventually destroy him, we are afraid. What can we do to help him?

There is no easy answer to this, because each situation is different and each person is different. That is one reason why you need to pray first of all for yourselves—that God will give you wisdom in dealing with this difficult situation. The Bible promises, "If any of you lacks wisdom, he should ask God, who gives generously to all without finding fault, and it will be given to him" (James 1:5).

That verse (and many others in the Bible) reminds us of a very important truth: God loves both you and your son, and God is deeply concerned also about your son's rebellion and its effects. God is "not wanting anyone to perish, but everyone to come to repentance" (2 Peter 3:9). Therefore pray for your son, because only God can convict him of his need to turn from his way of living and turn instead to Christ. I know that it may seem like a small and fruitless thing to pray, but "the prayer of a righteous man is powerful and effective" (James 5:16). Pray that he will see the destructive nature of what he is doing, and most of all pray that he will come to Christ for forgiveness and salvation.

Then take whatever steps you can to maintain contact with your son. You will especially need wisdom at this point. For example, your tendency may be to use the contact you have with him to let him know of your strong disapproval of what he is doing—and at this stage that might only alienate him and drive him further from you. At the same time, there may be times and ways you can use to help him see the outcome of what he is doing (perhaps by questions that lead him to see things for himself rather than giving him all the answers). But most of all let him know that you love him, in spite of what he is doing, and you want to welcome him back some day, just as the father welcomed the prodigal son (Luke 15).

I guess video games and other things like that are harmless, but our teenage son seems to spend almost all his time—and money—on them. So far we haven't said anything to him but I wonder if we are right to ignore this.

You have already answered at least part of your question by questioning whether your son's video game habit is really harmless; it may be more harmful than you realize. Not only is it taking a great deal of his time—which he could be putting to better use (including his homework)—but it is very possible that he also is not learning to develop personal relationships as he should with others. In addition, some psychologists have suggested certain young people may be influenced in a negative way by the violence that is part of many games.

No, you should not ignore this. Instead you need to talk frankly with your son, and then set down some guidelines about the amount of time and money he can spend on his interest. If you love your son, you want what is best for him; and he needs your loving guidance. It may be that you also need to talk with him about the whole subject of how he spends his time, and set down some guidelines about such things as his homework, what time he should be in at night, etc.

But more than this I hope you are encouraging your son spiritually. Your letter does not indicate if you and your family have committed your lives to Christ and are active in a church— but if you have never opened your heart to Christ you need to do so without delay. You son needs to see that Christ is real to you, and that He can make a difference in his life as well.

Then pray for your son. Encourage him to put Christ first in his life also, and to get involved in a church or interdenominational Christian youth group. The teen years are often difficult, but they are also decisive and you need to do all you can, under God's guidance and wisdom, to help him discover God's will for his life.

My husband is a man of strong opinions, and it seems like every discussion with our teenaged son ends up in a shouting match. This is turning our son against us more and more, but I don't know what to do.

Being a good parent is certainly one of the hardest jobs any of us has to do in life, but unfortunately many of us never give much thought to the way we act as parents and what the long-term effects may be on our children. You and your husband face many decisions as parents and you need God's wisdom— especially during your children's difficult teenage years.

There is another job that is also very hard for many of us—especially those of us who are men—and that is admitting that we don't have all the answers and we sometimes can be wrong. From what you say, your husband sounds like he may need to stop and think through his role as a parent, and how he should relate to your son. The Bible says to parents, "Don't keep on scolding and nagging your children, making them angry and resentful. Rather, bring them up with the loving discipline the Lord himself approves, with suggestions and godly advice" (Ephesians 6:4 TLB). I realize it may not be easy for you to get him to face this, but you should make it a matter of continual prayer and discuss it with him.

What should you and your husband seek to be doing with your son? First of all, you should be seeking to point him to Christ. He should see that Christ is real to you, and that you take seriously your role as parents under God. If you have never actually opened your hearts to Christ and asked Him to rule your lives you need to do that right now. Then encourage your son to seek God's will for his life, and let him know that you love him and want what is best for him.

One reason the teenage years are often so difficult is that a child is seeking to become more independent, and sometimes we as parents resent this. A teenager, however, needs to learn responsibility, and he will never really learn it if we continue to try to make all his decisions for him. He needs guidance, but he also needs a greater amount of freedom, and we need God's wisdom in deciding the balance.

5 | *I Am a Teenager . . .*

Did you ever get the feeling that nobody really cared for you or understood you? I am a teenager, and nobody seems to really understand what I'm going through—not even myself.

I am sure many young people your age go through the same feelings. But remember that every adult around you at one time was a teenager and went through the same problems you are facing. So don't feel that no one understands, even if they may find it difficult to communicate their love and concern to you.

There is one truth, however, which is even more important. In fact, it is the most important thing I could tell you. It is this: no matter how others may seem to misunderstand you or not care, God is not like them. God understands you perfectly—far better than you will ever understand yourself.

He also loves you with a love that is far deeper than anything you can imagine. How do I know that? I know it because God loved you so much that He was willing for His only Son, Jesus Christ, to come down from Heaven and die on the cross for our sins. "This is how God showed his love among us: He sent his one and only Son into the world that we might live through him" (1 John 4:9).

Have you ever realized that God loves you? And have you ever responded to that love? You are at a stage in life when you are making major decisions. But the most important decision you will ever make is this: Who will be Lord of your life? Will you decide to be your own ruler in life, running your own life without God? Or will you let God—who created you and keeps you every day—be Lord of your life and lead you according to His perfect plan?

Then I hope you will seek out the fellowship of other Christians. Get involved in a church where Christ is preached— preferably one that has a number of young people in it your own age. They can help you sort out some of your problems and help you grow spiritually. And they can encourage you so you know you are never alone because you are part of the family of God.

I am fourteen years old, and I have already run away from home several times. My parents have lots of problems, and sometimes I just want to get away. Please help me learn to do what is right.

First of all, I suspect you have already found out that running away from home does not really solve anything. It only creates another set of problems. And you may also have begun to realize that trying to live away from home at your age can be very dangerous, and get you involved in things that will harm you and change you for the worse.

I am sorry you are facing such an unhappy situation at home. I know it is a strain on you, and perhaps your question will help some parents realize what harmful impact their problems can have on their children.

The most important thing I can tell you right now is that God loves you, and He wants to help you in the midst of this situation. He created you, and He wants you to learn to turn to Him for the strength you need to do what is right. He also wants to help you to help your parents by praying for them and perhaps even encouraging them to deal with their problems in the right way.

Do you have a Bible? If so, begin reading in one of the Gospels (John is a good place to start). Notice how Jesus dealt with people, and what His attitude was toward others. Then realize that just as Jesus showed love to others, He also loves you. In fact (as you will discover), He loves you so much that He was willing to die on the cross so you could be forgiven of your sins and have eternal life. What He wants you to do is turn to Him and invite Him into your life as your personal Savior and Lord. Then He wants to help you each day.

Realize also that just as Jesus loved others—even when they were imperfect and hostile—so He wants you to love others, including your parents. Ask God to help you love them as you should. God loves you, and when you discover that great truth it will make all the difference.

I am a teenager, and I get very alarmed when I read the headlines every day about the future. It just looks like there isn't any hope for the future. Is there?

No one knows the future—except God. Yes, there are many dark clouds on the horizon of our world. Some people are even feeling that things are out of control and we are nearing the terrible times of which the Bible speaks toward the end of the world. Whether or not that is true, however, I want to point you to the only sure source of hope and strength as you face the future personally.

No matter what happens in our world, the most important thing you can do is trust God and commit your life to Him. God is ultimately in control of this world—although for a time Satanic powers have great strength. The Christian knows that there will never be perfect peace and happiness on this earth through human efforts alone. No political or economic solution will solve our problems completely. Why? The reason is that our basic problem is a spiritual problem—it is the problem of the human heart. The Bible says, "What causes fights and quarrels among you? Don't they come from your desires that battle within you?" (James 4:1). Only Christ can change the human heart—and He will, when we open our hearts and lives to Him as Savior and Lord.

The headlines each day warn you of the futility of man's efforts to solve his own problems apart from God. And they warn you as well that we need to trust Christ and commit our lives to Him. Have you ever turned your life over to Christ and committed your future to Him? If not, I urge you to do so right now.

Yes, there is hope for the future—hope in God. Some day Christ will come again, and all the sin and evil that infests our world will be taken completely away. That is our hope—and it can be yours as well as you turn to Christ.

I am eighteen years of age, am desperately in love, but my parents don't want me to get married because they say it is too early to know my own mind. They want me to finish my education, but I think love is greater than knowledge. What do you advise?

I have no doubt that you are in love, for love comes to the young as well as the mature. But I think your parents have a point and I think you should pray over this decision which can make or break your life.

The young person who takes a dim view of education is really curtailing his future earning power, and while I have heard of people saying they could live on love, I know of no documented record of anyone ever having done it.

What's wrong with going on to school and staying in love? True love can be a real stimulus to study and a moral balance wheel. After all, it has been the inspiration of some of our great literature, art, and music.

But you must remember that there are two kinds of love. First, there is physical magnetism which is the natural attraction of two people of the opposite sex. Then there is true love which has a spiritual basis. *If* your love is genuine, it can wait awhile. The Bible says: "Love suffereth long and is kind . . . seeketh not her own." Above all, make sure that you have the mind and will of Christ. Then your decision will be the proper one.

I'm in high school, and I'm afraid I've gotten in with the wrong crowd. I find myself doing lots of things (like drugs) that I never thought I would get involved in. I hate myself for this, but can't seem to get out of it. How can I get back on the right road?

I probably don't need to tell you that you are in a very serious situation, and it would be tragic if you were to ruin your whole life because of what you are doing right now. I pray that will not happen, and I am encouraged that you want to change. That is an important step.

No, you may find it impossible to break away from the life you are living in your own strength—but God wants to help you, if you will let Him. The Bible says, "I can do everything through him who gives me strength" (Philippians 4:13), and that is the key to changing your life—Christ, the One who gives you strength. That is why the first thing you need to do is honestly confess your sins to God, ask His forgiveness, and invite Jesus Christ to come into your heart by faith. You may not understand all the implications of that step of faith, but when Christ comes to dwell within you things will be different. The Bible promises, "If anyone is in Christ, he is a new creation; the old has gone, the new has come!" (2 Corinthians 5:17).

That doesn't mean, however, that suddenly all your temptations will disappear or that you don't need to take steps to fight against temptations. The opposite may be the result for a period of time, in fact, because Satan will do all he can to keep you from living for Christ.

That is why it is imperative for you to make a clean break with your past. If (as you suggest) there are friends who are dragging you down, you will need to find a new set of friends who will honestly help you. Look for other Christians your own age and find your new circle of friends among them. They will help you grow spiritually and become stronger in your faith, and they also will be able to help you when times of temptation come.

You are very important to God—He sent His Son to die for you. Give your life to Christ, and then look to Him each day for the strength and practical wisdom you need to live as you should.

I'm still a teenager, but I have gotten so mixed-up I'm afraid I've really messed up my life—an abortion, flunked out of school, can't get along with anyone, etc. I'd give anything to start all over again, but I don't think it's possible, do you?

Yes, I do believe it is possible for you to start all over again, and I sincerely hope and pray you will take the steps that are necessary. That does not mean it will be easy for you, but I want to assure you it is worth it. Your life is valuable—not only to you but to God—and it would be tragic for you to keep on the same road you are on because it will destroy you and keep you from true happiness.

The reason it is possible for you to start over again is that God can help you. I suspect you already know that you do not have the strength in yourself to change—but God can give it to you. He can give you a new purpose in life, and by His Holy Spirit He will come into your life and help you change your way of living.

Does this mean all your problems will vanish? No, not necessarily. But it does mean you will be headed in the right direction, and Christ will be with you. Each day you can turn to Him and commit that day into His hands. You can seek His guidance about what you should do.

At the same time, I believe there are several practical steps God would have you take. When you come to Christ, get into a church where Christ is preached, because you will need consistent Bible teaching and the fellowship of other Christians. Then take steps to get away from your old habits. The Bible says, "Submit yourselves, then, to God. Resist the devil, and he will flee from you. Come near to God and he will come near to you" (James 4:7–8). If at all possible, get back to school, also. But above all, let Christ's love surround you and change you, so that all you do the rest of your life is in response to His love for you.

I am in high school, and I think the thing that controls me most is my desire to be popular with other people. I have even stolen money to buy clothes and things so I will impress my friends. I know this is wrong, but how do I get out of this trap?

You are at the stage in your life when you are especially likely to be influenced by peer pressure (that is, the pressure to do things others your age do because you want to be accepted by them). But you need to learn to deal with these pressures because they can mold you into the wrong kind of person if you are not careful. In addition, as you have discovered, these "friends" can tempt you into doing things that are wrong.

Have you ever asked yourself why you are so concerned about popularity? I can think of several possible reasons, and maybe you can think of others. For example, right now you are changing in many ways—physically, emotionally, and mentally. This can be a little bit frightening, and you probably feel a need to be reassured that you are normal. You very much want to know that you are a useful person: a psychologist would say, I think, that you want to feel good about yourself and what you are. The approval of others can give you this assurance. In addition, like any normal person you don't like to be lonely.

The problem, of course, is that your desire to have the approval and friendship of others is causing you to do things that are wrong—and which really don't help you feel good about yourself either. My prayer for you is that you would turn your life over to Jesus Christ, because I know that He can help you deal with these things.

Then live each day for Christ. Turn from things you know are wrong, and seek His approval above all else. J. B. Phillips translates Romans 12:2 this way: "Don't let the world around you squeeze you into its own mold, but let God re-make you so that your whole attitude of mind is changed." Take your stand for Christ and seek to do His will, because that is the really important thing in life.

All my mother does is criticize me. She complains about my school work, my friends, my habits—everything. How can I get her off my back?

You are reaching a point in your life when you are naturally seeking to become more and more independent. This is not necessarily bad, because we each need to learn to make our own decisions as the years go by. But this time also can be a very difficult time for you because in your desire to become more and more independent, you can go to an extreme that is dangerous.

What am I suggesting? Simply this. Be on guard against an attitude or emotion in yourself that automatically resists or rejects anything your mother suggests to you, simply because she is your mother and you are trying to become more independent.

It is not easy for someone in your position to listen to your parents' advice without getting upset sometimes—but constantly you need to be on guard against this and evaluate carefully what your mother (or father) might be saying. For example, I get letters every day from young people who have gotten involved with "the wrong crowd." This crowd seemed to offer them excitement and adventure, but ended up getting them involved in things that were wrong or harmful. So learn to weigh carefully what your mother says. She may have much to teach you, and because she loves you, she wants you to avoid those things that she knows will harm you.

At the same time, I know parents can sometimes be too critical and never praise a young person, not even realizing what they are doing. They love their teenagers and are anxious to see they make right decisions. Have you honestly—and without getting into a heated argument—discussed your feelings with your mother?

You face many decisions in life right now, and you need Christ to help you and guide you. My prayer is that you will turn your life over to Him.

We are really worried about our daughter. She seems obsessed with keeping her weight down, and even does things that are harmful to her body to lose weight. Please pray for her.

Yes, I will pray for her. You must seek medical (and, if necessary, psychological) help for your daughter. Hers is an increasingly common problem in our society which tells girls, especially, that they have value only if they are thin and beautiful. Many have died from eating too little, hoping to be accepted.

But this also can be a problem that has a spiritual dimension as well. There may be various reasons why someone like your daughter becomes obsessed with keeping her weight down. For example, some people feel no one can ever love them unless they are a certain way physically. They may even feel that they cannot like themselves or have any self-respect unless they conform to our society's idea of an attractive person. But our society often puts far too much emphasis on such things. Yes, we should take care of ourselves physically. After all, the

Bible tells us we should take care of our bodies and we are to "honor God with your body" (1 Corinthians 6:20). Our goal should be to please God and honor Him, and not to spend all our time worrying about how other people will see or accept us.

There is something very liberating about realizing that God loves us just as we are. We don't have to wait until we are perfect in God's eyes apart from Christ. "But God demonstrates his own love for us in this: While we were still sinners, Christ died for us" (Romans 5:8).

This is why I hope you will urge your daughter to get the help she needs—and to give her life as well to Jesus Christ, who went to the cross to die for her sins and reconcile her to God. God in His mercy and grace accepts her just as she is and can help her become the person He wants her to be. Pray for your daughter, and pray that God will give you wisdom in dealing with her so she will see the harm she is doing to herself and seek instead to discover the joy of doing God's will every day and walking with Him.

I am a teenager, and I dream constantly about being a famous singer or actress so people will like me. Do you think daydreams like this are harmful?

It is good to think about the future—but in your case, I suspect there is a real danger that your daydreams may keep you from facing realistically the goals and plans you need to make for the future. In addition, you have responsibilities right now that you need to accept, and often daydreaming of this sort will make you neglect the duties you have right now in school and in your family.

There is another thing about your question which frankly concerns me, and that is the idea you seem to have that the most important thing in life is to be popular. Yes, we all want—and need—friends. But you need to be concentrating on ways you can build true friendships right now, not friendships that are based only on some superficial kind of popularity, but relationships where other people accept you for what you are. In addition, it is not good to always want to be the center of attention, or to think that that will really gain you true friends. Some of the most miserable people I have ever met have been people like you mention who are very popular with the public, but down inside are empty and miserable.

The most important thing you need to do right now is to set the right priorities for your life. What should your priorities be? First, you should seek God's will for your life above all else. God loves you, and He created you for a purpose. The greatest joy in life comes when you discover His purpose in life and then do it. Have you committed your life to Jesus Christ? Have you ever invited Him to come into your heart by faith and be your personal Savior and Lord? If not, I urge you to make that step of commitment right now. Then commit your future to Him and ask Him to show you His perfect will.

The Bible says, "The world and its desires pass away, but the man who does the will of God lives forever" (1 John 2:17). Make it your goal to love God and do His will. Then ask God to help you love other people.

My father has just remarried. The problem is that our stepmother treats my brother and me very differently from our own mother (who is divorced from my father and lives some distance from us). Sometimes I even feel like running away from home. How can I get along with her better?

First of all, nothing really would be solved by running away; you would only swap one set of problems for another—which would probably be worse and would definitely cause you much harm in the long run. But I believe with God's help you can work on this problem and things can be better.

You say that your stepmother treats you quite differently from your natural mother. But let me ask you a question: do you also treat her quite differently from your own mother? Rather than expressing any love or concern for her, do you instead constantly put her on the defensive or try to test how much you can get by with? Or are you constantly complaining or even comparing her openly with your natural mother? You see, you and your brother are probably not the only ones who are having a hard time adjusting to a new situation. Your stepmother also is undoubtedly still trying to find her place in the new family, and may feel quite insecure and uncertain in her new role. Sometimes the easiest thing to do in that kind of situation is to be stricter than might be the case otherwise, hoping to establish authority and control.

I want you to pray, therefore, that God will give you a genuine love for your stepmother. Pray also that He will help you express it as well, instead of bickering or trying to gain power. Most of all, pray that Christ will become the foundation of your family—and of your own life, if you have never trusted Him. The Bible says, "Let the peace of Christ rule in your hearts, since as members of one body you were called to peace" (Colossians 3:15).

Divorce brings many problems with it that are very difficult, which is one reason God's perfect plan for marriage does not include divorce. As you grow older pray that God will help you learn so that some day you will have a strong marriage built on Christ.

My husband and I are heartsick because our daughter—who is only seventeen—has just told us she is pregnant. We always thought her boyfriend was a nice young man and never suspected there could be any problem, but now he wants nothing to do with her. What sort of advice can we give her?

Unfortunately, this has become a very common problem today among teenagers. Perhaps your question will alert some parents to the need to talk honestly and clearly with their teenagers about the whole subject of morality and the need to resist the dangerous trend in our society that says premarital sex is not wrong.

This is a difficult time for her—as well as for you and your husband. She needs to know that you do not approve of what she has done, but that you still love her and want to help her. She needs your loving advice and wisdom right now. Claim God's promise that "If any of you lacks wisdom, he should ask God, who gives generously to all without finding fault, and it will be given to him" (James 1:5).

With all my heart I hope you will do all you can to help her resist the pressures she may feel to have an abortion. Some may try to persuade her that it is the easy way out, but it would be the wrong course of action. It would destroy that precious life within her, which would be wrong in God's eyes since that little life bears the image of God. In addition, every day I get letters from those who have had an abortion and now are riddled with guilt and depression over what they have done. There are countless childless families who want to adopt a child if it is not feasible for her to keep the baby after its birth.

God could use this experience in her life to make her realize her need of Christ—His forgiveness, His strength, and His direction. Pray for her, and pray also that God will give you and others natural opportunities to speak clearly to her about her need to commit her life to Christ as Savior and Lord.

We are a family of children whose mother recently died. Now Father is planning to remarry, and we don't believe we can ever get along with a stepmother. Can something be done to help us?

It is unfortunate that the word "stepmother" has fallen into disrepute. Some of the noblest women I know are stepmothers. In some ways the role of stepmother is much more difficult than being a mother. The love of her mate must be divided between many people, and she must do a tedious job of family "wire-walking."

You say that you know you can never get along with a stepmother. It is this preconceived sort of attitude that usually rules out any chances of happiness in a situation like yours.

I am deeply sympathetic with you children, for you have sustained a great loss. I suggest you think of the self-sacrifice of the woman who loves your father enough to share her love with his first wife's children, and who is willing to submerge her own identity, her own desires, and her own freedom in your family situation.

Would you try to tell parents that it is really hard to be a teenager? I don't think they understand what it means to feel like you are being tugged a dozen different ways at the same time, and it is really a confusing time for those of us who are in that stage of life.

Yes, I am sure parents—who were, after all, once teenagers themselves—can sometimes forget just what it was like during that stage of life. But I suspect also that there are often pressures on teenagers today that are more intense than those your parents experienced. For example, there are often enormous pressures on teenagers to experiment with drugs or sex. Parents need to understand these pressures, and do all they can to help their children resist them.

There are two things you especially need to keep before you. First, do all you can to keep the lines of communication open with your parents. They have experienced much in life, and you can profit from their wisdom. Don't just say "They wouldn't understand"—they might understand more than you think they do. But also you need to take time to listen to them and understand them. Communication is a two-way street.

Then I urge you to give your life to Jesus Christ if you have never done so. You need the strength that He gives to help you know what is right and to avoid what is wrong. You also need His guidance as you face the future. Remember: Even if no one else seems to understand, God knows you even better than you know yourself. Furthermore, He knows what is best for you because He made you and He loves you. "Remember your Creator in the days of your youth, before the days of trouble come" (Ecclesiastes 12:1).

Don't let yourself be tugged in directions that are wrong and will harm you. God has a perfect plan for your life, and the greatest joy in life comes from discovering His plan and doing it. Invite Christ into your heart by a simple prayer of faith, and then seek to walk with Him every day as you face the future.

Please pray for my little brother and me. Our parents have just told us they are getting a divorce, and I don't know what we will do. We even feel as if it somehow might be our fault. I am depressed and can't concentrate on my school work or anything, but mainly I just want them to get back together so we can be a family again.

One of the most tragic consequences of divorce is the effect it has on the children of the marriage. I am deeply sorry for the heartache you are experiencing right now. Perhaps your question will make some couple who is considering divorce stop and think about the consequences, and then work to rebuild their marriage with a stronger commitment to each other and to God—who gave marriage to us and intended it to be a life-long commitment.

First of all, it is natural for you and your brother to wonder if somehow you were the cause of this breakup—but you should not feel this way at all. The real problem, you see, is this: since your parents are telling you that they no longer love each other, you wonder if that also means they no longer love you. In the midst of a divorce action your parents may be preoccupied with their immediate problems, but that does not mean their love for you has faded.

Nothing that I can say will completely take away every hurt that you feel right now—but this could be an important time for you and your brother in another way. God loves you, and His love never changes. My prayer is that you and your brother will ask Jesus Christ to come into your lives, and that you will learn to trust Him every day. He understands your heartache and your fears about the future. "Cast all your anxiety on him because he cares for you" (1 Peter 5:7).

Then pray for your parents. It is a confusing time for them also, and the best thing that could happen to them would be to see that Christ makes a difference in your life and can make a difference in their lives as well if they will open their hearts to Him. And let them know that you love them both, and will continue to love them even in the midst of this tragedy.

Life in our small town is very dull. Any activity we get involved in is regarded as wild by the older people, and they say it isn't Christian. We kids get bored. Do you think that having a good time is wrong?

One of the reasons young people are bored is that there is not enough activity to consume their energy. If you are a normal young person, you want to give yourself to something and spend your energy on it. Many older people forget that they once were young, and that is why they fail to understand your desire for activity.

Plan some creative activity that will challenge the other young people. There are many wholesome games of competition that are enjoyable and clean. No, having a good time is not wrong. It is when we abuse and misuse what God has given us that it becomes evil. The Bible says that "God . . . richly provides us with everything for our enjoyment" (1 Timothy 6:17).

These gifts of God are for our use. To discern the true gifts of God, apply this standard to all activity: "Whatever is true, whatever is noble, whatever is right, whatever is pure, whatever is lovely, whatever is admirable . . ." (Philippians 4:8). These are the things the Christian should accept and enjoy to the glory of God.

How can I be a Christian and not be accused of being weird by the other kids in high school?

If you will keep the two things clearly separated you will find your problem so much easier. Being a Christian is the important thing and it involves a commitment of your life to Him as Savior and Lord. To be a true Christian means that we live by the ideals Christ would give us as the pattern for our lives. This means an attitude and a way of daily living that must be distinct from the world and those who do not know Christ. While some will think you "weird," do not let this disturb you, for just as many others will secretly admire you for your stand. But be sure that you do not assume a sanctimonious attitude toward others, or an attitude that you are better than they. Always remember that a Christian is only a sinner saved by grace and that we have no possible cause for boasting or pride. It is very possible that you will be persecuted by jokes and be misunderstood by some. If you accept this with patience and in a spirit of love, God can use this very thing to help you win some of your friends. Try at all times to show the joy and happiness in your life which a Christian should have. Actually, we are the only people in the world who have a right to be happy for we know where we are now, who is our Savior, and where we are going. Pray for your friends and love them. God will bless and use you to win them.

I have committed a horrible sin and I want to know if it means that I must go to hell. I am only fifteen years old but have committed adultery with a married man. Is it possible for God to forgive me when I really don't repent of my sins?

The reason that adultery is such a serious sin is that marriage is a picture of the relationship between God the Father, God the Son, and God the Holy Spirit. When we commit adultery, we are breaking our marital vow to "forsake all others until death do us part" and causing a rupture in a human relationship which God ordained. We also cause severe damage to many other people. Adultery, like all sin, is forgivable if placed at the cross of Christ. But you should know that even with forgiveness, the scars of this act may remain for a lifetime!

Many times adultery is condemned in the Bible, and this is the Christian standard. Under the law of Moses its punishment was death (Leviticus 20:10; Deuteronomy 22:22–24). As serious as this sin may be, God can forgive it. Read John 8:3–11, but do not forget that without repentance, there is no hope of forgiveness. Repentance will mean more than sorrow for sin. It will mean that with God's help you renounce it once and for all.

I was recently elected president of my class in high school. Many of the traditional activities I cannot take part in as a Christian. Do you think it wise for me to resign or continue in office?

You will have to make your own decisions all through life concerning doubtful practices. The office itself does not entail an activity of which you disapprove. It does put you in a place where you can bear a most effective witness to Christ. You are never responsible for activities the rest call for, for you have chosen to preside and guide but not to require them to do certain things. As long as you are able, take a clear position without compromise; let the office be a vantage point from which to proclaim the gospel with tact and force. Jesus said that the apostles should be "wise as serpents and harmless as doves." Do your work well and gain the admiration and respect of your class, and they in turn will accept your Christian influence. As the "salt of the earth" we must go everywhere with the message of Christ.

My mother is always getting after me because of the music I listen to. I guess some of it is kind of loud, but all my other friends listen to it so I don't see why she should be so upset.

I always get a lot of mail whenever I attempt to answer a question like this, because young people and their parents often have strongly differing opinions about modern music! Nevertheless, there are several things you ought to keep in mind.

Why do you suppose your mother sometimes gets so disturbed about the music you prefer? Yes, some of it may be because your music is different than what she knew when she was your age (although I suspect the music she listened to as a teenager might have gotten on her mother's nerves also!). But there may be other reasons that you need to listen to carefully. For one thing, she may be concerned because you may be inconsiderate of others, and play your music too loud or at the wrong time of day. You need to learn to be sensitive to others, not only when you play your music but in every other area of your life as well. Courtesy is not old-fashioned—it is something which should be part of our lives every day. Jesus said, "In everything, do to others what you would have them do to you" (Matthew 7:12).

Your mother also may be concerned, however, because she senses that some popular music can have a harmful effect on its listeners. For example, the words of some songs today glamorize immorality or drug experiences, and some even speak of Satanic themes. These ideas can mold your thinking and turn your heart from God's truth, and you should avoid music which by its words or rhythm intentionally stimulates wrong thoughts or actions.

The writer of Proverbs had some words of wisdom for young people: "Listen, my son, to your father's instruction and do not forsake your mother's teaching. They will be a garland to grace your head and a chain to adorn your neck . . . . For the Lord gives wisdom, and from his mouth come knowledge and understanding . . . . he is a shield to those whose walk is blameless, for he guards the course of the just and protects the way of his faithful ones" (Proverbs 1:8–9; 2:6–8).

6

Can God Help Me in My Job?

I am a nurse, and I get very discouraged and depressed because of all the suffering I see. For the first time in my life I am beginning to think about God. Do you think He can help me in my job?

I can understand why you become discouraged and depressed as you deal with suffering and death each day. Frankly, if I were not a Christian I too would get depressed because there would seem to be little hope in the world.

There is much we may not fully understand about suffering and why God allows it. The Bible speaks of evil as a "mystery" (2 Thessalonians 2:7). But there are several important truths I want you to know about. First, God loves us and He understands what it is like when we suffer. How do I know this? I know it because Jesus Christ suffered and died on the cross. Christ is God, come in human flesh to win our salvation. And Christ knows what it is to suffer. In fact, He suffered far more than we could ever suffer, because He took upon Himself the punishment and burden of our sins.

Then I want you to know that death is not the end, but the beginning of a new dimension of life—eternal life. Yes, there is hope for life beyond the grave, because Christ made it possible. By His death He made it possible for us to go to Heaven if we will turn to Him in trust and faith. By His resurrection from the dead He demonstrated beyond doubt that there is life after death.

Christ also is able to strengthen you and help you every day. He wants you to become His child, and He wants you to

94

be a blessing to other people, including those you work with every day.

I am deeply in love with a man who works where I do. He is quite a bit older than I am, and is married with several children. He claims that he loves me, but I am beginning to wonder because he is refusing to get a divorce. How can I tell if he really cares for me?

Let me be perfectly honest with you: your problem is that you are asking the wrong question. Instead of asking how you can find out if he loves you, you ought to be asking instead whether it is right of you even to be involved in this kind of relationship.

That leads me to this comment: it was wrong for you to get involved in this relationship and it is my sincere prayer that you will have the courage to break it off immediately. There are several reasons I say this. For one thing, it looks to me like this man is merely using you and does not really love you. I strongly suspect that if you were to marry him some day your marriage would be unstable and unhappy. (After all, if he is unfaithful to his present wife, what assurance would you have that he would not be unfaithful to you?)

But more than that, it would be morally wrong for you to continue that relationship and attempt to break up this man's family. The Bible tells us that God places a very high value on the marriage vow. God created the family, and "what God has joined together, let man not separate" (Matthew 19:6). The Bible also teaches that any sexual relationship outside of marriage is wrong.

Your letter suggests to me that you are searching—almost desperately searching, in fact—for love. But you are in serious danger of searching in the wrong place or the wrong ways for love, and ending up with only a cheap substitute which will never bring you happiness. How can you avoid this? First, by turning your life over to God, who loves you and wants to help you. Then, learn to walk each day with Him, committing every detail of your life into His hands, including your relationship with members of the opposite sex.

*I have been unemployed for eight months and it's terrible to feel
so useless. I have looked and looked, but there just aren't any jobs
available. How can I deal with this?*

Certainly one of the tragedies in any time of economic distress
is the widespread unemployment it causes. We should pray
for our world and its leaders, that they will have wisdom to
find solutions to this distressing problem. God did not intend
for us to be idle and unproductive, and there is dignity in
work.

Let me suggest several things to help you right now. First, I
hope you will not give in to despair and become depressed. Pray
that God will help you use this time in the best possible way.
The Bible tells us to "Be very careful, then, how you live—not as
unwise but as wise, making the most of every opportunity, because the days are evil" (Ephesians 5:15–16). Yes, it may be hard
for you to see it this way at first, but the time you have right now
can be an opportunity, and you have a God-given responsibility
to make the most of it as He wants you to do.

Let me suggest also that this could be a time of spiritual
growth in your own life. Your letter does not indicate if you
have ever given your life to Jesus Christ. If not, perhaps He
has let this happen to you to show you your need of Him. Open
your heart to Christ, and learn to walk with Him every day. If
you know Christ, ask Him to help you grow through this experience. Spend time reading and studying the Bible, mediating
on its meaning for your life. Spend time in prayer—not just for
your own needs, but for the needs of others as well.

Then realize that you can use this time to help others on a
volunteer basis. I don't know what opportunities there may be in
your church and your community, but pray that God will lead
you to ways you can help others. Often volunteer work leads to
employment.

*My biggest problem is the people I have to deal with at work. Some
of them seem like they will do anything to get ahead—even if it
means stepping on someone else. How should I react to these kinds
of people?*

It would be tempting for you to treat them exactly the same way they treat you and other people. The Bible says, "Do not repay anyone evil for evil. Be careful to do what is right in the eyes of everybody. . . . Do not take revenge, my friends, but leave room for God's wrath, for it is written: 'It is mine to avenge; I will repay,' says the Lord" (Romans 12:17, 19).

There are actually several principles indicated in these verses. First, the Bible teaches that those who selfishly step on others to get ahead will eventually find they have taken the wrong path. The reason is that any time we turn our back on God and do wrong, God will judge us for this action. Perhaps He will bring unhappiness to those who have done everything they could to be successful—only to find that once they were successful, their lives were empty and unhappy.

But another principle is that when we do good—even when others are doing wrong—God will bless us. That does not mean God will always bless us in material ways, although at times that is the case. (Your boss, for example, might be led to promote you because he saw you were a person of integrity who could be trusted.) But that is not always the case. God will bless you spiritually for your faithfulness.

If you know Christ and have committed your life to Him, let your life reflect His love for those around you. "Let your light shine before men, that they may see your good deeds and praise your Father in heaven" (Matthew 5:16). By your actions and your words you will be a witness to those you work with every day, and God will honor your witness for Him.

I just can't understand this person who works with me. She claims to be religious, but she has a bad reputation and even has shown up at work drunk once or twice. Frankly I get disgusted with her, although I guess I ought to try to help her.

Jesus said that "not everyone who calls me, 'Lord, Lord' will enter the kingdom of heaven." Many people think they are Christian because they were "born into a Christian family" or had their names placed on a church cradle roll at birth or have done good works or have not committed a crime. Your co-worker may not be a Christian at all in which case you should lovingly seek to share the gospel of Christ with her.

Your co-worker may, in fact, have received Christ at an early age and drifted from close fellowship with Him in recent years. This could have led to her "bad reputation" and drinking bouts.

My advice would be to try to get to know her better without judging her behavior. Find out first what she means when she says she is a Christian. Show her what Jesus said in John 3, that unless a person is born again, he or she cannot enter the Kingdom of Heaven or be declared a Christian. Next, find out whether she is having personal problems which have led to her drinking and other activities which have contributed to her bad reputation.

Only after you have done these things and demonstrated your care and concern for her as a person will you be able to point her to Christ's forgiveness and restoration. Most of all, pray for her and ask fellow Christians to do the same—and for you that you might be used of God to help her transform her life.

I am worried about my husband because he has lost his job and now he feels like he is totally useless and will never find work again. He is becoming more and more depressed, even though he is a very able person. How can I help him?

Losing a job can be a very traumatic experience. Often our self-esteem is tied to our work and when someone like your husband is laid off or fired, it can have a serious psychological effect.

In our culture, men and women often define themselves by the jobs they hold. Often I have heard people introduced by their name, followed closely by their job description. This usually happens when their work is in a field that is highly visible or exciting.

But a person's job tells you nothing about a person's character or value. Let your husband know that you consider him just as valuable, just as lovable, and just as much a man as when he held his job.

I have known many people who have lost one job only to find that this was God's way of re-directing their lives. You and your husband should ask God not only for his continued provision for you, but also for His direction to another job and, possibly, a new career.

This can be an important time for spiritual growth for both of you. Instead of focusing on your own vulnerability, focus on God's ability and strength. If your husband is not a Christian, this could be God's way of getting his attention and humbling him that he might consider his need for salvation and for God's direction in his life.

I have recently been fired after several years on my job. The boss said I didn't get along with people like I should, but I think he just had it in for me. I am angry because it was so unfair. There just doesn't seem to be any justice in the world.

I do not know the full circumstances of your case and cannot make a judgment about the fairness of what has happened to you. But when something like this comes into our lives, there are two things especially that I believe God would have us do

First, you need to examine yourself as honestly as you can to see if there is any basis for your boss's claim that you were not able to get along with people very well. This is not an easy thing to do, because often a person who has difficulty getting along with others tends to blame them for the problem instead of facing the truth about his own difficulties. None of us likes to admit we may have been at fault. I would encourage you to pray that God will help you see areas of your life that need improvement, including the way you get along with other people. If, for example, you always have the attitude that "I am right, and others ought to do things my way," you need to step back and realize that this can be offensive to others and that you need to learn to listen and be more flexible. The Bible says, "If it is possible, as far as it depends on you, live at peace with everyone" (Romans 12:18).

I also believe you need to be on guard against bitterness and anger. They will only destroy you. "See to it that . . . no bitter root grows up to cause trouble" (Hebrews 12:15). Even if you have been treated unfairly, don't let resentment turn you into a bitter person.

But most of all, use this as a time in your life when you re-examine your relationship with Jesus Christ. And don't forget to look for another job!

I am a fireman and have recently accepted Christ as my Savior. Some of my fellow firemen make fun of me, but others have congratulated me for taking a stand for Christ. What should I say to those who laugh at the reality of religion?

The first thing you must remember is that Jesus predicted we would be persecuted. He said that if they persecuted Him they would persecute us, too. They are really persecuting Christ in you, which is one of the proofs that Christ does, in fact, live in you.

Your example is Christ Himself. When He was ridiculed, He did not respond in kind. Neither should you. Your co-workers will be impressed that you do not respond as other men when mocked or challenged. They will soon wonder why you are different and you will have an opportunity to tell them with words what they have witnessed with their eyes.

As a fireman, you are called to rescue the helpless whose lives are in danger. This is a picture of what God has done for us. When we were lost and in danger of perishing in the fires of Hell, God sent His Son, Jesus Christ, to rescue us so that we would not have to face a fiery eternity. If someone in a burning home refuses your help, he will die. It is the same with God's offer of help. Perhaps this analogy will be useful to you as you make a stand for Christ in the fire station. Pray for Christ's patience under persecution and He will give it to you along with the power to witness to your co-workers.

Will God get me a job? I have been out of work for over a year, and before that I never worked much because jobs in my area demand more experience or training than I have. It gets very discouraging and I have almost given up trying to find anything, although I need to work.

One of the greatest truths of the Bible is that God is concerned about every area of our lives—including our jobs. He loves you, and He has a plan for you. That is why the Bible urges you to "Cast all your anxiety on him because he cares for you" (1 Peter 5:7).

The Bible tells us, "Trust in the Lord with all your heart and lean not on your own understanding; in all your ways acknowledge him, and he will make your paths straight" (Proverbs 3:5, 6). It may be, for example, that God wants you to get some new training; many communities offer a wide variety of opportunities for job retraining. Don't close the door on this possibility; these programs were designed for people in your situation. Federal and state governments and local colleges and universities have grant money and low-interest loans available for people who wish to improve their skills by taking classes for credit or for audit. You should consult your local, state or federal government education agency. Career counselors at your local college or university can help. Call them and ask for an appointment.

In the meantime I encourage you to make the best use of the time you have, and commit it to the Lord also. Perhaps you can help others who have special needs through one of the volunteer agencies in your community or through your church, for example. Let this be a time also when you draw closer to God through prayer and the study of the Bible, which is God's Word to us.

I am a Christian, a trained computer operator, and have a good job. My problem is that all day long I hear and talk about things that are either suggestive or downright vulgar. What should I do?

Make this a matter of definite prayer. God knows the situation and He loves all those people who are now indulging in vulgar talk. Tell Him you are willing to do whatever He leads you to do, then ask Him to show you what it is. It may be that God will give you the wisdom to talk to these people, not in a prudish way but by saying there are so many good and lovely things to talk about and by helping you to change the general habits of conversation in the office. Let those around you realize that their talk distresses you, but be sure you do this with both tact and patience. I know of instances where this very thing has transformed an entire office. Once it happened in a shop where one Christian man was used to change the entire atmosphere of the place. As a Christian, remember that you are both light and salt. Let your light shine and be sure that your life gives forth the savor of salt which is good. If you do this, your witness will certainly be blessed—to a few, or possibly to a large number. Consider also that God may not want you in this particular job. Trained computer operators should be able to find work.

I am a student nurse in a very large hospital. Most of the doctors treat all of us with respect and consideration but one of the most famous surgeons curses before us and makes vile jokes about the nurses working with him. I am a Christian and willing to take anything I should but this seems too much.

My advice would be for you to seek out the counsel of a senior nurse who is either a Christian or who shares your concern. Perhaps the two of you could then ask the doctor to discuss a matter of importance. Tell the doctor how much you respect him as a surgeon. Tell him you believe that in order to perform your task to the fullest and be of help to him, it is necessary for you to feel you have his respect as well. Tell him that as a professional, you know he would not knowingly say or do anything offensive to his support staff. Perhaps he is not aware of the injury he is causing you by cursing and making crude jokes about the nurses.

If he rejects your entreaty and continues cursing and making vile jokes, ask your nursing superior to intervene with the hospital administrator. While all Christians will suffer some persecution, there are regulations which protect people from this form of verbal harassment and the hospital ought to enforce them. Pray that your spirit in this will be a sweet one and that your ultimate goal might be to win this doctor to Christ.

I am interested in going into a small business for myself. If I do so, I will sometimes be involved in Sunday work. I would like to have your opinion on the use of Sunday for business purposes.

I wish it would be possible for all of us to reserve Sunday as the Lord's Day and as a true Christian Sabbath. This would give free opportunity for everyone to engage in Christian worship and activity. Nothing hinders the progress of the gospel in and through the church more than the increasing secular use of the Lord's day. If you can do so, you should reserve the one day in seven for unhampered worship and service for Him.

On the other hand, Christians are in constant danger of a legalistic attitude toward Sunday and toward other Christian observances. Jesus said that the sabbath was made for man, not man for the sabbath. We must not submit to a legalistic Christianity that is encumbered with commands and prohibitions. Our first and greatest commandment is to love God and to love our neighbor as ourselves. Therefore, you must make the final decision in this matter. You will ultimately be required to answer to God for the use you make of your money and of your time. Just remember, don't allow your proposed business ever to become an obstacle to your devotion and service to Christ.

I am a Christian and a worker in the church. I want my life to be an example for the Lord. I work as an accountant for a large business firm. Recently, I was approached by the owner of a large night club and gambling house to become their accountant. I would have the same work I now have with a greatly increased salary. Would you advise such a change?

The question is really whether you think Christ would feel comfortable in an environment where men and women are consuming alcoholic beverages, gambling away their money, and engaging in conversation that is often filled with the baser things of life. It is a relevant question for, as a Christian, Christ lives in you and you carry Him wherever you go. The Bible tells us to "come out from them and be separate" (2 Corinthians 6:17). While separation does not mean disengagement from the world, there are certain activities and places that God clearly wants us to avoid not only to protect ourselves from spiritual harm but so that the witness we have will not be tarnished. Suppose other Christians see you working in such an establishment? Won't it then be easier for them to rationalize doing something similar or even worse? If you are in need of a higher income, ask God to supply your needs according to His will for your life.

Can a Christian be a member of a labor organization? I have been advised not to join, but unless I do I will continue to be out of work.

A labor union as such is not evil. In fact, some have had definitely beneficial effects on the entire history of labor and industry.

Admittedly, some unions have fallen into the hands of unprincipled and unscrupulous men who have brought disrepute on the entire movement. In unions, as in business or politics, this has happened because men with high standards and Christian convictions have withdrawn and turned the entire movement over to the forces of evil.

Now, at last, many good Christians are aware of their former errors and are taking places of responsibility in the world, not willing that wicked men should have control. Take your place and accept responsibility, but never with the intent of compromise or participation in the evil practices. The Bible does forbid our being unequally yoked together with unbelievers, but only where that yoke forces us to partake in their wickedness. Commit yourself to Jesus Christ, and then go on to extend the gospel and Christian standards. Remember that Jesus said: "Ye are the salt of the earth," and also that "Ye are the light of the world." We cannot do our duty unless we invade the world for Christ.

I am a Christian businessman, but somehow I never prosper as many others do who are not Christians. In fact, God seems to overlook their wickedness and prosper them. This troubles me, though I don't intend to forsake my faith because of it. Is there any explanation that will put my mind at rest in the matter?

There have been others who have had the same dilemma. One who spoke with authority, David the Psalmist, was confronted with the problem and it troubled him for a long time. Not until he got a vision of the final judgment did he see the issue. What you are doing is looking at the matter without any perspective.

When David finally got the right point of view, he wrote it down for our help and said: "Behold, these are the ungodly, who prosper in the world; they increase in riches. Verily I have cleansed my heart in vain." In other words, he felt for a moment that righteousness did not pay. Then he said, "When I thought to know this, it was too painful for me; until I went into the Sanctuary of God; then understood I their end" (Psalm 73:12–13, 16–17 KJV).

God's standards of justice and economics are frequently at odds with our own. Jesus said, "In the world you will have tribulation. But be of good cheer, I have overcome the world." He was speaking to those who believe in Him.

Many of the wicked are receiving their wages now. Many Christians who may not be succeeding according to the world's standards now, will reap great rewards in Heaven if they remain faithful to Christ and "store up treasure in Heaven where moth and rust cannot corrupt and thieves cannot break through and steal."

While things may seem unfair now, ultimately God's economy and justice will prevail.

7 | *Do I Really Need the Church?*

I have a friend who laughs at religion, because he says it is only for weak people. He says if you are intelligent and mentally balanced you won't need to have a crutch like religion, because you will be able to make it through life on your own. How can I answer him?

In a sense, your friend is right. We are all weak in that we have all sinned and fallen short of the glory of God. None of us can get to Heaven on our own and that is why, even while we were yet weakened by sin, God sent His Son to die for us. Tell your friend that as long as we think we are strong our true weakness will never be revealed and, as a result, our greatest need for forgiveness of sin and a home in Heaven will never be met. Ask your friend whether he has ever tried to lift an object only to find out he was not strong enough to do it. Tell him that sin is such a weight (and thinking we have not sinned is part of that weight) that we can never lift it ourselves. Then pray for your friend and ask him how he came to believe as he does. Has he ever considered what God has to say or has he reached his conclusion without evidence? Then give him the names of some of the most famous men and women in history who have been Christians (beginning in the Bible and through modern times) and ask him if he thinks they are weak. Remember what the Lord said to Paul: "My power is made perfect in weakness" (2 Corinthians 12:9).

I wish you would urge churches to pay more attention to older people. There are several of us who are senior citizens in our church, and no one seems to pay us any attention.

I think it would be good for you and others who are in your situation to talk frankly with your pastor about your concern. I suspect he is probably not aware of this, and would very much appreciate your honesty. As you talk with him, don't just complain because you feel that you are left out. Instead, tell him that you want to help in whatever ways you can so that the church can have a more effective ministry with older people.

Then it would be important for you to reach out to other older people in the church and see what you can do together to help each other and have fellowship with each other. In other words, don't just leave everything to the initiative of others— think about what you can do on your own as well. I suspect there are many people in your church who are lonely—and not just older people. Be sure you are friendly and reaching out to others.

Above all, remember that you have much to give your church, and it is unfortunate that those who are younger tend to forget this. Some of the greatest saints I have ever known were those who had walked with Christ for many, many years and were therefore a great inspiration to others. Do you show by your love and your cheerfulness that Christ is your Lord? If not, the first step you need to take is to recommit your life to Christ in a fresh way, asking Him to draw you nearer to God and make you more and more like Christ.

God bless you and make you a living example of Christlike living to others.

Not long ago two people came to our door to talk to us about their religious beliefs. They almost talked us into joining their church, but how can I know their beliefs are true?

There are several cults that specialize in this type of approach, and I think you should be very cautious about being convinced by what they say. (There are also, of course, churches in your community which may seek to make contact with people in this way, and whose beliefs are in line with the historic Christian faith.)

There is only one ultimate guideline for religious truth, and that is God's Word, the Bible. The problem, however, is that you may not know what the Bible teaches, and groups like this (if these people are from one of the cults with which I am familiar) often claim to believe the Bible and act as if they knew its teachings thoroughly.

Let me give you three key questions that will be helpful in determining whether the group is biblical or not. First, what do they think of the Bible? Very often non-Christian sects will claim to believe the Bible, but they also emphasize the writings of someone else as well, such as their founder. Or they may have their own translation of the Bible which they claim is more accurate—although it is not recognized by any other group or by recognized Bible scholars. The Bible, and the Bible alone, is God's Word, and no additional so-called Scripture is necessary to understand it or add to it. It is God's complete and final revelation of Himself to us.

Then, what do they think of Christ? This is ultimately the real issue both for them and for each one of us. Do they see Him as a great religious teacher only, or somehow divine but not fully God? The Bible stresses repeatedly that Jesus Christ is God Himself, come down from Heaven in human form. Our cry should be that of Thomas when he saw Christ after the resurrection: "My Lord and my God!" (John 20:28).

Finally, what do they teach about salvation? Salvation comes to us as a gift of God's grace through faith in Christ. It is never through Christ and anything else—it is Christ alone who saves us. And that is what you can discover for yourself.

Our church is a large one, and sometimes I just feel lost in the crowd. I'm very lonely, but sometimes no one even says hello to me after the service. Should I change churches?

I do not know your situation completely, but I would hope you do not change churches until you have tried several things that might very well overcome this problem you feel.

Yes, a large church can sometimes be intimidating or cold to someone when that person first comes into it. But did it ever occur to you that maybe there are people sitting next to you who are also waiting for someone to take the initiative? Thus you can make it a point to speak to others. And if your church has the custom of having the pastor stand at the door after the service, or at the front of the church, take the initiative to speak to him and let him know of your concern.

Also, I strongly suspect that this church has many, many activities in addition to the regular Sunday morning service, and you need to get involved in some of them. There probably is a Sunday school class, for instance, that is made up of people who have a similar background to yours in terms of age, etc. Often it is in this kind of situation that you really get to know people. Again, you may find there are people there who are also lonely and yet are afraid to reach out to others.

I hope, however, that the church you attend—whether this one or a new one—will be one where you can not only have friends but where you can grow spiritually. In church we come together with other believers to worship God, but we also come together to learn more about God and His Word.

We need the fellowship of other believers. That is why the Bible urges us, "Let us consider how we may spur one another on toward love and good deeds. Let us not give up meeting together as some are in the habit of doing, but let us encourage one another" (Hebrews 10:24–25).

I grew up in a church, but when I reached my teenage years I dropped out. Now that I am married and have a family I wonder if maybe I ought to give the church another try. What do you think?

You are probably realizing that you have many responsibilities you never had before, and now you sense your need for God's help. In addition, the other members of your family also need the help and guidance of God.

By all means I hope you will return to church. But more than that, I want you to realize that your real need is to come to know God personally—and you can know Him. In other words, there is nothing magical about going to church, if your church-going becomes merely a habit that you perform. The message of the church should be centered in Christ, and without Him your church-going can easily become a dull routine.

The Bible says that God loves you and created you, and the most important thing you can do in life is to come to Him and turn your life over to Him. He wants to forgive you of your sins, and He wants to make you part of His family. He wants to be part of your life every day—in fact, He wants to be the foundation of your life (and the lives of your family as well). You have a responsibility to your children, to help them know what is right and wrong, and most of all to teach them about God's love for them so they will want to seek His will for their lives.

How can you come to Christ? First, confess to God that you have left Him out of your life—although He has been taking care of you all these years. Then open your heart to Christ and invite Him to come into your life by faith.

Then seek to live each day for Christ. An important part of that is growing in your relationship to Christ by having fellowship with other believers and hearing His Word taught, which is why the church is important.

Recently a man in our church has been accused of some illegal or questionable actions in connection with a large business deal. People in our church feel that we should not have anything to do with him, while others feel we ought to try to help him in some way. What is your opinion?

I do not know all the facts, of course, but in general the Bible clearly stresses that we need to reach out to people who are in need. This man is hurting, I strongly suspect, and he needs the love and support of those who are his fellow believers. The Bible says, "Carry each other's burdens, and in this way you will fulfill the law of Christ" (Galatians 6:2).

Even if this individual has done something wrong—which has apparently not been proven at this point—you have a responsibility to help him see the seriousness of what he has done and encourage him to repent of it. In 1 Corinthians, Paul had to deal with a man who had committed an open, blatant sin—and who apparently felt no sorrow for it. Only then did Paul instruct the church to remove him from its fellowship. Later, when he repented, Paul urged that he be restored to fellowship at once (1 Corinthians 5:1–7; 2 Corinthians 2:5–10). The Bible commands, "Brothers, if someone is caught in a sin, you who are spiritual should restore him gently. But watch yourself, or you also may be tempted" (Galatians 6:1).

I cannot help but feel that there may be some in your church who are more concerned about the public reputation of the church than they are about the man who needs your love and support and wisdom. Certainly we should be careful, so that outsiders have no legitimate reason for thinking we are not concerned about purity of life. But Christ was known as a friend of sinners (Matthew 11:19), because He went out of His way to demonstrate His love for those who have sinned. We should be thankful for this, because we have all sinned and we all need His grace.

I would hope that your church would not only seek what is right in this situation, but that it might cause each Christian in your fellowship to think more deeply about the love Christ calls us to demonstrate to others. "All men will know that you are my disciples if you love one another" (John 13:35).

I feel like an oddball in our church, because I am almost the only single person around. I don't feel like I have much in common with all of the married couples my own age. What do you think I should do?

First, you can accept your situation and work to improve it so that your church begins to reach out to other singles, and you can take steps also to establish firmer friendships with those in the church who are married. Or second, you can seek out a church where you feel more comfortable because of its ministry to singles.

I cannot tell you which choice is right for you; you certainly should make it a matter of prayer and seek God's will about it. But look at each of these choices: you could work to improve the situation in your church—and this is probably the way you should go if at all possible. For one thing, you should talk frankly with your pastor about your concern. You may be surprised to find that he is very sympathetic to your feelings and will appreciate your willingness to mention the problem to him. He may in fact ask you for suggestions on ways the church can help—so be prepared with some specific suggestions! Many churches today are beginning to reach out to singles, and you actually may have an excellent opportunity to be used of God in your church to reach out to single people who need Christ. In addition, he may be able to suggest ways in which you can be of service in the church, and this is often an excellent way to establish friendships.

It may be you will come to the conclusion you would be happier, and would grow spiritually in a great way in a church which has others who are single. But remember most of all that you need other Christians and you need to grow in your relationship to Christ. Even if your present church is not ideal according to your wishes, ask God if He has a ministry for you there and if you can grow spiritually there. "But grow in the grace and knowledge of our Lord and Savior Jesus Christ" (2 Peter 3:18).

There is a woman in our community who runs around openly with a married man. She is forty and he is thirty. On Sunday she goes to church and pretends to be the best one there. People are getting tired of the way she acts. Don't you think someone should talk to her?

The Bible prescribes a formula for dealing with the situation you describe. First, the pastor or someone who is a member of the church should go to her and confront her in private with her sin. Then, if she does not repent, two or three others are to confront her in private. If she will still not repent, she is to be taken before the entire congregation and if she still refuses to repent, she is to be put out of the church.

The emphasis is on repentance, not judgment, except as a last resort—and even then God still cares about her redemption and restoration. I would be especially careful that you and your fellow church members do not exhibit a "holier than thou" attitude. This could be destructive to her and to you as well, for there but for God's grace go you and every other church member. Most of all, pray for this woman and the man she has been seeing (and his wife and family) that they might acknowledge their sin and be cleansed by the blood of Christ.

Why do you find such difference of opinion and such strong feelings on the part of some Christians about some matters of faith and church procedures?

The Christian faith is so great in its implications that it is difficult for man to see it all. It is something like a diamond with many facets and we see only a part of the diamond at one time. Another reason is that there are times when we magnify some particular point beyond its significance. There are things about the Christian faith which are essential; there are others which are important in varying degrees but which have no bearing on one's personal salvation.

Then too the frailty and perversities of human nature may cause us to interpret certain truths from a purely human viewpoint, thereby losing their spiritual significance. While your question is interesting, let me suggest that you will be wise to look, not at the differences in the church but at the things on which historic Christianity has always agreed; the deity of our Lord, His death for our sins, His resurrection, and His coming again among them. If we agree on the things about which the Bible is very clear, we can agree to disagree on many minor points.

Why do you always say that a new Christian should immediately unite with a church?

Why should a newborn baby have a home? It is as simple as that. A child can be born outside the home, and a person can become a Christian outside the church, but nurture and care is essential to the development of both. These can best be provided in the home in the case of the child, and in the church in the case of a Christian.

Only the church provides the nurture for spiritual growth. Here we are taught to grow in the Word, and here we have the help of other Christians when we are tempted to stumble. The church is a storehouse of spiritual food whereby the inner man is fed, nourished, and developed into maturity. If it fails, it is not fulfilling its purpose as a church

Years ago someone in my church hurt me very much and I left. I haven't been back to church since. I know this is wrong, but don't you think it is possible to be a good Christian and not attend church?

You need to deal with the hurt you feel. No matter what the facts of the case, you need to forgive the person who hurt you. That is never an easy step to take when we feel someone has wronged us, but the Bible is clear: "Bear with each other and forgive whatever grievances you may have against one another. Forgive as the Lord forgave you" (Colossians 3:13).

The verse I have just quoted gives the key to forgiving others. It says you should forgive in the same way the Lord forgave you. How has Christ forgiven you? He forgave you totally and completely out of His grace and mercy. He did not forgive you half-way, nor did He forgive you because somehow you were able to earn His forgiveness. He forgave you because of His love for you, and in turn you are to forgive others—whether they deserve it or not in your eyes.

Then get back in church. You need the fellowship of other believers, and you need to take your stand publicly for Christ. You need the encouragement of other believers, and God does not want you to be a spiritual infant all your life. Take seriously what God has commanded for us: "Let us not give up meeting together, as some are in the habit of doing, but let us encourage one another" (Hebrews 10:25).

Not having been a Christian for long, I wonder if you can tell me how to choose a church? I don't want to get into one that does not preach the gospel faithfully.

As you say, I would select a church which preaches the gospel faithfully. However, sound theology, as fundamental as it is, is only the first step. I would also choose a church that endeavors to practice what it preaches, and translates its beliefs into everyday life. I would choose a church where there is a degree of love and acceptance toward other Christians. I would choose a church that opens its arms to everyone with a spiritual need, regardless of their social standing, and that has a concern for the social sins of the community. I would choose a church which has a missionary vision and spirit, one which is willing to cooperate in every worthwhile effort to bring Christ to the world. And last, I would choose a church that is worthy of my tithes and offerings, and where I could find opportunity to use my talents and capabilities for the glory of God.

Some time ago I made a pledge to the church for missions. I made it large, mainly to impress people, and now I can't pay it. What are the legal problems involved? Can I be made to pay or what should be my course of action?

I am quite confident that no church group that is sincerely seeking to follow Christ would attempt to force collection of such a promise. But you still must answer to God. Actually your promise was supposedly made to Him. What do you intend to do about it? I see only one course of action now. Either you must make a public statement of your false intentions when you made the pledge or ask for the time to honor it. If you did this, you would have a clear conscience toward men, if not toward God. Then you should in repentance turn to God, asking forgiveness in Jesus' name, and He who forgives every sin will also forgive you.

My friends claim I am not a Christian because I do not attend church. Can one be just as religious and good if he is not a member of a church?

I suppose it could be said that going to church will not make one a Christian. But of this we are even more sure: refusing to fellowship with believers will not make you one either.

You could subscribe to the principles of the Rotary Club without being a Rotarian. But it seems to me that if you sincerely wanted to be a good Rotarian or a good Christian you would do well to fellowship with those who have kindred goals and motives.

The church is the family of believers. Christ died, not only for the individual, but for the church. The Bible says: "He loved the church, and gave Himself for it." If Christ loved the church enough to die for it, we should love it enough to associate ourselves with it.

By joining a good spiritual church, we are letting the world know where our loyalties are. Even you admit that your friends say you are not a Christian because you do not belong to church. If we really believe in Christ, the least we can do is to identify ourselves with others who believe. In this way your faith is strengthened, and your witness is buttressed.

Our church is so well organized that there seems to be no place for the freshness of spontaneity, or individual expression. Sometimes I feel that I can't see Christ for the trimmings. Am I wrong in feeling this way?

No, I don't feel that you are wrong. I think perhaps you have a point. I'm sure your pastor would welcome any constructive suggestions you may have along this line.

Most ministers regret that their membership does not participate more actively in the life of the church, and I am sure your minister would be for any sanctified "spontaneity" you may bring to the life of the church.

I hope the day will never come when the church abandons the "class meeting" and the prayer service. In these services everyone who so desires should have an opportunity for expression. The old-fashioned "testimony" meeting should be revived, for through this medium we can share with others our faith and our triumphs as well as our needs and mistakes.

But this is important: although opportunities for expression may be limited within the church walls, there is plenty of opportunity to witness to your neighbors and friends to the saving power of Christ. In fact, it is much more effective to witness to those who need Christ, rather than to those who already know Him. More power to you! Be spontaneous and expressive in your Christian witness.

Our church is planning a building program that I think is beyond our financial ability. My friends are enthusiastic. Should I stand in opposition and still work in the church or should I leave as a matter of conscience?

As church members we may not always find ourselves in total agreement in matters of policy. As long as there is not denial of the essentials of our faith, and as long as your friends do not cease to be your friends simply because you disagree, I would continue to work with them. There is no moral deviation here, but a matter of business judgment. We need to be able to disagree in love and still work together to bring men to Jesus Christ. State your objections and continue to work with them as friends and as bothers and sisters in Christ. Time will show who was right. You will have your friends and your church.

I was raised in a family with very strong church ties. Now I am married and living in a community where there are no congenial churches. Do you think that my husband and I should try to start a new church?

Most of the major denominations have basically the same Christian doctrines. It is true that some are much closer to their original beliefs than others and for that reason congregations and ministers differ greatly. I would suggest that you make a study of the basic beliefs of the churches in your community and then join the one you feel most closely resembles your ideal. Remember that there is no perfect church and no perfect congregation. It can well be that God is opening up for you a new opportunity to serve Him through a church which needs your witness and help (or perhaps through a church that is just getting started). Remember, also, that we sometimes confuse our prejudices with our beliefs. In any case you should join a church where you find spiritual help and strength each week and where you can join in the program of the church in reaching out to the unchurched in your community. It is impossible for me to answer your question in more than broad generalities because there are many details I know nothing of and also because this is a personal problem and God alone can lead you to a final decision which is right. If you and your husband make this a matter of prayer and be sure to follow God's leading in the matter, you will make no mistake.

We have recently moved into a new community where there is no church of our denomination. There is a church here with which we can agree with few reservations. Should we drive a great distance to a church of our own denomination, or could we serve where we are? They have asked me to teach a Sunday school class.

I believe in denominational loyalty, but I also believe that Christians should witness where they live. Unless you show an interest and love for those in your community, people might suspect that you are religious snobs—which of course you are not.

You say that you agree with the doctrine of the local church with few reservations. I have found that nonessentials separate people more often than essentials. In reading the history of denominations, it is interesting to note that the great divisions have always resulted from somewhat minor differences. It is more important to maintain a church attitude in spite of the differences between us. Some people call that "compromise"—others see it as Christian charity.

I have made up my mind to fellowship with all those who love Jesus Christ with all their heart, and are seeking to win men to Him.

I have sometimes been criticized for doing this, but I would rather lose a few friends than the blessing and favor of my Lord. If you feel that you can be a blessing to these people who don't see quite eye to eye with you on every point, by all means serve where you will be the greatest blessing.

Some time ago I served as treasurer of our church. From time to time I took small sums of money, intending to repay it as soon as possible. Now another man has been elected to the office and I am ashamed to tell him what I did, but I must repay the amount to balance the record. Can you help me with a suggestion?

I would suggest that you take the pastor of the church into your confidence. Your problem is certainly one that has some spiritual implications, and you can probably be sure that he will not betray your confidence.

There is no question about what must be done. It is merely a matter of procedure, and it would be the proper policy to confide in your pastor. He should be the kind of person you need to include in such a problem. In fact, he has much at stake in every such problem. The Bible tells us that we should submit to those who have such responsibility: "They keep watch over you as men who must give an account. Obey them so that their work will be a joy, not a burden, for that would be of no advantage to you" (Hebrews 13:17).

I get tired of preachers always begging for money for their pet projects. Our pastor has been preaching about it a lot, and it seems like many of the preachers I see on television take a lot of time to urge people to give money. What do you think of this?

While it is true that some ministers may seem to constantly plead for money, particularly on television, it is also true that many others do not. When Jesus told us that it is more blessed to give than to receive, He was making an important point. God does not need our money. He owns everything, including "our" money. What He wants to discover is where our central focus of worship lies. Is that focus on God or is it on our money? Some people use a preacher's request for funds as an excuse not to give because such persons really worship their bank account more than they do God. Make sure that is not your attitude.

The Bible indicates that God is more interested in our attitude when it comes to giving. We should give wisely, making sure that the recipient is a good steward of God's money. Ask for a financial statement so you can make sure that the money is being used for the intended purpose. Then talk with your pastor about your concerns. Jesus said, "Give, and it will be given to you. A good measure, pressed down, shaken together and running over, will be poured into your lap . . ." (Luke 6:38).

I hate to admit it but I find church and sermons boring. I try to pay attention, but it just doesn't work. I know I ought to go to church, but why bother if I am not getting anything out of it? Is there something wrong with me?

There may be several reasons for your problem—which unfortunately is shared by many people. But the gospel should never be dull, for it is the most exciting and relevant news we could ever receive. When we find it dull, it is a warning sign that something is going on inside us and we need to take action to correct it.

Some problems may be on a practical level. For example, many of us are so used to the fast pace of television that we find it hard to concentrate on a longer message, such as a sermon. To overcome this, let me urge you first of all to pray before each service, asking God to speak to you and keep you alert. Then be sure you get enough rest; some people work so hard at their weekend recreation that they have little energy left for the Lord's Day! In addition, take notes on your pastor's sermons, jotting down the main points. This will help you concentrate and also will help you remember the sermon's teaching during the week.

There may be a spiritual problem behind this also. If you are just going to church out of habit instead of from a personal commitment to Christ, it is not surprising you find church boring. Have you ever committed your life to Jesus Christ, deliberately and consciously turning your life over to Him and determining to follow Him as His disciple? The true child of God will have a hunger for worship and God's Word. "I will praise you with an upright heart as I learn your righteous laws" (Psalm 119:7).

I live in one of our large cities, and I have become very concerned because there are so many people in our city who don't even have enough food to eat. Do you think churches ought to do more about this project?

Yes, churches and individual Christians should certainly be concerned about this problem, and should be doing all they can to help alleviate it. Jesus stated that His true followers would be those who care for the hungry and others in need (see Matthew 25:31–46). The Bible also says, "Suppose a brother or sister is without clothes and daily food. If one of you says to him, 'Go, I wish you well; keep warm and well fed,' but does nothing about his physical needs, what good is it?" (James 2:15–16).

I would encourage you to find out more about programs in your community to help those who are hungry or homeless; you may discover many churches are already deeply involved in some of them. Recently I have been in several of our major cities and have visited a number of church-sponsored programs for feeding the hungry. In many of our crusades in recent years we have collected truckloads of food for the hungry.

If God leads you to become personally involved in a church-sponsored program to help those who are hungry in your community, pray that He will use you not only to meet the physical needs of people but to minister to their spiritual needs as well. Jesus fed the hungry, but He also declared, "I am the bread of life. He who comes to me will never go hungry" (John 6:35).

Part II

Spiritual Concerns

I'm Afraid My Life Is Ruined

I am afraid my life is ruined. I think I have herpes. Why would God punish me so much just for being sexually active?

Your doctor can advise you about the seriousness of your condition and exactly what you can expect in terms of its damage to your health.

Although God has allowed this to happen to you, I want you to realize that you are the one who is responsible, and not God. I believe venereal disease (and there are many forms of it, including other new strains that defy medical treatment) is one way God warns us about the seriousness of sexual license. Sex is not given to us by God for our own selfish pleasure or gratification. It was instead given to us by Him as a sign or symbol of the oneness that should characterize married love. Any sexual act outside marriage is wrong—not because God wants to destroy our happiness, but because He knows that sex only reaches its highest joys within marriage. Love without commitment is not true love. We defile one of God's greatest gifts when we treat sex as something casual. "Marriage should be honored by all, and the marriage bed kept pure, for God will judge the adulterer and all the sexually immoral" (Hebrews 13:4).

I am not in a position to advise you medically, of course, although at present there is no medical cure known for the venereal disease you mention, Herpes Simplex II. It is a disease that has swept our country, however, and I believe this is an indication of the widespread moral laxity we have seen in our country in recent years.

Therefore I urge you to turn to Christ. By a simple prayer

of faith you can invite Him into your heart, and then each day you can learn the joy of walking with Him and seeking to do His will.

I have recently become fascinated with the subject of predicting the future, and have bought several books on fortune-telling. Do you think it is possible for someone to know what the future holds?

Only God knows the future, and you should not allow yourself to get involved in any scheme or teaching which claims to have accurate knowledge of the future. (I am not talking about projections which some social scientists or others might make based on present trends, but about those who claim to have supernatural abilities to predict the future precisely.) At best, such schemes are mere guesswork; at worst, they may be involved in dangerous occult practices. The Bible clearly warns against such things (e.g., Deuteronomy 18:9–13).

Have you asked yourself why you have become interested in this subject? I cannot help but feel you are searching for certainty about the future, and about your own life as well. Use your fascinations to find out what Christ has to say about the future.

The greatest discovery we can ever make in life is not some supposed "truth" about the future, but the joy of peace with God. God loves you, and He wants to come into your life and establish a personal relationship with you if you will but open your heart to Him.

Then learn to trust the future to Christ. We may not know everything God has in store for us, but when we know Christ we know that God is in ultimate control and we need not fear the future. "If God is for us, who can be against us? . . . For I am convinced that neither death nor life, neither angels nor demons, neither the present nor the future . . . will be able to separate us from the love of God that is in Christ Jesus our Lord" (Romans 8:31, 38–39).

I have just been through my sixth surgery in the last year, and all I seem to have ahead of me is more pain and sickness. I have always felt that God was good to us, but now I am beginning to wonder if God really cares. Why must I suffer?

There is no easy answer to the question of suffering and why some people seem to have especially heavy burdens of pain to bear. Some day—in Heaven—we will understand everything fully. "Now we see but a poor reflection; then we shall see face to face. Now I know in part; then I shall know fully, even as I am fully known" (1 Corinthians 13:12).

God cares because He knows what it is like to suffer. God came down on this earth in the person of His Son, Jesus Christ, and He suffered the horror of a cruel death on a cross. His death was even more terrible because He was perfect and did not deserve to die. The Bible says, "He was despised and rejected by men, a man of sorrows, and familiar with suffering" (Isaiah 53:3). His suffering was more intense than anything you and I could ever know, because the sins of the whole world were being placed on Him. He did this willingly, because He loves us and wanted to do everything possible to bring us forgiveness.

God is with you in the midst of your suffering. He has not abandoned you, because "God has said, 'Never will I leave you; never will I forsake you'" (Hebrews 13:5). Do you remember Job in the Old Testament? It seemed that virtually everything that could go wrong did go wrong for him. He lost his children, his possessions, and his health. And yet he knew that God could be trusted even in the midst of his circumstances.

Perhaps God can use you to help someone else who is suffering. Turn your eyes away from your situation, and by faith turn to Christ. Open your heart to Him, and thank Him that He loved you enough to die on the cross for you. Then you will join the countless millions throughout the ages who have discovered that "You will even be able to thank God in the midst of pain and distress because you are privileged to share the lot of those who are living in the light" (Colossians 1:11–12, Phillips Translation).

How can I believe God loves me when He destroyed our entire crop?

When a ship's carpenter needed timber to make a mat for a sailing vessel he did not cut it in the valley, but up on the mountainside where the trees had been buffeted by the winds. These trees, he knew, were the strongest of all. Hardship is not our choice, but if we face it bravely it can toughen the fiber of our souls.

Even if you can't understand why your crop was destroyed you can still trust God. From disaster He can bring victory. A fire sweeps over a hillside, burning the pines like matchsticks; but God has planted spruce seeds there, and in the sunlight they push up, making a new forest. A tornado destroys a community. Then men and women arise to meet the challenge, building a more beautiful city. History has proved that God can build upon the ruins. But He needs the hands of consecrated men and women. Christ did not promise His followers ease or comfort. He said again and again: "Take up the cross and follow me."

This experience could be your steppingstone to finding Christ as your Lord and Savior. That could be why it happened. When I was in Korea following the war there a young GI who had lost both eyes said to me: "I'm glad I came to Korea, because losing my eyesight brought me to Christ!" He had found Christ better than eyesight!

I have been trying to be a Christian, but I'm not having much success. I will do well for a while, then suddenly I will give in to temptation and be right back where I started. Do you have any secret on how I can be a better Christian?

Be clear about what a Christian really is—and then be sure you are one. What is a Christian? Many people think a Christian is a person who lives a moral life and tries to follow the Ten Commandments and the moral teachings of Jesus. Certainly a Christian will want to live like this—but simply trying to live a good life does not make a person a Christian. Instead, the Bible says a Christian is a person who has committed his Life to Jesus Christ, and is trusting Him alone (and not his good deeds) for salvation. Have you realized you are a sinner and cannot save yourself by your own good deeds? Have you realized that Christ died on the cross for you, and He offers you His salvation as a free gift, if you will only receive it? If you have never opened your heart and invited Jesus Christ to come into your life, do so today.

Then be clear on what God has given you to grow spiritually. Just as God has given us food so we can grow physically, so He has given us spiritual "food" so we can be strengthened spiritually. What is that "food"? First, it is the Bible, which is His Word. Are you spending time reading and thinking about His Word? He also has given us prayer, and fellowship with other Christians. Make use of these each day, and He will strengthen you spiritually.

Can God forgive an unwed mother?

Not only can God forgive an unwed mother, He can also forgive an unwed father as well as married and single persons, whether they are parents or not. But His forgiveness does not come cheaply. It cost Him the life of His Son, Jesus Christ. The wonderful news is that God's forgiveness is available to all who ask for it. But you must ask.

God does not forgive everyone automatically. That would devalue the sacrifice of Christ on the cross for your sins and mine. Before asking for God's forgiveness there is something important you must do. You must repent, that is, turn from the behavior and lifestyle which led you to become an unwed mother. Then God will forgive you and give you the strength you need for you and your child to face the future with Him.

I have a brother who has some brain damage because he got involved in some heavy drugs. I know you believe that Jesus Christ came to take away the consequences of sins that we commit. Do you think if he invited Christ into his life that God would take away that damage?

First of all, the Bible does not promise that all of the consequences of sins we have committed in the past will automatically vanish. Sin is a terrible and destructive thing, and sometimes we have to pay the consequences for our foolishness and our refusal to obey God. King David in the Bible sinned greatly when he committed adultery with another man's wife. God forgave him when he truly repented and asked God for forgiveness—but the child born of that illicit union still died as an act of God's judgment on David.

I therefore do not want to hold out a false hope to your brother, promising that if he invites Christ into his life all of the results of his drug habit will definitely vanish. At the same time, I know that God "is able to do immeasurably more than all we ask or imagine, according to his power" (Ephesians 3:20). There are times when God works in ways that are beyond our human understanding to bring healing and restoration, although none of us can predict when this will be the case. This much is certain: your brother needs Christ.

Your brother needs forgiveness for what he has done, and he needs strength that Christ can give him every day. He needs hope for the future. God has graciously spared him, and God can use him if he opens his life to Christ.

Encourage your brother to come to Christ. It is the most important decision any of us will ever make. What has happened to your brother is tragic, but God wants to help him and make him His child through faith in Christ.

I know God is mad at me because of the way I have been living. How can I get Him back on my side? My life is on a deadend road unless I change, I know, but how can I win God's approval when I have so many bad things against me?

Suppose you owed someone a very large sum of money. What could you do? One possibility would be to pay them back. But what if you did not have the money, and had no prospect of ever getting it? Then your only possibilities would be to undergo bankruptcy and suffer the loss of everything you had, or else to go to him and ask to have the debt forgiven. But in human experience that kind of forgiveness is very rare.

But that is what God offers you—free and full forgiveness for your sins! You see, you cannot "buy" God's favor, nor can you somehow do enough good deeds to balance off your bad deeds. Why? Because God is holy, and even one sin is an offense to Him. "Your eyes are too pure to look on evil; you cannot tolerate wrong" (Habakkuk 1:13). No, the only hope is if God will forgive you. But is that possible? Yes! It is possible because Jesus Christ, the righteous Son of God, took upon Himself the punishment you and I deserved for our sins. "God made him who had no sin to be sin for us, so that in him we might become the righteousness of God" (2 Corinthians 5:21).

Don't turn your back on God's forgiveness any longer. Instead, realize that your only hope is in Christ and open your heart to Him by faith. "For the wages of sin is death, but the gift of God is eternal life in Christ Jesus our Lord" (Romans 6:23). How can you receive Christ? Simply tell Him that you know you are a sinner, and you need His forgiveness. Then turn from your old way of living and with God's help begin to follow Christ every day.

God is on your side. God is not mad at you, but at your sin. You don't need to win God's approval. Christ did that on the cross.

I am the mother of one illegitimate child and am expecting the second one. Recently I was converted to Christ. When can I begin the new life and how can I leave the old life behind with two children born in sin?

When a group of Pharisees brought a woman to Jesus who had been taken in the act of adultery, Jesus asked them to cast a stone at her, whoever was without sin (John 8:1–11 KJV). When it appeared that there was no sinless one to cast the first stone, they departed. Then Jesus said to the woman, "Neither do I condemn thee: go and sin no more." Repentance and faith are genuine and valid when the sinner enters a new way of life. There may be the reminders of the past with you, but you can have this assurance that there is no sin that cannot be forgiven to those who desire the new life that comes about through our faith in Jesus Christ. Begin by being the best mother you know how to be, praying for your children and bringing them up in the knowledge of Christ. The time will come when they will recognize the transformation wrought in your life.

Would it be wrong for me to pray that God would take my life? I am tired of living, because no one cares for me, including God. My ex-husband abused me mentally and physically for years, and I feel worthless and useless. I yearn to be happy, but I know now it will never happen.

Yes, it would be wrong for you to ask God to take your life—because He wants to help you discover there can be happiness and joy in life for you, if you will turn to Him.

You have been painfully scarred emotionally by your past, and God knows that and understands your feelings. Those experiences have taught you to believe that you are worthless and no one cares—but they have not told you the truth! In spite of what has happened to you, God loves you and you are very important in His eyes. Although elsewhere in your letter you indicate you have never given much thought to God, you have never been far from His thoughts, and He has a plan for your life. God says in His Word, "'For I know the plans I have for you,' declares the Lord, 'plans to prosper you and not to harm you, plans to give you hope and a future. Then you will call upon me and come and pray to me, and I will listen to you. You will seek me and find me when you seek me with all your heart'" (Jeremiah 29:11–13).

By faith accept God's love by inviting Jesus Christ to come into your life. You can do this by a simple prayer, telling God you know you need Him and that you want to turn your life over to Him. You might also consider getting into a support group for abused women. Then take time each day to read the Bible to discover how much God loves you. "This is love: not that we loved God, but that he loved us and sent his Son as an atoning sacrifice for our sins" (1 John 4:10). Knowing God cares will make all the difference.

I feel so lonely that sometimes I just want to end it all. I yearn to have close friends—I am in high school—but it is impossible. You see, my parents are divorced and my mother is an alcoholic, and friends would just laugh at me if I took them home. Would God forgive me if I just ended my life?

My heart goes out to you, and I know you have been carrying a heavy burden. However, I urge you as strongly as possible not to be tempted by the thought of suicide. There are people who care for you and want to help you, and your situation—although it is not easy—is not impossible. With God's help you cannot only come through this but you can become a strong and joyful person.

God understands your situation, and He understands your feelings as well. Perhaps the most important thing I can tell you is that God loves you, and He wants to come into your heart and help you. The Bible promises, "Cast your cares on the Lord and he will sustain you; he will never let the righteous fall" (Psalm 55:22). You see, Jesus Christ came into this world to take away our sins and to restore us to God. As we commit our lives to Him, God accepts us and adopts us into His family, and He becomes our daily companion and friend. Ask Christ to come into your life today by a simple prayer of faith.

Then I would encourage you to step out and make friends. Find a church which has an active program for young people; there may also be a Christian group like Campus Life or Young Life in your school. There you will not only meet people who will be genuine friends, but you will find spiritual encouragement. Share your burden also with an adult, such as a church youth leader. With Christ there is hope for the future.

I am old and virtually alone now. I have a number of relatives, but they don't pay any attention to me because we never got along. Pray for me, because I am unhappy and the future is not very hopeful either.

Loneliness is certainly one of the most common and serious problems in our society, and yet God made us with the plan that we would find happiness in our relationships. Yes, I will pray for you, and I encourage you to be praying also for yourself.

One thing you should be praying for is wisdom about ways you can overcome your loneliness. For example, your letter does not say why you never got along with your family.

Can you honestly say it was all their fault? Or did you contribute to these problems by stubbornly insisting on your own way when you should have been more willing to adjust to others? Has an unforgiving spirit on your part kept those splits alive? Pray that God will help you face those questions honestly, and then deal with them by seeking His forgiveness and the forgiveness of any you have hurt across the years. Even if your forgiveness does not heal the split, you still need to get rid of any bitterness or resentment you have in your heart. "Be kind and compassionate to one another, forgiving each other, just as in Christ God forgave you" (Ephesians 4:32).

Then do what you can to reach out to others around you. Don't let self-pity paralyze you, but realize there are probably people all around you who are also lonely and yearn for someone who will be a friend to them and care for them. Most of all, realize that Christ is with you if you have committed your life to Him, and you are never alone or without hope when you know Christ.

I believe I am a Christian, but I always seem to be faced with strong temptation. Is there any way to overcome such temptation?

God never promised to remove temptation from us, for even Christ was subject to it. The Bible says that He was tempted in all points like we are, yet without sin (Hebrews 4:15). There is really no good reason why you should seek to escape, for such times of testing have beneficial effects: "Tribulation worketh patience; and patience experience; and experience hope; and hope maketh not ashamed . . . ." There is a sense of achievement and assurance that results from victory over temptation that cannot come to us otherwise. Temptation really shows others what kind of people we are. It does not make us Christian or un-Christian. It does make the Christian stronger and cause him to discover resources of power. It also makes evident the false profession and hypocrisy of the non-Christian. You can benefit from what might be tragedy if you will only discover that in just such a time of temptation, Christ can become more real to you than ever, and His salvation will become more meaningful.

l thought I was off drugs but I'm not. I went through a rehabilitation program, but two weeks after my release I am back in the same old habits. I think I could have made it if I hadn't gone back to my old friends, who have dragged me down. Please warn people about this, because I know my habits are going to destroy me.

One reason I have reprinted your letter is that it might serve as a warning to someone who is facing a similar situation. Peer pressure—the pressure from one's "friends" to act the way they want you to act—can be very strong and harmful. The Bible warns, "Do not set foot on the patn of the wicked or walk in the way ot evil men. Avoid it, do not travel on it; turn from it and go on your way. For they cannot sleep till they do evil; they are robbed of slumber till they make someone fall" (Proverbs 4:14–16).

But don't give up or assume there is no hope for you. Yes, you have fallen—but with God's help you can get back on the right path and get free of the drugs and other habits that threaten to destroy you I do not promise that it will be easy, but God wants to help you and He will if you will let Him.

What must you do? First, admit that you cannot lick this problem by yourself, and ask Christ to come into your life to help you. God loves you, and Christ died on the cross to take away your sins. He also rose from the dead and sends His Holy Spirit to live within us so we can receive His power. Then make a clear and definite break with the past, including your "friends" who are dragging you down. Seek a fellowship of Christians where you can find new friends who will encourage you and help you spiritually. Some of them, you may find, have been through the same struggles you are facing.

I am facing surgery next week and I am scared to death. The doctor suspects there might be cancer. I have hardly been sick a day in my life, but suddenly I am faced with the possibility of losing my health. Can you give me any words of encouragement?

Death is something every one of us must face sooner or later. It is frightening.

Have you ever thanked God for the years of good health He has given you? Perhaps you have taken good health for granted, but it has been a gift from God. Perhaps you have even taken God for granted, or thought very little about Him and the place He should have in your life. But just as He has been with you in the past, so He is with you now as you face this situation.

Let this be a time, therefore, when you discover God's love and nearness. Let this also be a time when you realize—perhaps for the first time—that life for every one of us is short, and the most important thing you can do is to prepare for eternity. The Bible reminds us, "There is a time for everything, and a season for every activity under heaven: a time to be born and a time to die . . . God does it, so men will revere him" (Ecclesiastes 3:1–2, 14). The Bible also promises, "Because of the Lord's great love we are not consumed, for his compassions never fail. They are new every morning; great is your faithfulness" (Lamentations 3:22–23).

Give your life to Jesus Christ. He died on the cross for you, and He offers you forgiveness and eternal life if you will trust Him as your personal Lord and Savior. No, you do not know what the immediate future holds (nor do any of us, no matter how healthy we seem to be). But when you have committed your life to Christ, you know He is with you every moment of the day. Don't let another day go by without turning your life over to Him.

I don't have any problem feeling close to God when things are going smoothly in my life, but when things get rough then God seems far away. Is this a common problem?

Yes, it is a common problem—in fact I am sure almost every believer has experienced it. But God does not change just because circumstances change, and we need to learn to trust Him in every situation.

Do you remember the incident of Jesus' life when He had stayed behind to pray while His disciples went on in a boat across the Sea of Galilee? During their journey a storm arose and they were very afraid. Suddenly Jesus came to them, miraculously walking on the water toward their boat. Then we read

that Peter, in a burst of faith and in obedience to Jesus' command, "got down out of the boat and walked on the water to
Jesus. But when he saw the wind, he was afraid and, beginning
to sink, cried out, 'Lord, save me!'" (Matthew 13:29–30). Peter
was all right as long as he kept his eyes on Christ, but when he
turned away and concentrated on the storm then he was in
trouble.

We are often like Peter. As long as things are smooth in life
we have no trouble, but when the storms come we take our eyes
off God and become filled with doubts and fears. But notice
that Peter knew what to do when he had failed—he turned
back to Christ and began to trust Him again.

You need Christ every day, and in every circumstance.
And He can be trusted no matter what happens. He is God, and
He knows what is best for us in every situation. Like a child
who turns to his father when he is afraid, so we need to turn to
Christ when we have times of need.

God can be trusted—and that is the basic issue. If you can
trust Christ for your eternal salvation, can't you also trust Him
in the midst of life's problems? Of course you can! "If God is for
us, who can be against us? He who did not spare his own Son,
but gave him up for us all—how will he not also, along with
him, graciously give us all things?" (Romans 8:31–32). Trust
God and the promise of His Word, because He is worthy of
your trust.

*I just feel like I am a total failure. My husband has left me (and my
three children) for another woman. I just don't feel like there is anything left for me and sometimes I even think I ought to end it all.*

I know you feel that there is little hope for the future, but this is
not true. Don't let your emotions mislead you into doing something that would be so final. Certainly if you were to decide to
"end it all" you would have chosen the wrong path, and my
prayer is that you will find in God the strength you need to
bring you through this experience. Think of your children! How
tragic it would be for them to have neither a father nor a mother.

It is important for you to be honest in dealing with your
feelings of failure. You feel rejected right now, and you feel that

somehow there must have been something wrong with you to
have caused your husband to abandon you. But your husband is
the one who has to bear responsibility for what he has done,
and that has nothing to do with your value. I know that you
may be thinking of things you wish you could have done differently during your marriage. Learn from those experiences—but
don't believe that they make you worthless. God says you are
valuable. You are valuable to your children, and you are valuable to God. God loves you, and the proof of your value to Him
is that He was willing to send His only Son into the world to
die on the cross for you.

Then you need to begin to look to the future and not concentrate on the past. I know that may not be easy, and you may
even shrink from it because you feel the future is bleak. But
listen! You are not alone as you face the future—God is with
you. God has a plan for your life, and the greatest thing you
can do is discover His plan and commit yourself to Christ. The
Bible says, "You have made known to me the path of life; you
will fill me with joy in your presence, with eternal pleasures
at your right hand" (Psalm 16:11). Begin afresh by committing
your life to Christ and He will help your life each day with the
joy of His presence.

*I wish I had time and space to tell you all the harm that has been
done in my family because of one relative who seems to spend her
time gossiping about other family members—and usually without
knowing the full facts. Does the Bible condemn gossiping?*

Yes, the Bible has some strong things to say against gossiping.
The Old Testament commands, "Do not go about spreading
slander among your people" (Leviticus 19:16). Among the sinful
actions condemned in the New Testament are hatred, discord,
dissensions, and factions (Galatians 5:19–20)—all of which are
a result of malicious gossip. Those who seek to follow Christ are
commanded instead to "rid yourselves of all malice and all de-
ceit, hypocrisy, envy, and slander of every kind" (1 Peter 2:1).
Among the seven sins which are said to be "detestable" to God
are "a lying tongue . . . a false witness who pours out lies

and a man who stirs up dissension among brothers" (Proverbs 6:16–19).

Gossiping is certainly one of the most common sins—so common, in fact, that most people do not take it as seriously as they should and instead tolerate it in their lives. But you have put your finger on one of the reasons gossiping is wrong: it destroys relationships between people. "Consider what a great forest is set on fire by a small spark. The tongue also is a fire, a world of evil among the parts of the body. It corrupts the whole person, sets the whole course of his life on fire, and is itself set on fire by hell" (James 3:5–6).

The practical problem you face, however, is how to deal with this relative of yours. Pray for her. This is a spiritual problem most of all, and she needs to yield her whole life—including her tongue and her thoughts—to Jesus Christ as Lord. Then pray that God will give you both wisdom and an opportunity to confront her—lovingly but firmly—with the facts about her gossiping and the damage she is doing. She may not even be aware of how serious a matter this really is. This will not be easy, but in the long run it is far better to do this than allow her to continue to destroy the reputation of others. You may actually find that she will appreciate your honesty and your concern for her, and will—with God's help—come to grips with this problem.

Many years ago I did a very foolish thing. I left my first husband and married another man who was much older than I. I hurt an awful lot of people, and now that I am elderly I am very, very lonely, with no one who really cares about me. I wish you would warn young people about the cost of doing foolish things like this.

I am sorry that you have had to learn through experience that when you break God's laws you end up instead being broken by them. You are—as you know—paying the bitter price for your foolishness and disobedience. My prayer is that your testimony will perhaps touch someone who right now is being tempted to take a similar path. As the Bible says, "Sin pays its servants: the wage is death" (Romans 6:23, Phillips Translation). There is a terrible price to be paid for following the temptations of Satan, both in this life and in eternity.

But I want to say something else very important to you. It is not possible to go back and change the past; what is done is done. But has it ever occurred to you that God still loves you, in spite of what you have done? You may feel that God is just like all the people you have hurt, and that He really could not care for you or love you because of what you have done. But that is not true! You have committed many sins—but every one of those sins was placed on the back of Jesus when He died on the cross. He endured the loneliness of the cross so that you could be forgiven of your sins and reconciled to God. Wouldn't it be wonderful to be able to look yourself in the mirror each day and know that you are completely forgiven, and you are a child of God? Wouldn't it be wonderful as you approach the end of your life, to know that you have the hope of eternal life in Heaven because of what Jesus Christ has done for you?

It is not too late to open your heart to Jesus Christ, and my prayer is that you will make that commitment today. Christ died for sinners—including you. Accept Jesus' invitation: "Come to me, all you who are weary and burdened, and . . . you will find rest for your souls" (Matthew 11:28–29).

I have a friend who used to be very active in church, but now she has turned her back on that and says she doesn't believe in anything. She is a very miserable person and I would like to help her, but she gets very agitated whenever I begin to bring up the subject. How can I help her?

I firmly believe that your friend knows in her heart what she has done and she is trying with all her might to flee from God. But she cannot flee from Him. The Bible says, "Whither shall I go from thy spirit? or whither shall I flee from thy presence? If I ascend up into heaven, thou art there: if I make my bed in hell, behold, thou art there" (Psalm 139:7–8 KJV).

Furthermore, I am encouraged by the fact that she is miserable—because that shows she is under conviction by God and is sensitive to Him, even though she is trying to flee from Him. The person who is in the most serious spiritual condition is the person who has become totally insensitive to God and can no longer hear the voice of God calling him back to repentance and faith.

You can help your friend first of all by praying for her. She needs to realize in a new way that God loves her, and although she has sinned by deliberately turning her back on God, He wants to forgive her and welcome her into His family. You should also pray that God will help you talk with her in a loving and gentle way that does not make her defensive or angry. She needs to know that you really care for her, and that you want to help her. She needs to sense in your life something of the peace and joy that Christ gives to those who follow Him.

I cannot help but feel that your friend also may have substituted religious activity—like going to church—for a sincere and genuine personal commitment to Jesus Christ. Without a personal commitment to Christ, being active in church can become empty and meaningless. Your personal example of faith and trust in Christ may be the most important way you can help your friend turn to God.

9 I Feel So Empty Inside

I don't understand myself. I have everything I ever thought I wanted, but down inside I am just existing. I am bored with life and feel empty inside. What is wrong with me? How do I get out of this feeling?

We not only have a body and a mind but we have a spiritual side to us as well, because God created us with a soul. Most people spend their lives feeding their bodies and their minds—and yet starve their souls. When they do, their lives are incomplete and empty, no matter how prosperous they may be outwardly.

But what does your soul yearn for? It yearns for God—and only God can satisfy that inner longing. You see, God created us originally so we could have a personal relationship with Him. But when we leave Him out of our lives, there is a blank space in our hearts that will not go away, because only He can fill it. As St. Augustine said centuries ago, "You have made us for Yourself, O God, and our hearts are restless until they find their rest in You."

Not only do we need God, but God actually wants us to come to know Him. He wants to enter our lives and fill them, and He wants us to know the joy of His presence. That is why Christ came into the world. "For Christ died for sins once for all, the righteous for the unrighteous, to bring you to God" (1 Peter 3:18).

What must you do? First, turn to God and confess your sins to Him—including your sin of leaving Him out of your life. Then ask Christ to come into your heart by faith. He has promised, "I

142

stand at the door (of your heart) and knock. If anyone hears my voice and opens the door, I will go in and eat with him, and he with me" (Revelation 3:20). You can know God's presence right now if you will open your heart to Christ.

Last year I was going through a painful divorce. This man in my office was going through the same experience, and naturally we were drawn to each other. Well, one thing led to another and he asked me to move in with him, promising we would get married when the divorces were finalized. But now he only laughs at the idea of getting married, saying he isn't ready. Now I realize I made a mistake, but I don't know how to get out of it. I don't know where to turn.

We live at a time when divorce no longer has the social stigma it once had. It used to be that no one could be elected president if he had been divorced. That is no longer true. Regardless of what our society thinks of divorce, God's opinion has not changed. God says He "hates" divorce.

It is understandable that you would be lonely and wish to reach out to someone else for comfort and assurance that you are a valuable person. But just as it was not God's intention for you or this other man to be divorced, you should also realize that your decision to live with him merely compounded an already serious situation. This man's lack of commitment to his wife has led him to think that he need not be committed to anyone. In your own pain you are now finding that the happiness you sought has eluded you. It is because you have been searching for it in the wrong place.

The Bible is very clear about how we should live. It says "Flee from sexual immorality" (1 Corinthians 6:18). But God does not want you to keep on living this way, without any secure foundation in life. He loves you and He wants you to get on the right road in life—which is His way of living. The Bible warns, "There is a way that seems right to a man, but in the end it leads to death" (Proverbs 14:12).

Now is the time for you to face your need of Christ and turn to Him for forgiveness and new life. By faith ask Him to come into your life as your Lord and Savior. Then with His help turn from sin—including this relationship. It may not be easy, but God will bless you if you will put Him first.

How do you deal with a person who says their church is the only one which is right, and if you do not belong to it you cannot get to Heaven? I have a friend at work like this, and it has made things difficult because she is constantly trying to get others to come to her church (although it is a small group that I think may even be a cult).

The Bible teaches there is only one thing that saves us and gives us eternal life, and that is our relationship to Jesus Christ. We are not saved by our church membership (important as that is to our spiritual growth), nor are we saved by our own good deeds or religious actions. Only Christ can save us, as we turn to Him in faith and trust Him as our Lord and Savior. The Bible says, "Salvation is found in no one else, for there is no other name under heaven given to men by which we must be saved" (Acts 4:12).

Pray for your friend. Down inside she has a deep insecurity and a spiritual hunger for God—a hunger that cannot be satisfied in a lasting way by church activity alone. Then ask God to give you opportunities to talk with her about Christ and encourage her to read the New Testament on her own. (Many cults claim to believe the Bible, but in fact they distort its clear message and discourage people from reading it on their own.)

Most important, be sure of your own relationship with Christ. Are you trusting Him for your salvation, and have you committed your life (and your eternal salvation) into His hands? If you are unsure of your own relationship to God, turn to Christ in faith and trust without delay. "For God so loved the world that he gave his one and only Son, that whoever believes in him shall not perish but have eternal life" (John 3:16).

Is there any difference between pride in one's accomplishments and personal pride, such as one's appearance? According to the Bible it seems to be sin; but without pride there seems to be no reason for careful grooming, good housekeeping, etc.

Nowhere in the Bible do I read that God puts a premium on slovenliness. However, the Bible places the emphasis on spiritual slovenliness, rather than physical. It is possible for a person to be impeccable in his attire and person, and yet be slovenly in his morals and conduct. On the other hand, a person of modest means may not be put on the "best-dressed" list but his or her character can be irreproachable. God says, ". . . man looketh on the outward appearance, but the Lord looketh on the heart" (1 Samuel 16:7 KJV). But at the same time, I believe that a neat, clean, well-groomed Christian is more impressive than a slovenly one. It would be poor policy to keep the inside of our houses immaculately clean, but let tin cans and garbage accumulate in the yard. By the same token, if Christ has cleansed our hearts, the least that we can do is to keep our bodies, which are the temples of the Spirit, clean, neat, and presentable.

I do want to do right but sometimes I am too weak to overcome temptation. What hope is there for me?

You are exactly where all of the rest of us are. None of us is strong enough to overcome temptations, regardless of how good our motives may be. That is the reason God sent His Son into the World—to take away the guilt and penalty of our sins and to give us the strength to overcome temptation. May I suggest that your trouble is probably too much looking inside at self and not enough looking outward and upward to Christ who wants to help you? The Bible says: "There hath no temptation taken you but such as is common to man; but God is faithful, who will not suffer you to be tempted above that ye are able; but will with the temptation also make a way of escape, that ye may be able to bear it" (1 Corinthians 10:13 KJV). When temptations come let me suggest that you ask God for strength and also to show you the way He has prepared for your escape.

One other word of counsel: be very sure that you do not deliberately place yourself in a position to be tempted. All of us are not subjected to the same weaknesses and temptations. To one, alcohol may be the temptation; to another it may be impure thoughts and acts; to another greed and covetousness; to another criticism and an unloving attitude. Regardless of what it may be, be sure that Satan will tempt you at your weak point, not the strong. Our Lord has given us an example of how to overcome the devil's temptations. When He was tempted in the wilderness He defeated Satan every time by the use of Scripture. The psalmist tells us how to do this when he says: "Thy word have I hid in mine heart, that I might not sin against thee" (Psalm 119:11 KJV).

A few months ago I think I became a Christian. I'm not really sure though, because the decision didn't solve any of my problems. In fact, I have had more trouble since then. Isn't Christianity supposed to solve problems for you?

The Bible does not promise that God will get us out of trouble or solve all of our problems. What it does promise is that God will give us the power to overcome our problems and will sustain us in our troubles. In 2 Corinthians 12:9 God says to Paul, "My grace is sufficient for thee, for my strength is made perfect in weakness."

Faith in Jesus Christ solves the problem of sin. This is really man's greatest problem, and from sin come all the other problems. Salvation is not like aspirin, dulling the nerves to feeling. Salvation goes to the root of the problem and makes a new person out of you. "God made him who had no sin to be sin for us so that in him we might become the righteousness of God" (2 Corinthians 5:21).

I'm crippled with arthritis and I'm useless. What's the good of living?

Christ died for you—that makes you worth a great deal. God doesn't think you're useless. He needs all kinds of people to do His work. He needs the quick and the slow. He needs the strong and the weak. I know a boy without any arms who paints with his toes. The lad's courage has inspired many to forget their handicaps. If you are cheerful and patient when in pain, you are witnessing for Christ.

A retired minister spends three hours each day writing friendly notes to those in trouble. His message brings courage and comfort to thousands every year.

God has something special for you to do. Ask Him to show you how you can serve Him, and He will.

We can't understand why illness comes, but when we suffer we must still trust our Heavenly Father. Then we have more time for prayer than ever before. Pray for others as well as yourself. Pray for those in positions of authority. Pray for peace and justice. Even when lying flat on your back, you can pray. This is one way you can now labor for Christ and His kingdom.

I was involved in a religious cult until a few months ago. I have broken free of it but now I am still confused about God. I would like to know God personally, but I don't know where to look.

The Bible promises you, "Ask and it will be given you; seek and you will find; knock and the door will be opened to you. For everyone who asks receives; he who seeks finds; and to him who knocks, the door will be opened" (Matthew 7:7–8). The One who spoke those words was Jesus Christ, and He wants you to discover the truth. Where can you find God? You can find God in only one way and that is through Jesus Christ. He is the One to whom you must look. Why is this true? Because Jesus Christ is God Himself. He came down on this earth in human form so we could know what God is like. And He showed us that God loves us, because He went to the cross and died for our sins. He proved that He was God's only Son who is worthy of our worship and our lives, because He rose again from the dead.

Jesus declared, "I am the way and the truth and the life. No one comes to the Father except through me" (John 14:6). That is a staggering claim—but millions of Christians throughout the ages have discovered it to be true. God "wants all men to be saved and to come to a knowledge of the truth. For there is one God and one mediator between God and men, the man Christ Jesus, who gave himself as a ransom for all men" (1 Timothy 2:4–6).

The rising number of religious cults (which claim to have the truth about God but actually do not and enslave a person in their doctrines) is one of the most alarming signs of our time. They and their leaders remind me of those about whom Paul warned Timothy: "They are the kind who worm their way into homes—never able to acknowledge the truth . . . men of depraved minds, who, as far as the faith is concerned, are rejected" (2 Timothy 3:6–8). I am thankful you have broken free of this group, because you would not find God and His will for your life through its teachings.

Yes, you can know God personally by turning to Christ and accepting Him in faith as your Lord and Savior. Then get into the Word of God, the Bible, and get help from other Christians so you can grow spiritually.

Our oldest son was killed in an automobile accident just a few months before graduating from college. It all seems so senseless, and frankly it has even shaken my faith in God. Can you help me understand this?

Whenever I receive a letter like yours I always wish I had an easy explanation I could give that would cover all situations and answer all questions. But we do not always understand completely why things happen to us that are seemingly so senseless or evil. The Bible talks about "the mystery of iniquity" (2 Thessalonians 2:7 KJV), suggesting that there is indeed a mystery to some of the things that happen to us.

At the same time, we need to remember that we live in a world badly stained and twisted by sin. The world was not this way when God created it; instead, "God saw all that he had made, and it was very good" (Genesis 1:31). But then sin entered the world when the human race turned its back on God and chose instead to go its own way. And although we cannot fully understand it now, that rebellion has had terrible consequences for the human race, bringing heartache and death in its wake.

The loss of a child is very painful and God allows us a grieving process so we can withstand that pain. He knows your pain and your hurt and anger.

As you consider this, I also want to remind you of something else very important. You are deeply hurt, but I want to assure you that God knows exactly how you feel. How do I know this? I know it because God's only Son, Jesus Christ, also died. He suffered and died on a cross, so you and I could be reconciled to God. God understands your heartache—and He wants to surround you with His love if you will let Him.

There is a verse in the Bible that says "Whatsoever is born of God doth not commit sin." I used to think of myself as a Christian, but I know that I have sinned. Does that mean that I am not a child of God?

You are probably referring to the Scripture found in 1 John 3:9. Many people are confused by the verse. What it actually means is that whatsoever is begotten of God does not sin as a way of life or he does not continually practice sin.

Don't let your failures or your weaknesses discourage you. If in your heart you desire to live in fellowship with God, and if you have confessed Christ as your Savior, you have the assurance that His blood does cleanse from all sin. I like the way The Living Bible cites this verse: "The person who has been born into God's family does not make a practice of sinning, because now God's life is in him; so he can't keep on sinning, for this new life has been born into him and controls him—he has been born again."

I have been a Christian for several years. Although I still love Jesus and feel sure that I am His child, I know I am not making any definite progress. I seem always to be treading water or marking time. Is there any simple answer to this problem that you can give?

No complete answer to so complicated a problem can be given, but I can offer some specific suggestions.

1. Never forget that the real source of all spiritual growth and progress is the Bible. Unless you systematically study the Bible, you cannot hope to make any true progress.

2. Prayer is important. It is a vital part of your life with God. Prayer is your true desire, expressed or hidden. If you desire what is promised in the Bible, then there is communication with God.

3. Obedience is the key to Bible knowledge. You don't read the Bible to satisfy curiosity but to find the practical answer to a real problem, and when you find the answer, you act decisively upon it.

4. Praise is essential. For every known blessing, give praise to God both privately and when fitting, publicly. Praise is the action that puts you before others as an example. Do not avoid this public display of your love for God.

If one is a Christian and God directs and allows everything that happens to you, what takes place between God and you when you sin?

I believe your question can best be answered by a rather simple illustration. I ask you this question: What happens to the father-son relationship in everyday life when the son does something that is displeasing to the father?

The Bible does not tell us that we are going to live free from sin as long as we are in this body. The Bible says: "If we claim to be without sin, we deceive ourselves and the truth is not in us" (1 John 1:8).

Actually what will happen is that there is a rupture that takes place in our fellowship, and this fellowship is not completely restored until confession of that sin is made. In other words, we may still be sons of God without enjoying the fellowship that sons rightfully should have. There are thousands of Christians who do not have the joy and peace that fellowship with God brings. There is no joy or ecstasy quite like that of daily fellowship with God. Try it!

I am a very old man and have lived a wicked life. I would like to turn to God now but am afraid He won't accept me at this late hour. Besides, I am no longer able to do anything to merit His favor. Can you help me?

Don't you know that the desire to know the Lord indicates the Spirit of God is now speaking to you? If He were not, you would not have this desire. Your age is not the most important consideration in this matter so long as there is the desire. I recently heard of a 94-year-old lady who came to Christ.

Jesus once gave a parable to show that it makes no difference providing you respond to the invitation when it is given. That parable is found in Matthew 20:1–16 and ends with the familiar verse: "So the last will be first, and the first will be last."

There is a good reason why this is so. Salvation does not depend on your personal merit but on the merit of Jesus Christ. In a lifetime we could not store up sufficient merit to enter heaven. Concerning this Paul once wrote: "Where, then, is the boasting? It is excluded. On what principle? On that of observing the law? No: but on that of faith" (Romans 3:27). I encourage you, then, to respond to the urge to trust Christ, for He is able to save all who come unto God by Him.

I don't agree with you when you make such general statements about everybody being a sinner. There are many wonderful people in the world who certainly aren't that bad.

The Bible says so: "All have sinned and fall short of the glory of God" (Romans 3:23). If there were no other reason, that in itself would be sufficient. But there is a second reason also. Human nature is best explained when you accept this view. The wonderful and good people you mention are without a doubt as good as you say when judged by human standards. It is when we make the comparison with the holiness of God that we realize the truth of this statement. Any person who is not fully as good as Jesus Christ is a sinner. He alone is the world's only example of One who was without sin. Other people, even the good and wonderful ones you may have in mind, have their weak moments when they fall below their own faulty standards. That is why we all need a sinless Savior. Of Jesus, the Bible says: "God made him who had no sin to be sin for us, so that in him we might become the righteousness of God" (2 Corinthians 5:21).

I was reared in a Christian home where the Bible was clearly taught and believed. Since I have grown up I have seen older people converted and how they rejoiced. I have never had this kind of feeling. Is it because I have been taught about Jesus and "good" all my life?

There are perhaps two reasons why you have never experienced this "joy" you have observed in other people.

First, if you accepted Christ in early life, the transition from innocent childhood to a believing Christian was not nearly so noticeable as it is in a mature person whose conscience has been weighed down with years of accumulated guilt. To illustrate: let us say that a farmer and his son were walking home from the cornfield. The boy carries a few ears in his hands, but the father bends beneath the weight of a hundred-pound sack of corn. Now suppose a friend comes down the road with a wagon and offers to carry father and son home. He carries the load of each, but it is obvious that the father would be the more relieved and grateful of the two. The child coming to Christ, because his burden of sin is light, may not experience the overwhelming joy of the confirmed sinner who finds relief from his guilt through Christ. His load was greater—thus his joy is greater.

The other reason could well be that you have trusted in your good upbringing rather than in the person of Christ. Only you can decide which applies to your case.

How can a person know for sure if he is a Christian?

The Bible suggests ways in which we can have the assurance of our salvation.

We know because of a change that takes place. The Bible says: "Therefore if anyone is in Christ, he is a new creation; the old has gone, the new has come" (2 Corinthians 5:17).

We know by the presence of God's Spirit in our lives. "Hereby know we that we dwell in him, and he in us, because he hath given us of his Spirit" (1 John 4:13 KJV).

We know we are Christians if love is the dominating force in our lives. "Beloved, let us love one another: for love is of God; and every one that loveth is born of God, and knoweth God . . . for God is love" (1 John 4:7, 8 KJV).

We know we are Christians when we find it in our hearts to obey God. "And hereby we do know that we know him, if we keep his commandments" (1 John 2:3 KJV).

And last but not least, we know because we receive Christ. "As many as received him, to them gave he power to become the sons of God, even to them that believe on his name" (John 1:12 KJV).

I hear people talking about inner peace, and that is certainly what I wish I could have. I even go to church sometimes but I still feel like I am missing something. Is it really possible to have peace in our hearts?

Yes, it is possible to have peace in our hearts. Christ promised His disciples, "Peace I leave with you; my peace I give you. I do not give to you as the world gives. Do not let your hearts be troubled and do not be afraid" (John 14:27).

How does Christ's peace come to our hearts? Notice that Jesus did *not* say that He will necessarily give us peace by taking away all our problems and difficulties; in fact, He spoke those words to His disciples just a few hours before He was to be arrested and put to death on the cross. Instead, Christ can give us peace even in the midst of the storms of life. Let me suggest three kinds of peace that Christ gives to us when we open our hearts to Him and trust Him.

First, there is the peace of forgiveness. We have sinned against God, and although we may try to hide it, we feel guilty and know we deserve only God's judgment. But Christ came to give us peace with God. "Therefore, since we have been justified through faith, we have peace with God through our Lord Jesus Christ" (Romans 5:1).

Second, there is the peace of Christ's presence. When we come to Christ, God the Holy Spirit takes up residence in our lives. Think of it! God Himself comes to dwell within us. Even when we do not feel His presence He is still there, and by faith we can be certain of that fact. Jesus promised, "Surely I will be with you always, to the very end of the age" (Matthew 28:20).

Third, there is the peace of God's strength. We can't live as we should—but God will help us when we turn to Him for strength. The apostle Paul knew Christ's strength, as have Christians throughout the ages: "I can do everything through him who gives me strength" (Philippians 4:13).

How can you know God's peace? By opening your life to Christ by faith and yielding your life to Him as Savior and Lord. As you take that step and learn to trust His Word, the Bible, every day, you will know the joy of His peace.

Outwardly I suppose I am a good person, but I would die of embarrassment if anyone could read my thoughts. I admit I have bad thoughts about other people—anger and things like that. I don't like this but I can't seem to control them. Do you have any answer for this? Or is everyone like this down inside?

I suspect we all have felt like you do from time to time—and with good reason, because our thoughts are the most reliable indication of what we are really like. And when we face our thoughts and our motives honestly, we have to admit we are not as good as we would like other people to believe.

One of the greatest truths of the Bible is that God wants to change us—not only our outward actions, but our innermost thoughts. One reason is this: He knows that when we do wrong it is because we have first allowed evil thoughts to control us. Jesus said, "For out of the overflow of the heart the mouth speaks. The good man brings things out of the good stored up in him, and the evil man brings evil things out of the evil stored up in him" (Matthew 12:34–35). And God can change us—both outside and inside—if we turn our lives over to Christ and allow Him to work in our hearts.

Begin by giving your life to Jesus Christ and asking Him to come into your heart and mind. Then learn each day to walk with Him and allow Him to fill your life. Have you ever seen a bucket filled with stagnant, smelly water? The only solution is to empty it and clean it—and then fill it with fresh water. That is what Christ will do if we commit our lives to Him and let His Word, the Bible, fill our hearts. "Do not conform any longer to the pattern of this world, but be transformed by the renewing of your mind" (Romans 12:2).

How can I feel close to God? I have a friend who is constantly talking about how real God is to her, and I wish that was true for me, but it isn't. Is there a secret to knowing God, or is it just something you have to hope will happen to you?

Have you ever thought about the way a friendship develops between two people? First they have to be introduced to each other; you can't be a friend to someone you have never met! Then you have to spend time with each other and talk to each other. Without time together a relationship can never become deeper.

It is the same way in our relationship with God. God loves us, and He wants to be our friend—in a far deeper way than any human friend. Have you ever been "introduced" to Him, by turning to Him and asking His Son, Jesus Christ, to come into your heart and take away your sins? If not, open your life to Him and commit yourself to Him. Then learn to spend time with God and talk with Him every day. How do you do that? You do it through the Bible, which is God's Word and is His way of speaking to us. Then pray to Him, thanking God for all He does for you and sharing your burdens and concerns with Him. Jesus said, "I have called you friends, for everything that I learned from my Father I have made known to you" (John 15:15).

Each day spend time alone with God. It may only be a few minutes at first, but as you realize His love for you and come to understand that He is with you every moment, then your closeness to Him will grow and you will realize you can turn to Him at any moment. Even when you may not feel His presence, by faith you know that He is still with you for He has promised, "Never will I leave you; never will I forsake you" (Hebrews 13:5).

Somewhere along the line I feel like we have missed the boat. My husband and I are middle-aged, and we have been very successful materially. Every one of our children has gotten into some kind of difficulty (like drugs), and we are empty inside. Where do you think we went wrong?

The Bible gives us a formula for training our children but it also gives them a free will to make the choice between following the ways of men or the way of God. From your question it appears that you may have set the pursuit of material gain ahead of pursuing God's will and way for your lives and that of your children.

I would suggest that you first earnestly seek God's forgiveness for your failure to be the kind of parents God wanted you to be. Then, go to your children individually and confess to them. Tell them you are sorry for putting material things ahead of them and ask their forgiveness. Do not expect it immediately, for there is much healing that will need to take place.

Then, determine that Christ will be at the center of your life and marriage from this day forward. If you must relinquish some of your lifestyle in order to make things right with God and with your children, do so. You have again proved the Scripture which says, "What shall it profit a man if he gains the whole world and loses his own soul?"

Above all, keep in mind that nothing is too hard for God, including the redemption of yourselves and your children.

What exactly is an atheist? Is it a person who doesn't know whether or not God exists? If so, I guess I am one because I have a lot of doubts and wonder if we can really know anything about God. I would like to know God is real, but I don't.

The term "agnostic" would more accurately describe you. An atheist does not believe in God; an agnostic is not sure whether or not God exists. The word literally means "one who is without knowledge"—that is, a person who says he does not know whether or not God is real.

But can you come to know about God? Yes! And not only can you know that God exists, but you can come to know Him by having a personal relationship with Him. You see, God has not left us to wander around guessing whether or not He exists or what He is like. Instead—and this is very important for you to understand—God has shown Himself to us. How has He done this? He has done it in a way that staggers our minds. He did it by actually taking upon Himself human flesh and becoming a human being. Do you want to know what God is like? Examine Jesus Christ, because Christ was God in human flesh. "He is the image of the invisible God . . . . For God was pleased to have all his fullness dwell in him" (Colossians 1:15, 19). Christ confirmed that He was the Son of God by rising from the dead after His death on the cross.

I invite you to look with an open mind and heart at Christ as He is found in the New Testament. When you do, you will discover that God loves you, and He has done everything possible to remove the barriers between God and humanity. Then commit your life to Christ and discover for yourself that "to those who believed in his name, he gave the right to become children of God" (John 1:12).

I know preachers talk a lot about repenting of sin, but what exactly do you mean by that? I know there are a lot of things wrong in my life, but if I have to wait until I get rid of all of them before God will love me, then I guess I don't have a chance.

The word "repent" is used frequently in the New Testament, and it literally means "to have a change of mind" about the way we are living. Jesus said, "I have not come to call the righteous, but sinners to repentance" (Luke 5:32).

In other words, to repent is to face the fact that we are sinners and the way we have been living is wrong in God's eyes. It means we also have a new attitude toward sin—no longer loving it or excusing it, but realizing that it is wrong and displeases God. When we truly repent we actually want to turn from sin, and with God's help we will turn from it. Repentance is not merely feeling guilty for our sins, or sorry because we know we have done wrong. Repentance means we actually turn from sin as best we know how, seeking God's forgiveness and strength.

But repentance is only one side of the coin. Yes, we are to repent. But the good news of the gospel is that God will forgive us when we repent! God loves us, and Christ died on the cross to take away our sins. "The blood of Jesus, his Son, purifies us from all sin" (1 John 1:7). When we repent and then accept Christ into our lives by faith, God forgives us and makes us His children. He receives us just as we are.

Have you realized your own need of repentance and faith in Christ? Don't let pride get in the way. Instead, confess to God that you know you are a sinner and you are sorry for your sins and repent of them, and then ask Christ to come into your life as your Lord and Savior.

Do you know exactly when you became a Christian? I have friends who say they do, and that everyone should be able to remember it, but it makes me feel strange because I can't. Does this mean I'm not really a Christian? I grew up in a Christian home and as long as I can remember I have felt that God loved me and I trusted Christ for my salvation.

Yes, I can recall very vividly the night I made my decision to follow Christ. I was seventeen at the time, and a visiting evangelist was holding a series of meetings in my home town of Charlotte. After a time of spiritual struggle I went forward and made a public commitment to follow Christ.

My wife, on the other hand, cannot recall a time when she did not believe in Christ and trust Him for her salvation. Her parents were godly missionaries in China, and from her earliest years they had taught her about Christ and the way He loves us and died for our sins. Her experience was somewhat like that of Paul's young helper Timothy: "From infancy you have known the holy Scriptures, which are able to make you wise for salvation through faith in Christ Jesus" (2 Timothy 3:15).

The point is that people come to Christ in different ways. The central question is not how or when we came to Christ, but that we are sure to have come, and that we are trusting Him alone for our salvation. Tragically, many people grow up in a religious background and go to church all their lives, and yet their religion is only a habit and they are not truly trusting Christ alone for their salvation. Thank God for your background and your trust in Christ, who died on the cross for you. And be sure you are continuing to grow in your relationship with Him through His Word and prayer every day.

Some time ago I read one of your answers concerning evil thoughts. I, too, am troubled over this because the more I try to dismiss them from my mind, the more they trouble me. In fact, the problem grows worse as I try to overcome it. I am a Christian and wish to please God. Is there any answer to this problem?

It is known that we cannot always control the thoughts we have. In fact, you will find that your desperate attempt to dismiss them from your mind is exactly the thing that keeps them active. It is just like most spiritual struggles.

They are not overcome by our own self-will and determination. The best resolution will not overcome the enemy. Only when we admit our helplessness, and call upon God to deliver us, will we find deliverance. As long as you try by your own strength, you will fail, but when you draw upon the resources of His strength, you will find relief.

You are worried about the wickedness of these thoughts. As long as you disapprove of them, you are well, but when the time comes that you approve of them and affirm them with your will, then you are certainly in a low spiritual condition. Paul once wrote: "Finally, brethren, whatsoever things are true, whatsoever things are honest, whatsoever things are just, whatsoever things are pure, whatsoever things are lovely, whatsoever things are of good report; if there be any virtue, and if there be any praise, think on these things" (Philippians 4:8 KJV).

I watched you the other night on television as you spoke about loneliness. I guess that is my biggest problem. I have a good job and everything, but I just about go crazy when I come home to the four walls of my apartment. Please pray for me.

I believe loneliness is one of the most critical problems in our nation today. There are some things in our society—such as the fast pace of city living—that truly make many people lonely in the midst of a crowd.

There are two things I especially want to tell you. First, no matter what your situation may be, God is always with you. You are never completely alone when you know Christ. The Bible promises, "God has said, 'Never will I leave you; never will I forsake you'" (Hebrews 13:5). No matter where you go or what you do, God is there and by faith you can reach out to Him. This is one reason I am convinced the first step in solving your problem is for you to ask Jesus Christ to come into your heart by faith. Jesus stands at the door of our hearts and promises, "If anyone hears my voice and opens the door, I will come in and eat with him, and he with me" (Revelation 3:20).

The second thing I want to urge you to do is to take definite, practical steps to establish friendships with others. Church is an excellent place to do this—not only in Sunday morning worship, but especially in the many other activities most churches have. (You also need the fellowship of other Christians to grow spiritually.) Ask God to lead you to a church where Christ is preached and where you can find friends.

Also take other steps to reach out to others. Are there others at work who are also lonely? Are there others in your apartment building who seem to have few friends? It may not be easy for you at first, but learn to be a friend to others. A good way to start is to do something practical for someone else who has a need.

I am an entertainer and work at night. I do feel my need of God, but lately I have taken to drink. I sometimes feel that life is so futile and empty. Is there any help for me?

You are right to be concerned about the direction of your life and my first advice to you would be not to seek solace in alcohol. Alcohol obscures good judgment and leaves you unable to think clearly or understand what God is trying to say to you.

The fact that you are reaching out indicates that you are troubled about where your life might lead. Life *is* futile and empty without Christ. God made us to have a relationship with Him and we try to fill the void God wants to fill with

Himself, with success, fame, money, lust, and all sorts of other false gods that never satisfy.

The Bible says "Him that cometh unto me I will in no wise cast out" (John 6:37 KJV). What you must first do is come to God. Confess your sin to Him and receive Jesus Christ as your Savior. Then consider the kind of "entertaining" you have been doing and ask yourself whether this is God's will for your life. Find others who desire to live for God and begin spending time with them and reading God's Word.

10 | *Does Prayer Really Make a Difference?*

Do you think prayer really makes any difference about how things turn out?

Yes, I am convinced that prayer makes a difference. Let the Bible answer your question: "The prayer of a righteous man is powerful and effective" (James 5:16). God always answers prayer—not sometimes, but all the time.

We may not always understand how God answers our prayers—at times He says "yes," while at other times He answers "no" or "wait." But one of the greatest privileges of the child of God is the privilege of coming directly to God in prayer. This is possible because Jesus Christ has reconciled us to God through His death on the cross. We are separated from God, but Christ took away our sins and when we come to Christ by faith we are united with God. "Therefore, since we have been justified through faith, we have peace with God through our Lord Jesus Christ, through whom we have gained access by faith into this grace in which we now stand" (Romans 5:1–2). Yes, we have access to God through Jesus Christ.

Does that mean we can ask God for anything at all—no matter how selfish it might be—and He will automatically give us our request? No, what we should seek when we pray is God's will, not our own. (That does not mean, of course, that we are not to bring our own concerns to God in prayer—quite the opposite. But our desire is to see God work in accordance with His perfect will.) The Bible says, "This is the assurance we have in approaching God: that if we ask anything according to His will, He hears us. And if we know that He hears us—whatever we ask—we know that we have what we asked of him" (1 John 5:14–15).

Is prayer a central part of your life? Pray for your own needs. Pray for the needs of others. Praise God in prayer, and pray for His guidance in your life. "Devote yourselves to prayer, being watchful and thankful" (Colossians 4:2). Remember, Christ prayed repeatedly, and if He—the sinless Son of God—needed to pray, how much more should we learn to "pray continually" (1 Thessalonians 5:17).

What do people mean when they end a prayer "in Jesus' name"? I have never really understood this.

In order to understand the meaning of this you have to know something about the meaning and importance of a name in the ancient world.

To people in Jesus' time, a person's name was very important. (This was true in Old Testament times as well.) The reason is that a person's name was seen as summarizing or indicating a person's true character or nature. You could almost say that a person's name gave a picture of his personality. A name was not simply a sound or a word—it had meaning. (We have lost that idea today, but at one time it was true in English also; e.g., someone named "Armstrong" had strong arms.)

Let me give an example from the Old Testament to show you what I mean. On one occasion, David had difficulty with a man named Nabal. The word "Nabal" in the original Hebrew language means "fool"—and that was exactly what this man was. He refused to help David although David had helped him. Nabal's wife, however, urged David not to harm her husband in spite of his mistreatment of David. She said, "Pay no attention to that wicked man Nabal. He is just like his name—his name is Fool, and folly goes with him" (1 Samuel 25:25). His name—fool—indicated the whole character or personality of the man.

Now think about the name of Jesus. "Jesus" in the original language of the New Testament means "The Lord Saves." Its full meaning is given by the angel to Joseph: "You are to give him the name of Jesus, because he will save his people from their sins" (Matthew 1:21).

Therefore, when we pray "in the name of Jesus" we are recalling who Jesus is and what He has done for us through His death and resurrection. We are recalling that He has made our prayers possible because He has saved us, reconciled us to God, and is our mediator. We cannot come before God in our own merit, because we are sinners. But Christ has taken away our sins and made forgiveness possible. To pray in Jesus' name—as we should—is to acknowledge our need of Christ and our desire to seek His glory and His will alone in our prayers.

Do you think it is possible for God to get angry with us because we pray too much about a particular problem we have? I worry about bothering Him too much with my problems.

No, the Bible tells us to persist in prayer and to pray about everything. God does not always answer the *way* we think He should, or *when* we think He should. (We should be grateful for this—He knows far better than we do what is best!). But, the Bible tells us to "always keep on praying" (1 Thessalonians 5:17 TLB). Jesus, in fact, told a parable about a persistent widow who constantly begged a judge to act on her case, which He eventually did. (You can read it in Luke 18:1–8.) One reason Jesus told this parable was to encourage us to pray frequently.

There are, however, two things I would like to add as footnotes, so to speak. First, be sure that you are not trying to change God's mind about something which He has already answered. In other words, it is possible that God will answer a prayer of ours with a "no" rather than a "yes." Are we willing to accept His will? Remember that God answers prayer in one of three ways as far as time is concerned: yes, no, and wait. In prayer we seek above all else to have God's will done, and when He has acted we must not second-guess Him or try to get Him to change His perfect will.

Second, remember that there are times when we ourselves are to act as well as pray. That is, we become the answer to our own prayers. For example, on one occasion Jesus told his disciples to "Ask the Lord of the harvest, therefore, to send out workers into his harvest field." In the very next verses we find that the disciples themselves were sent out to do God's work. They became the answer to their own prayers! (See Matthew 9:38, 10:1.)

Prayer is one of the privileges of the child of God, made possible because Jesus Christ has opened up the way to our Father. God loves you, and He wants you to "not be anxious about anything, but in everything, by prayer and petition, with thanksgiving, present your request to God" (Philippians 4:6).

I have a friend who tells me that if I just pray and read my Bible every day my problems will work out. I'm not so sure it's that simple, are you?

No, the Bible does not promise that if we are committed to Jesus Christ all of our problems will vanish. We should commit our lives to Christ because He is "the way and the truth and the life" (John 14:6), and not because we hope to escape all the problems of this life. Yes, when we come to Christ many of our problems are solved. For example, if we truly understand what Christ has done for us on the cross we do not need to be burdened with a load of guilt any longer, because He has washed away our sins. But we may find new pressures that come because we are seeking to be faithful to Christ.

Look at the example of the apostle Paul, the greatest follower of Jesus Christ the world has ever known. And yet His life was often marked by difficulties and circumstances that were far from pleasant. (You can read about some of his troubles in 2 Corinthians 11:23–33.)

That does not mean, of course, that it makes no difference whether or not we believe in Christ—not at all! Yes, you may face problems in your life just as other people do, but there is a difference—Christ is with you! He can strengthen you in the midst of difficulties you have in your life, and He can give you wisdom in dealing with them. He also gives you hope, because you know that this world is not the end of everything. Some day we will go to be with Christ in Heaven, where "There will be no more death or mourning or crying or pain, for the old order of things has passed away" (Revelation 21:4).

In one way, therefore, your friend is pointing you in the right direction. God will not necessarily remove all your problems when you give your life to Christ, but through praying to Him and through studying the Bible every day (and trusting its promises) you will grow closer to Christ and know in a fuller way "the peace of God, which transcends all understanding" (Philippians 4:7)—no matter what circumstances you face.

For months I have been praying that God would change me and make me a better person. Nothing seems to happen however. What do you think is wrong?

I cannot help but wonder if you feel somehow that God should reach into your life and miraculously change you all at once—almost like a bolt of lightning striking you. But that is not the way God usually works. Think of it this way—it took a while for you to become what you are. It will take a while for God to change you.

Indeed, you need to realize that God also expects us to do our part. I do not know what specific problems you face in your life that you want God to change. But let's say, for example, that you have a particular problem with your tongue. Perhaps you say things that hurt others and cause them to resent you, or you have problems because you gossip easily about others. How do you think God will deal with that problem?

First, God will want you to see the seriousness of this problem. He wants you to know that a sharp or undisciplined tongue is a sin which not only hurts your relationships with other people but is wrong in His eyes. "The tongue also is a fire, a world of evil among the parts of the body. It corrupts the whole person, sets the whole course of his life on fire, and is itself set on fire by hell" (James 3:6).

Then God wants you to commit this problem to Him, repenting of it and admitting that you need His strength to combat it. "Repentance" means that you deliberately turn from it and with God's strength fight it in your life. It means you will avoid situations where you know you will be tempted to fail—and this requires discipline on your part. It also means that you will seek to use your tongue to honor Him as well as to refrain from evil. In addition, God has given you the Bible, and your daily study and application of its teaching to your life is crucial.

How can I get close to God? Praying to Him sometimes feels like praying to a brick wall; and although countless prayers of mine have been answered, it seems that my prayers just slide into the blackness of I-don't-know-where. Do you think you could possibly help me?

I'm afraid you are trying to use God as a genie, as a kind of Aladdin's lamp. You say that countless prayers of yours have been answered. That seems to me like a pretty good average. God answers all our prayers, but in His wisdom, He sometimes answers them with a "no."

Prayer is not our using God; it is more often employed to get us in a position where God can use *us*.

Many years ago, I watched the deckhands on the great liner, *United States,* as they docked that ship in New York Harbor. First, they threw out a rope to the men on the dock. Then inside the boat the great motors went to work and pulled on that great cable. But oddly enough, the pier wasn't pulled out to the ship; instead, the ship was pulled snugly up to the pier.

Prayer is the rope that pulls God and man together. But it doesn't pull God down to us: it pulls us up to Him. We must learn to say with Christ, the Master of the art of prayer: "Not my will, but thine, be done" (Luke 22:42 KJV).

Is it always necessary to pray for long periods of time to maintain a spiritual outlook?

It is not the length of the prayer that is important. Do you think God is persuaded by long prayers or by the earnestness with which we pray? Put it on the level of the human: What makes the strongest impression on you? Is it the long but indifferent request or the terse but earnest plea of one who has a strong desire? I am sure you can see that it is the condition of the heart and the definiteness of the request that makes the difference. Jesus said, "When ye pray, use not vain repetitions, as the heathen do" (Matthew 6:7 KJV). The simple and direct request in Jesus' name will accomplish far more than millions of half-hearted and indefinite words. Finally, pray expectantly. God knows when you pray without hope of an answer. You cannot pray unless you pray with hope.

It is interesting to note that Jesus often prayed all night in private but His public prayers were very brief.

Is it more meaningful to kneel while you pray? Is it just an expression of humbleness, or are one's prayers more likely to be heard when kneeling?

It is not the posture of the body, but the attitude of the heart that counts when we pray. The Bible speaks of bowing in prayer, kneeling on one's face before God, standing, sitting, and walking. The important thing is not the position of the body but the condition of the soul. If the heart is attuned to God, one can pray in any posture imaginable.

Jesus prayed sitting, standing, kneeling, and in a prone position. Moses often fell on his face to pray. Daniel frequently kneeled. The disciples were sitting in the upper room when the Holy Spirit descended upon them in answer to prayer. Ahab prayed with his face between his knees.

There are times when I like to kneel in prayer. There are other times when it seems more natural to sit or stand. I don't believe there is any special virtue in any particular posture. God doesn't look upon the outward appearance, but upon the heart.

My problem is that I cannot concentrate when I pray. In other matters I am quite able to keep my mind from wandering but not when I kneel to pray. Is there something wrong with me?

There is not necessarily anything wrong with you. This was the problem the disciples had in the Garden of Gethsemane.They went to sleep when they had been commanded to "watch and pray." Of all the activity of the Christian life, prayer is the most difficult. The Bible even points this out, saying that "We know not how to pray as we ought."

Someone has said: "Satan trembles when he sees the weakest saint upon his knees." When we get to Heaven, I am convinced we will be amazed at our prayerlessness. Prayer can move mountains. Thus Satan will do all in his power to distract you. You may never be entirely free from distraction in prayer, but you can improve your concentration by quoting psalms and using prayer helps. Remember also that prayer is a two-way conversation. Be still and listen for the voice of God. Most of us want to do too much talking in prayer. God has promised special help in the matter of prayer: "In the same way, the Spirit helps us in our weakness. We do not know what we ought to pray, but the Spirit himself intercedes for us with groans that words cannot express" (Romans 8:26). No matter what your problem, don't get discouraged. Continue to pray.

I have a lot of problems I would like to see solved. Is it really true that if you have enough faith then all your prayers will be answered? How can I get that kind of faith?

Being a Christian does not guarantee us a trouble-free life. Jesus "was despised and rejected by men, a man of sorrows, and familiar with suffering" (Isaiah 53:3). The apostle Paul frequently encountered troubles and difficulties as he worked for Christ.

But God does promise several important things. He promises that in the midst of troubles He will be with us to help us and strengthen us. He may give us special wisdom to deal with a situation. He may give us a special measure of spiritual courage and strength. "Fear not, for I have redeemed you; I have called you by name; you are mine. When you pass through waters, I will be with you; and when you pass through rivers, they will not sweep over you . . . . Do not be afraid, for I am with you" (Isaiah 43:1–2, 5).

Then He promises to give us peace in the midst of life's storms. When we learn to trust the future into His hands, then we know that we do not need to be anxious and worried about the outcome. "Do not be anxious about anything, but in everything, by prayer and petition, with thanksgiving, present your requests to God. And the peace of God, which transcends all understanding, will guard your hearts and your minds in Christ Jesus" (Philippians 4:6–7). God hears our prayers, and we can have confidence that He will answer in the right way.

Finally, God gives us hope for the future. Even when our lives seem to be engulfed with troubles, we know there is a bright future ahead in Heaven for all those who know Christ. Then there will be no more pain or troubles, and we will be with Christ forever.

I know you urge people to take time each day and spend it in prayer and Bible study, but somehow I just can't seem to get going on it. Why do you think it is important? I do go to church several times a week and feel I am getting closer to God through the Bible teaching I get there.

It is good you are gaining spiritually from Bible teaching in your church. But God also wants to bless you spiritually as you meet with Him every day. This need not be a complicated or lengthy time, but each of us can profit from time alone with God. Let me suggest four guidelines that might help you get started.

First, have a purpose. Many people don't take time—even just a few minutes—for prayer and Bible reading each day because they don't see its importance. Such a practice, however, can strengthen you spiritually. It also can help others as you take time to pray for them. Remember too that God wants our fellowship.

Second, have a time. I have found unless I deliberately plan a definite time for Bible study and prayer, other things all too easily intervene and crowd it out. We can always find time for things we think are really important. Set aside a time when you are alert and will not be disturbed, even if it is only a few minutes at first, and discipline yourself to give it priority.

Third, have a plan. Spend a few minutes in prayer— thanking God for His blessings, bringing your needs to Him and remembering the needs of others. Many find it helpful to keep a list of the people for whom they are praying. Then spend time in reading the Bible. Don't feel that you necessarily have to read a long section—it is far better to read a few verses and get their meaning than to read a larger section and not get much out of it. Start in a book (such as the Gospel of John) and move through it day by day.

Finally, understand and apply. What is this Bible passage saying about God, or about how we should live? And in what ways should my life be different as a result of what God has shown me here?

Yes, it is important to talk to God each day, and allow Him to talk to us through His Word. And when we know Christ we can have fellowship with Him at any time.

11 I Want to Know God's Will

I am a new Christian and I honestly want to know and do God's will, but how can I know what His will for me really is?

There are many ways by which God leads us but it is only when we have minds and hearts surrendered to Him that we sometimes hear His voice. God speaks to us through the Holy Spirit, sometimes while we are praying. I know a man who was faced with a very difficult problem. He was an earnest Christian and he prayed about this particular problem and while he was praying he had a clear sense of the answer, so much so that he got up from his knees and wrote it down. Later in the day, during a conference in which the problem was under discussion, he read this statement. Immediately the entire group, although they had differed sharply one with the other, felt this was the answer and unanimously agreed. As a result, an issue which had divided Christians for months was resolved in absolute harmony.

God sometimes leads men through the words or acts of other people. He often gives direct leading as we pray about it and read our Bibles. There are times when a group of individuals may come to a conclusion which indicates how one of them should act. The important thing is to be willing to do God's will. When that is true, God will surely make it known. Many Christians have experienced the fulfillment of the words of the prophet Isaiah: "And thine ears shall hear a word behind thee, saying, 'This is the way, walk ye in it, when ye turn to the right hand, and when ye turn to the left'" (30:21 KJV). Another promise is found in Proverbs 3:5–6: "Trust in the Lord with all thine heart; and lean not unto thine own understanding. In all thy ways acknowledge him, and he shall direct thy paths" (KJV).

I have no patience with people who get intoxicated, but do you think a little social drinking to promote good fellowship does any harm?

Of course it does. Can you be blind to the fact that one drink often leads to another? In every city I visit someone asks me to pray for a husband, or wife, or son who started as a social drinker and now has become an alcoholic. Today you think you have perfect self-control. But if you make a habit of drinking what will you do when you face anxiety or disappointment?

You also have some responsibility for the welfare of your neighbor. Your example may lead him into a habit he cannot break. If you encourage him to do anything which brings about his downfall, you are guilty. And don't forget that alcohol is the cause of many of our traffic accidents (estimates of alcohol-related highway fatalities hover at around 50 percent). A man who commits murder on the highway because his responses are slow, or he doesn't see where he's going, is guilty in the sight of God.

Our bodies are the temples of our souls. We must treat them with respect. The Bible says: "Whether therefore ye eat, or drink, or whatsoever ye do, do all to the glory of God" (1 Corinthians 10:31 KJV). This is a command no Christian should ignore.

My wife and I are having an argument about something and I wonder what your opinion is. She says that watching some of the shows on television that have a lot of violence or sex can be harmful, but I'm not sure it really makes much difference, since those shows are just fictional stories.

The fact that the shows are fictional does not mean they cannot excite our imaginations or stir our desires—sometimes in a wrong way. We need to be careful, therefore, what we allow to enter our minds.

The Bible makes it clear that what we see and what we think about can have a powerful influence on our lives. That is why the Bible urges us to turn our minds away from things that feed our hearts in a wrong way and instead turn our attention to those things which are good. "Set your minds on things above, not on earthly things. . . . Put to death, therefore, whatever belongs to your earthly nature: sexual immorality, impurity, lust, evil desires and greed" (Colossians 3:2, 5). The reason for this is that God's will is for us to be pure, and to be guided by Him.

Your question makes me wonder, however, if you have ever honestly examined your own life and asked yourself if your priorities are right. Are you honestly concerned about God's will for your life, or are you somehow seeking to keep Him at arms' length so you can run your own life without Him? God created you, and He sent His only Son to die on the cross so you can be forgiven of your sins and become His child forever. If you have never committed your life to Christ, turn to Him and invite Him to come into your heart as your Lord and Savior. Make Him Lord of every area of your life—including your time, your imagination, and your marriage.

Then seek God's will for the way you spend your time. Yes, we all need times of relaxation—but these should become times that strengthen us spiritually as well as physically, rather than tear us down. Remember the Bible's command: "Do not conform any longer to the pattern of this world, but be transformed by the renewing of your mind" (Romans 12:2).

I feel very much like I would honestly like to do God's will in my life—if only I knew what it was. It seems like it would be far more worthwhile to do God's will rather than do things that don't make any difference, but how can I know what His will is?

I am thankful that you realize the most important thing in life is doing the will of God. It would be tragic to look back over our lives and realize that nothing we ever did had any truly eternal significance. But we can know the will of God, because He has a perfect will for each of us and He wants to show it to us.

How does one discover the will of God for his life? First of all, God has revealed His will to us in the Bible. That does not mean the Bible will necessarily give precise, detailed guidance for each day—but it gives something very important: principles by which our lives are to be lived. And every day of your life you will know the will of God in many, many situations because you know the truth of God's Word.

For example, perhaps there is someone near you (such as a neighbor or a relative) who is facing some particular problem right now. Is it God's will for you to try to help that person? Yes, it probably is, because God's Word tells us that we are to "Love your neighbor as yourself" (Matthew 22:39 RSV). The Bible also teaches us that we are to demonstrate our love for others through our actions. "If anyone has material possessions and sees his brother in need but has no pity on him, how can the love of God be in him? Dear children, let us not love with words or tongue but with actions and in truth" (1 John 3:17–18).

I could give many other examples, but the important thing is that you allow your life to be saturated with the teaching of God's Word. I heard someone say long ago that if we are ignorant of God's Word we will also be ignorant of God's will, and that is true. At the same time, when we are open to His will we find He also will direct us through circumstances and through the inner promptings of the Holy Spirit. But that directing is never in conflict with the written Word of God.

In science class at school, all living things are classified as animals. Are human beings actually animals, or does God classify them differently?

Biologically, man is an animal. That is to say, he does not make his own food by photosynthesis. He is thus distinguished from plant life. But he is more than an animal. He has three attributes which four-footed animals do not have: reason, conscience, and will. Animals are motivated by instinct. Their behavior patterns are instinctive, not intelligent. Since their responses are instinctive, they have no conscience. A dog probably feels no more remorse after biting a man, than he does when chewing a bone. Then again, an animal's decisions are not volitional, but instinctive. He has no will, but acts instinctively, according to set, inner urges.

Why is man different than the other animals? Because he was created in the image of God. He was directed with three attributes as we have said. The first man, Adam, used all three of these attributes. First, he reasoned that his own judgment was as good as God's, and he ate the forbidden fruit. In that act, the will of man came into play, for he could have decided either way. Then, after he broke God's command, he felt conscience-stricken and ran away to hide in the garden. Strangely, this man-animal has been following that same pattern through the centuries. Within these God-given attributes are life or death, happiness or sorrow, and peace or conflict. If he dissipates the powers which God has given him, he is of all creatures most miserable. But if he uses them properly, he can make of his world a paradise.

What Christian grace in my heart can make me a better Christian and a better witness for Christ?

The greatest Christian grace is love—not the sentimental feeling often called love today but that deep regard for the welfare of others which will prompt us to help them when they need help; to be sympathetic when sympathy is needed; to make us say kind things about people instead of being critical; to make us long to win them to Christ if they are not Christians.

Love is at the very heart of everything that comes from God, for He is love. It was love which prompted the sending of His Son into the world to die for our sins. It is love which is mentioned first when the apostle Paul enumerates the fruits of the Spirit (Galatians 5:22). It is love which must characterize our attitude to God and man, if we are to fulfill His law. In Matthew 22:37–38 we read: "Thou shalt love the Lord thy God with all thy heart, and with all thy soul, and with all thy mind. This is the first and great commandment." Following this, Christ said: "The second is like unto it, Thou shalt love thy neighbor as thyself" (Matthew 22:39 KJV). After that, Christ tells us: "On these commandments hang all the law and the prophets." It is God's love which should constrain us. The Bible says: "This is love: not that we loved God, but that he loved us, and sent his Son as an atoning sacrifice for our sins" (1 John 4:10). If you have a loving heart, you will bear fruitful witness for Christ.

For the benefit of those who are confused, would you explain your position on tithing? Should we give a tenth of our gross income or a tenth of what we have left after expenses are paid?

I can only tell you my personal convictions in the matter. If I were to wait until all expenses were paid before I tithed my income, there would be none left for the Lord. Income means, "what comes in," and if we give one tenth of our income to kingdom work, then we must give a tithe of our gross.

The trouble with too many of us is that we try to see how little we can get by with rather than how much we can do for God. Even the federal government recognizes tithing and charitable giving as a citizen's duty and allows such to be deducted from income tax. I have had many people tell me that nine tenths of their income went farther with God's blessing on it than ten tenths of it did without His blessing. We have found that true in our own experience. Did not God say, "Bring ye all the tithes into the storehouse . . . and prove me now herewith, saith the Lord of hosts, if I will not open you the windows of heaven, and pour you out a blessing, that there shall not be room enough to receive it" (Malachi 3:10 KJV).

I worry about the attitudes that our children seem to have toward money and possessions. We were always taught in my generation to work hard and save all we could—I still have memories as a child of the Great Depression. But our children seem to want all the possessions they can get and even go deeply into debt to get them, and this worries us. I guess this doesn't sound like a spiritual problem, but I wonder what you think?

Our attitude toward money is very often a sign of what we really think is important in life. Your question does, therefore, deal with a spiritual problem because it touches the whole question of what you and your children consider central in life.

Look carefully at something Jesus said in the Sermon on the Mount. He declared, "Do not store up for yourself treasures on earth, where moth and rust destroy, and where thieves break in and steal. But store up for yourselves treasures in heaven, where moth and rust do not destroy, and where thieves do not break in and steal. For where your treasure is, there your heart will be also" (Matthew 6:19–21).

Was Jesus saying we should never work hard or save money? No, this was not His point; the Bible commends such things as honest work and thrift, and warns us of the dangers of debt. His point instead was that money and things can easily take the place of God in our lives. We begin to think that our real security in life comes from our bank account, and we turn away from trusting God. Jesus was also warning against a spirit of materialism which puts things and the pleasures of life in place of God. The Bible teaches as well that we would use our money not only for ourselves but to help others.

How do your children observe your attitudes toward money? Do you tithe to your church? Are you frugal, but not stingy, with the money God has made it possible for you to have? A generous spirit on your part will serve as an example to your children, and while they are responsible for their own attitudes about money, you can help shape those attitudes by the way you live.

Immediately after graduating from college I went into the Army and am due to be discharged in a few months. I honestly want to serve God but I don't know what He wants me to do.

I am convinced that anyone who honestly wants to know God's will for his life will be led to a clear understanding of God's plan for him. This has its foundation in a personal faith in Jesus Christ as Savior. In the Irish Channel there are a series of lights which the pilot of a ship must line up before entering one of the harbors. In determining God's will for our lives, once we have given our hearts to Christ, there are certain factors which converge in giving us spiritual leading. First, there is the inward impulse coming from the leading of the Holy Spirit. Then there is the Bible which corroborates our sense of divine guidance. Finally, God often uses a trend of circumstances through which He indicates His leading. In this connection Proverbs 3:5–6 is a wonderful promise. "Trust in the Lord with all thine heart; and lean not unto thine own understanding. In all thy ways acknowledge him, and he shall direct thy paths" (KJV). Here is a definite promise. Believe it and act on it. God will not fail you.

I have a brother who is on drugs, and I am afraid he is going to just get in deeper and deeper if somebody doesn't help him. I would like to help him, but I don't know how. What do you suggest?

The first thing you need to do is to pray that God will give you (and others in your family and among his friends) wisdom in dealing with this. Remember the promise of God: "If any of you lacks wisdom, he should ask God, who gives generously to all without finding fault, and it will be given to him" (James 1:5).

At some time your brother needs to be confronted in a loving way with the problem he is facing. Often a person in his situation may think his habits are hidden from others, and he may try to deny that he is having a problem with drugs. But if you are certain of this, you owe it to him to let your concern be known in an open and frank way. Before he will seek the help that he needs, he has to face the fact that he has a problem. He also needs to sense that he has the support of those who love him. Simply condemning him for his actions will probably only alienate him. He needs to know you love him so much that you will not stand by and allow him to destroy himself.

Get professional help. You do not indicate your brother's living situation, but if he is still at home I believe your parents should insist on his getting help. Your pastor may be able to help you at this point and you and your parents should seek his counsel and the counsel of others who might be able to help.

Most of all, pray for your brother. Pray that he will find strength to fight this problem, and pray that he will come to grips with his need for God. God will not only help him, but Christ can give him the meaning and sense of direction in life that he will never find through drugs.

Is it wrong to have questions about God and religion? I have a lot of questions about things I don't understand, but I wonder if maybe I ought to just try to put them out of mind.

Our minds are limited, and we will never fully grasp the greatness of God. Only in Heaven will we receive the answers to some of the questions we have now. "Now we see but a poor reflection; then we shall see face to face. Now I know in part; then I shall know fully" (1 Corinthians 13:12).

But that does not mean you should try to bury your questions or not seek answers to problems that are keeping you from a full relationship with Christ. Faith does not mean that we have no understanding. We can't know everything, but that doesn't mean we can't know some things about God. Even more importantly, we can come to know God in a personal way.

I know it may seem hard for you at first, but the most important step you can take is to open your heart to Jesus Christ and let Him come into your life by faith. You may reply that it is hard to take that step when you have so many questions. But let me stress one very important thing: God can be trusted. God does not lie, for He is perfect and holy. And He has said that if we turn to Him in faith He will accept and forgive us. If anyone in the universe can be trusted, it is God! Let your prayer be the cry of one man who came to Jesus but was nevertheless still plagued by some doubts: "I do believe; help me overcome my unbelief" (Mark 9:24).

Then seek answers to the questions you have. The most important resource for you—or anyone else—is God's Word, the Bible. Get into the Bible on a regular basis and ask God to help you understand it and apply it to your life—not just to answer your questions but to help you become the person God wants you to be. Then don't hesitate to ask other believers about questions you have and books they would recommend. But when you come to Christ, I suspect many of your questions will fade because you will come to realize the greatness and love of God.

I recently met a girl in one of my college classes who claims she is a witch, but she denies she has anything to do with the worship of Satan or anything evil. This seems weird, but I am fascinated and wonder what you think.

I know that someone like this girl would claim there are various kinds of occult practices, and that she is involved in practices which have nothing to do with satanism. But the Bible—as well as the history of occult practices—shows this is not true. Ultimately all occult practices have their origin in Satan rather than God. They are a false substitute for the worship and service of God, and as such they are wrong.

That is one reason why the Bible constantly tells us we should avoid any type of occult practices. This could include not only the type of thing this girl is involved in, but any type of fortune telling, sorcery, charms, spiritism, or any other occult practice or belief. These were all common in the ancient world, but God's people were commanded not to have anything to do with them. "Let no one be found among you . . . who practices divination or sorcery, interprets omens, engages in witchcraft, or casts spells, or who is a medium or spiritist or who consults the dead" (Deuteronomy 18:10–11). When those who were involved in occult practices in Ephesus turned to Christ, they immediately burned their occult books (see Acts 19:19).

We have seen a great upsurge of interest in the occult in recent years. I have asked myself why that is the case, and I am convinced it is because of a deep spiritual hunger on the part of many people. I suspect you are like this, and that down inside you are searching for the meaning of life. But you will not find the true meaning of life in this way. You will find it only in Jesus Christ, the Son of God, who loves you and wants to come into your life.

Don't get fascinated by practices which you think will lead you to God. Instead, you can know God personally by giving your life to Jesus Christ.

Part III

Psychological Problems

12 | *I Feel So Guilty*

I used to go to church a lot, but I have done something very wrong and now I don't go to church because it just makes me feel guilty over what I have done. Can you understand why I react this way?

Yes, I can understand why you react this way—but I want to point out a very important fact. You are not solving your real problem; you are only avoiding it. What you need to do is face this problem and deal with it.

What is your real problem? The problem is not your guilt feelings, although they are kind of like a medical thermometer that tells you something is wrong. The problem is that you have done something wrong and you need God's forgiveness. No matter how much you hide or suppress your guilt feelings, you still are guilty of wrongdoing and you need to deal with the fact of that guilt.

But here is the most important truth you can know: you don't need to carry the burden of your guilt any longer! The reason is that God wants to forgive you and lift the burden from you. Can that be possible? Yes! It is possible because God loves you, and in His love He sent His only Son into the world to die as a perfect sacrifice for your sins. On the cross Christ took upon Himself the burden you are now carrying—the burden of sin and shame and guilt (not just for this one sin that you have done, but for every other sin you have ever committed). The Bible says, "He himself bore our sins in his body on the tree, so that we might die to sins and live for righteousness; by his wounds you have been healed" (1 Peter 2:24).

God's salvation is a free gift, offered to you in Jesus Christ. You could never take your own sins away—but Christ could, and He did. There is no reason for you to bear the burden of guilt any longer. Turn to Christ in repentance and faith, and accept His forgiveness as you invite Jesus Christ into your heart. There is no greater joy than knowing your sins are forgiven, and that can be your experience right now through Christ.

Years ago I was "the other woman." My husband was married to another woman, and he left her for me. We have a good marriage, but now I find myself feeling very guilty over what I did. I realize now I have messed up the lives of a lot of people. What can I do?

One of the greatest tragedies of a marriage breakup is what it does to other people—children, close relatives, etc. I am afraid people today tend to overlook that dimension, and seek only their own selfish desires without regard to the hurt they bring to others. Perhaps your letter will make someone who is in the position you once were stop and think.

You cannot undo the past. But the most important thing you can do is to seek God's forgiveness for what you have done. When David sinned by committing adultery with another man's wife—something clearly forbidden by the Ten Commandments—he tried (like you) to avoid facing his responsibility. But the time came when he was confronted with his sin. He knew he had greatly wronged many people, but he also knew that his greatest sin was against God. That is why he confessed, "Against you, you only, have I sinned and done what is evil in your sight. . . . Surely I have been a sinner from birth" (Psalm 51:4–5).

Yes, you have sinned—against others and against God. That is why you feel guilty. But I want to tell you something very important: God loves you in spite of what you have done, and He sent His only Son Jesus Christ into the world to die in your place. By turning to Him in repentance and faith, you can be forgiven by God and you can become His child. Open your heart to Him as your Savior and Lord. Then you can say with David, "Blessed is he whose transgressions are forgiven" (Psalm 32:1).

Then I suggest you think of some practical ways you can seek the forgiveness of others you have wronged. It will not be easy, but it might be you should write some letters, for example, telling others that you have wronged them, and not only have you sought God's forgiveness for this but you seek theirs as well.

About a year ago I had an abortion. It was against everything I believed in, and since then I am filled with guilt and hatred for myself. How can I expect God to forgive me when I can't even forgive myself?

God's forgiveness for us is not conditional on our forgiving ourselves. The Bible says that "While we were still sinners, Christ died for us" (Romans 5:8). This means that even before we were interested in repenting and asking God to forgive us of our sins, God had already taken the initiative.

I want you to know that the child you aborted is with God in Heaven at this moment. Now God wants to forgive you if you will ask Him to do so. I know of many young women in your situation who believed the lie that the baby they carried was nothing more than an inconsequential piece of tissue and who came to realize the truth too late. Many are now active in telling other women in similar circumstances about their experience and helping others not to make their mistake. Perhaps this is what God has in mind for you.

I was raised in a Christian home and my parents always tried to teach me what was right. But when I got older and left home I left all that behind me and decided I didn't need it. Now I realize I was wrong to do this, and I feel very guilty over it. But is it too late? I think it is, and that He has turned His back on me, just as I have done to Him.

Think for a moment how wonderful you would feel if you could go to bed tonight and know beyond doubt that God has forgiven every sin you had ever committed. And that can be your experience, because God loves you and is ready to receive you back to Himself.

Jesus Christ has already done everything that is necessary to bring you complete forgiveness. When He died on the cross

He took upon Himself your sins and my sins. No, He did not deserve to die, for as God's Son He was sinless. But Christ willingly took your sins upon Himself, and He willingly took upon Himself the punishment you deserved for those sins. The debt that you owe God has already been paid by Christ! "In him we have redemption through his blood, the forgiveness of sins, in accordance with the riches of God's grace that he lavished on us . . ." (Ephesians 1:7–8). If you had been the only person in the world who needed forgiveness, Christ would still have been willing to go to the cross for you. God loves you that much.

God has promised, "If we confess our sins, he is faithful and just and will forgive us our sins and purify us from all unrighteousness" (1 John 1:9). That promise is to you, no matter what you have done in the past. Don't let the past keep you from Christ any longer, but get on your knees, confess your sins to Him, and then receive Christ and His gift of forgiveness today.

I admit I haven't been a perfect person by a long shot, and down inside I have a lot of guilt over things I have done that I know are wrong. How can I know God will forgive me? I want to make a new start in life, but I am afraid I will only fail.

God has given you feelings of guilt to persuade you to change your way of living, and to seek the relief of His forgiveness. And His forgiveness is real; God would not have given these feelings to you if He did not also offer you forgiveness.

How can you know God's forgiveness? You have already taken the first step by facing honestly your sin and your inability to do anything about it. Now turn to Christ for forgiveness. You see, Christ came to take away our sins. As God's Son He was perfect and without sin, but He willingly took upon Himself the sin and the punishment you and I deserve when He died on the cross. He died in your place, so that you might be forgiven. "Here is a trustworthy saying that deserves full acceptance: Christ Jesus came into the world to save sinners" (1 Timothy 1:15). Why did God do this? He did it because He loves you.

Christ has done everything necessary to bring you forgiveness, and He offers it to you as a free gift. What must you do? Like any other gift, God's gift of salvation must be received.

This may seem like a simple question, but why do I feel guilty when I do something I know is wrong? I don't claim to be a very religious person, although I believe in God, but I can't get away from feelings of guilt when I do wrong. Is this just a psychological thing, as some of my friends suggest, or is there more to it?

The reason we feel guilty is that we *are* guilty. You see, God has made this world so that some things are morally right and other things are wrong—and when we go against His rules for living we are guilty of breaking His laws. Furthermore, God has made us with a conscience, so that when we do wrong we know it and are sensitive to it. This is one of the things that makes us different from plants and animals.

But let me pursue this just a bit more. Why did God make us so we would have feelings of guilt when we disobeyed Him? One reason is so that we would realize our need of Him. When you put your hand on a hot stove you immediately feel pain. God gave you the ability to experience that pain, and He did it for a purpose—so you would move your hand and not hurt yourself. Now guilt is something like that. It is a kind of "pain" that God gives us when we sin, so we will realize what we are doing is not only wrong but it will hurt us. Its purpose is to drive us from sin and help us realize we need God.

Have you ever honestly faced your own need of God? You need His forgiveness for your sins, and you need His help every day. More than that, you need the eternal life He alone can give. "God has given us eternal life, and this life is in His son. He who has the Son has life; he who does not have the Son of God does not have life" (1 John 5:11–12). Open your heart to Christ today.

13 | *I'm Angry*

I know it will probably offend you, but I am angry at God. I have just lost my wife to cancer, and I find myself overwhelmed with resentment and bitterness—even though she was a fine Christian and I know she is in Heaven.

Be thankful that your wife knew Christ and is now in Heaven with Him—where pain and death will never touch her again. Be thankful that God is with you right now, and that He loves you and wants to help you. God is still in control—even if you do not understand all that happens in this sin-scarred world. Like Paul we can be "sorrowful, yet always rejoicing" (2 Corinthians 6:10).

Then confess to God how you really feel. He already knows it, of course, but you need to be honest with Him and face your own need of repentance and healing. You need to admit your need of His comfort for your grief. Remember that Christ died on the cross for you—and that means God knows what it is to grieve. Christ is "a man of sorrows, and familiar with suffering" (Isaiah 53:3). Open your life in a fresh way to Christ by faith, for He wants to help you.

This is not an easy time for you—but you can come through this experience with a deeper sense of God's love. Christ came "to comfort all who mourn . . . to bestow on them a crown of beauty instead of ashes, the oil of gladness instead of mourning, and a garment of praise instead of a spirit of despair" (Isaiah 61:2–3).

I am of a different racial background than most of the people where we live. Frankly, I have seen a lot of prejudice and while I try to overlook it it is hard not to be angry. Can you understand how I feel?

190

Yes, I certainly can. One reason is because I have seen far too much prejudice in my lifetime. Early in my ministry I determined that our crusades would not be segregated. I also have been in foreign countries where I was no longer of the same race as most people, and at times I have sensed that hostility some have against my own race. Racial prejudice, I have come to realize, is found in many parts of the world—and is sometimes very intense.

A Christian who is seeking to live as Christ wants him to live will realize that racial prejudice and hatred are wrong. The apostle Paul had grown up being very proud of his racial heritage, but when Christ came into his life he began to see people differently. He began to look at them the same way God looks at people, and reached the point where he could say, "So from now on we regard no one from a worldly point of view . . . . All this is from God, who reconciled us to himself through Christ and gave us the ministry of reconciliation" (2 Corinthians 5:16, 18). God had given him a new love for others, and Paul became the great apostle to people who were not of his race.

At its heart, racial hatred is a spiritual problem caused by sin. We would support laws and other measures that promote racial harmony, but at the same time the deeper problem of hatred is a spiritual one which can only be fully solved by God. Christ can change a person's heart, replacing hatred with love and indifference with compassion.

Don't let hatred control you, no matter what others do that causes you to get angry. You would only become guilty of the same sin that afflicts them, and nothing would be solved. Instead, open your life to Christ and let Him give you a new love for others. Let Him show you ways you can help bridge the gap between peoples, and let Him help you in every area of your life to live for Him.

Three months ago I was in an auto accident, and it has left me with a physical handicap that will be with me all my life. I don't understand why God let this happen to me. I am in college and this has wrecked my plans for the future. I admit I am angry at God, and I can't help it, although I know you would say that is wrong.

Have you ever stopped to ask why you were spared—when so many people die each year in automobile accidents? And have you ever actually thanked God for sparing your life?

I do not know why God allowed this accident to happen to you—any more than I know why He spared you. But I do know this: God cares for you, and He wants to help you in the future. You can go through life constantly asking "Why?"—but what good will that do? It will only twist you and hurt you, and cut you off from those around you. The Bible warns, "Resentment kills a fool, and envy slays the simple" (Job 5:2).

Don't cut yourself off from God's help. Instead, open your heart to Jesus Christ and ask Him to come into your life and help you. Some of the finest people I have ever met have been those who were handicapped, and yet they had discovered the secret of walking with Christ every day and knowing His strength and joy. This can be your experience as well, if you will commit your life and future into His hands. "I can do everything through him who gives me strength" (Philippians 4:13).

I have so many problems that I just feel like God has turned His back on me. I know that is not supposed to be true, but it's hard for me not to be angry at Him.

I know it is often hard for us to face problems in our lives that are very difficult and not ask why God has allowed them. It is only a step from that to anger and bitterness, feeling somehow that God has abandoned us or is punishing us unjustly. But that is not true, and we need to learn to look beyond the immediate problems we face to God Himself, learning to trust Him in every situation.

Let me give an example from the Bible. There came a time during Jeremiah's day when his nation was devastated by a foreign invader. In many ways the nation was not innocent, for the people had turned their backs on God. But it still came as a shock to Jeremiah, seeing the nation and its beautiful capital city of Jerusalem destroyed. Yet in the midst of the pain he felt, he learned to look to God because he knew that God still loved His people and was near to them. Listen to what Jeremiah wrote: "Yet this I call to mind and therefore I have hope: Because of the

Lord's great love we are not consumed, for his compassions never fail. They are new every morning; great is your faithfulness" (Lamentations 3:21–23).

God loves you, in spite of the problems you may not be able to understand. And He has not abandoned you. How do I know He loves you? I know it because He was willing to let His only Son go to the cross and die as a sacrifice for your sins and mine. If He did not love you, Christ would never have died to make it possible for you to know God and go to Heaven when you die. But He loves you, and the greatest thing that could happen to you right now would be for you to reach out in faith and accept God's love in Jesus Christ.

You may not understand why some things happen to you—but you can learn to face each day with the certainty that Christ is with you even in the midst of the storms of life.

I know we are supposed to love other people, but it is hard for me not to be angry at my husband's brother and sister. His mother is quite elderly and lives with us because she has a lot of health problems. But they never come to visit her or offer to help in any way. We can afford to care for her, but in principle I think they ought to be more thoughtful, don't you?

Yes, they should be more thoughtful. After all, when they were children she took care of them for many years, and it is sad that they do not do more to express gratitude for all she did for them. Some day they also will probably be elderly and less able to take care of themselves. How will they feel when their children—who are undoubtedly observing them and noting the way they treat their mother—pay no attention to them in their time of need?

The Bible says much about our responsibility toward our parents. One of the Ten Commandments declares, "Honor your father and your mother" (Exodus 20:12). The Bible also states, "If anyone does not provide for his relatives, and especially for his immediate family, he has denied the faith and is worse than an unbeliever" (1 Timothy 5:8).

This kind of thoughtlessness and ingratitude points to a spiritual issue. When we are selfish and treat others selfishly, it indicates that we have not allowed God's love to touch us and control us. When we have no regard for our parents, it is a sign that we also have no regard for God, our heavenly Father. Pray for your relatives, not only that they will show more love for others but that they will come to know Christ and experience His love and forgiveness.

At the same time, do not let bitterness or anger destroy you. Perhaps you need to take the initiative and invite your relatives over to your house from time to time—not to argue, but to let them know they are welcome. "Do not repay anyone evil for evil. Be careful to do what is right in the eyes of everybody. If it is possible, as far as it depends on you, live at peace with everyone" (Romans 12:17–18).

Recently my husband took a new job in another city. I have always been close to my family where we used to live, and now that we have moved to a new city I am depressed and angry at him for doing this to me. Do you think I would be justified in telling him we either move back or else I leave and go back without him?

You have a responsibility to be the best possible wife you can for your husband. When you were married you took a vow—not only before others but before God—to be committed to each other, no matter what circumstances might come your way.

God wants to use this time to help you grow spiritually and emotionally. Have you ever thought about this and asked God to help you? You need to ask Him not only to help you adjust to your new situation, but also to learn whatever lessons He wants to teach you during this time. Do you remember the story of Abraham in the Old Testament? He had a very successful and happy life in the city where he grew up, but the time came when God called Abraham to leave that city and go to a new place. The Bible says, "By faith Abraham, when called to go to a place he would later receive as his inheritance, obeyed and went, even though he did not know where he was going" (Hebrews 11:8). Abraham learned to trust God, and God rewarded his trust.

If you have never given your life to Christ, now is the time for you to make that important decision. Then ask God to show you practical ways you can overcome your feelings and become adjusted to your new neighborhood. Get involved in a church where Christ is preached—it will do much to help you overcome your loneliness. Paul said, "I have learned the secret of being content in any and every situation . . . I can do everything through him who gives me strength" (Philippians 4:12–13). This can be your experience as you yield your life to Christ and grow closer to Him each day.

I find it hard not to be angry at God. I lost both my sister and my mother to cancer during the last year, and I miss them very much. Why did God let this happen to them? They both had faith that God would heal them but He didn't, and I don't understand that.

I know this is a difficult time for you and inevitably you ask the question, "Why?" We are limited as human beings, and we don't always understand fully why some things happen to us. We often presume that this is a better place and a better life than what God has in store for us in Heaven where there is no pain, no suffering, and no more death. If you can focus more on what Heaven must be like and on a God who loves your sister and mother so much that He brought them home to be with Him, rather than see them suffer, you will begin to feel much better about God's graciousness toward them and toward you.

The Bible teaches that God is a loving God, and he also is in ultimate control of this universe. The Bible also teaches that evil is real, and calls death an "enemy" (1 Corinthians 15:26). These things are true—even if I cannot fully understand them or reconcile them.

You can have one of two reactions to what has happened, and I want you to think about them carefully and not let your emotions cloud the truth. On one hand, you can react against God, blaming Him for what has happened and becoming bitter and angry. If you do this, you will be saying that God is unloving and unfair, and is even wrong in what He does.

On the other hand, this event can bring you closer to God. How can this happen? It can happen if you realize that you need God right now. You need His love and compassion, and you need His hope for the future. You need the inner peace that He alone can bring—and will bring to you if you learn the secret of trusting Him.

Look beyond your present grief to Jesus Christ. God knows what it is like to suffer and even experience death—because His Son died on the cross. He did this so you could have forgiveness and eternal life. Do you want to know—really know—that God loves you? Look at Christ. "This is how we know what love is: Jesus Christ laid down his life for us" (1 John 3:16). Your mother and sister were evidently women of great faith, and right now they are with Christ in Heaven, completely free of the pain and sorrow of this life. Don't let bitterness grow and poison your life, but turn to Christ and renew your commitment to Him.

I admit I am angry at God, because I have had a physical handicap since birth and it has always cut me off from normal life. Why did God do this to me? I'll never be able to hold down the kind of job I would like or anything. You can't begin to understand how frustrating it is to be stuck in a wheelchair most of the time.

Most of us who have never faced the difficulties you face cannot fully understand the frustration you feel; one reason I have printed part of your letter is to encourage all of us to be more sensitive to those who have any kind of handicap.

One of the most striking things about Jesus was the way He demonstrated His concern for those who were sick or handicapped. "People brought to him all who were ill with various diseases, those suffering severe pain, the demon-possessed, the epileptics and the paralytics, and he healed them" (Matthew 4:24). And I encourage you to bring your own personal burdens and hurts to Christ, for He loves you and He wants to help you. We may not fully understand why God allows suffering and handicaps. You can either allow anger and bitterness to control you the rest of your life, or you can accept your limitations. We are all limited in some way, but with God's help we can discover the joy of living life to its fullest potential.

Anger and bitterness will distort and destroy you; in their own ways, they will make you even more handicapped than you are. But Christ wants to take all that away, and He will help you adjust and gain victory over the things that will hold you back.

14 I'm Getting More and More Depressed

Please help me, because I am getting more and more depressed. I have been in love with a man who is much older than I. He has a family, but always claimed that he loved me. Now he has turned his back on me and I just don't know what to do.

I hope you will not think that I am insensitive to your emotions, but very frankly you should be thankful this has happened to you. You have been spared even greater heartache down the road, I strongly suspect, because if you had eventually married this man you would probably not have had a secure and happy relationship. After all, if he was willing to sneak away from his family and his wife for you, what guarantee would you have that he would not do the same thing to you?

There is only one right thing to do, and that is to leave this behind you and get your feet on the right path. What you have done is wrong in God's eyes, because marriage is a very sacred thing to God. It would have been a terrible thing for you to be responsible for breaking up this man's family—terrible for them, and terrible in the eyes of God.

Your question suggests to me that you have never really considered your own need of Christ in your life. Down inside you are looking for love and happiness—but you will never find it in this way. However, God loves you, and He wants to come into your life and give you a joy and peace that you could never experience any other way. Jesus said, "Peace I leave with you; my peace I give you" (John 14:27).

God created you, and God loves you. His only Son, Jesus Christ, loved you so much that He gave His life on the cross so you could be saved from your sins and become a child of God. When you accept Christ into your life, something wonderful and supernatural happens. God Himself comes to dwell within you! You become part of His family, and you can know the joy of His presence every day. You can commit every area of your life to Him, because He has a perfect plan for your life. Get on your knees right now and invite Jesus Christ into your heart. It will be the most important decision you will ever make, and will get you on the right path.

I am haunted by my past. I was a soldier in Viet Nam, and like a lot of others who were there I will never get over the memory of some of the things I saw. I also got into some things (like drugs) that have been hard for me to shake. I have been involved in several rehabilitation programs that have helped me some, but once again I have become so depressed I can't even hold a job or anything. Please pray that God will help me somehow.

God has an amazing way of taking things that are painful or even wrong in our backgrounds, and helping us overcome them so that we are no longer slaves to them. I pray that this will be your experience.

That is why I encourage you to turn to Christ for the help and forgiveness you need. What can God do for you? First, He can bring you freedom from guilt, for He alone can forgive you of your sins—and one thing that is haunting you from the past is your sins. You see, sin separates us from God. But God loves us, and He wants to forgive us and bring us back to Himself. And He has done everything necessary to make our forgiveness possible, by sending His only Son, Jesus Christ, to die on the cross in our place. The Bible promises that in Christ we have "the forgiveness of sins, in accordance with the riches of God's grace" (Ephesians 1:7).

Then God also wants to give you a new purpose and strength for living. He wants you to find His will for your life—and there is no more exciting adventure than knowing God and following His will. He can also guide you to some practical programs that can help you deal with your problems. When we know Christ, we have an anchor that will keep us secure no matter what storms come our way.

Our son has a slight physical disability, and we are worried because he is very self-conscious about it and is getting more and more withdrawn. The problem is his classmates make fun of him because he is different and can't do all the things they do. Should we be concerned about this or will he grow out of this attitude, do you think?

Yes, you should be concerned and should do all you can to help him overcome it. Otherwise he is in danger of developing negative attitudes about himself and about others that could handicap him the rest of his life. Modern psychology is discovering a truth the Bible taught long ago—that the early years of a child's life are extremely important in shaping his character and direction.

Talk frankly with your son's teachers about this problem; they are probably unaware of it, and will want to do all they can to help your son. They also need to help his classmates be more sensitive—not just toward your son, but toward all who are handicapped in our society. In addition, do all you can to encourage your son and let him know that you love him just as he is.

Beyond this, however, encourage your son to commit his life to Jesus Christ. One of the most important truths any of us can discover is that we are important and valuable to God—no matter what other people may think about us or what other problems we may face. "Fear not, for I have redeemed you; I have called you by name; you are mine. When you pass through the waters, I will be with you" (Isaiah 43:1–2). How do we know this is true? We know it because Jesus Christ was willing to go to the cross and die on our behalf. Pray for your son, that he will realize he is never alone if he knows Christ.

I've always believed in God, but since our precious baby lived only a week, I'm despondent. I can't seem to pray any more. How can I find courage to go on?

I wish I could sit down and talk to you and give a full hour to answering your question. A situation like yours puts Christianity to the supreme test. Don't imagine that you are the only one who has had moments of spiritual darkness. Even the saints had their dark days. But they found God again. You can too. Do these four things:

1. Each morning kneel and thank God for all the joy He has brought through the years. Surrender your day to Him. Ask Christ to guide and direct you. Then all through the day think of Him as walking by your side.

2. Read your Bible. There you find words of wisdom and comfort, as "For now we see through a glass, darkly; but then face to face: now I know in part; but then shall I know even as also I am known" (1 Corinthians 13:12 KJV).

3. Seek opportunities to help those in need. There is someone who needs your love and care. Ask God to show you who it is.

4. Hold fast to your belief in Eternal Life. Death is not the end, but the doorway into Heaven.

This is a difficult hour for you. Remember that Jesus did not promise that His followers would escape suffering and heartache. No, He promised instead that they would have peace in the midst of pain, and be given a divine strength to support them in hours of weakness. The Bible says: "This is the victory that overcometh the world, even our faith" (1 John 5:4 KJV).

My wife is going through chemotherapy as a followup to the cancer surgery she had several months ago. The whole process has been difficult for her physically, but the surprising thing is that her spirits are very high—while I have been getting more and more depressed. I try to hide it from her, but it is only getting worse. Maybe her faith has something to do with her attitude, but whatever it is I wish I had what she has.

From what you say elsewhere it is clear that your wife has a strong faith in Christ, and God has given her an extra measure of strength for this difficult time. My prayer is that you also will come to know Christ so you can share together the joy of belonging to Him.

Why is your wife's faith making the difference? One reason is that when we know Christ we know we are never alone,
no matter what problems or suffering we face. "Where can I go
from your Spirit? Where can I flee from your presence? . . . if
I make my bed in the depths, you are there . . . even there
your hand will guide me, your right hand will hold me fast"
(Psalm 139:7, 8, 10). Another reason is this: she knows this life
is not all, and that some day she will go to be with God in
Heaven throughout eternity. And she knows in Heaven "There
will be no more death or mourning or crying or pain, for the
old order of things has passed away" (Revelation 21:4).

Right now God is seeking to get your attention. Don't turn
your back on Him. Instead, confess to God that you know
you are a sinner and need His forgiveness, and then ask Jesus
Christ to come into your life as your Savior and Lord. When
you do, you will begin to see life (and death) in a new light,
and Christ will replace your despair with hope and the light of
His presence.

*I guess I would have to say I have never been happy at any time
in my life. My father was always too busy making money and my
mother always nagged me. My marriage has not been happy, and I
find myself getting increasingly depressed. Maybe if I tried God it
would help.*

I am sorry your life has been filled with so much unhappiness.
Some of your feelings, I suspect you know, probably come from
your childhood experiences, and parents need to realize how
much their behavior affects the lives of their children for years
to come.

Yes, God can help you in this situation, and He wants to
help you because He loves you. Throughout your life you have
felt that people did not really love you—and whether you realize it or not, you probably have felt down inside that you were
not worth loving and that life was hardly worth living. But I
want to tell you good news—God loves you! How do I know
that He loves you? I know it because Jesus Christ, God's only
Son, was willing to die for your sin so that you could become
part of His family. If you had been the only person with sin in

the whole world, Christ still would have gone to the cross as a sacrifice for your sins. That's how much He loves you!

This is why one of the most important things you can do is to begin to see yourself the way God sees you. You cannot be the same once you realize God's love is focused on you. "How great is the love the Father has lavished on us, that we should be called children of God! And that is what we are!" (1 John 3:1).

Yes, God has done everything possible to wash away your sins and bring you into a personal relationship with Himself. But you must respond to His love. How can you do that? By accepting Jesus Christ into your heart by faith, asking Him to come into your life and become Lord of your life. God is only a prayer away, and He stands ready to receive you. Then get into the Scriptures, and see what they say about God's love for you. God wants to change you and give you an inner peace you have never known—and He will, as you turn in faith to Him.

A couple of months ago I took an overdose of pills because I was very depressed. I am better now, but lurking in the back of my mind is the fear that I will lose control and try to do it again. How can I get over this fear?

As I am sure you have discovered, there are many causes of depression. From a medical point of view I am sure your doctor would strongly urge you to seek professional help immediately if you find your depression is returning. But I also believe you can receive help from God to deliver you from your fears and strengthen you spiritually and emotionally.

This is why the most important thing I can tell you is to learn to trust God in every circumstance, and to keep your eyes on Him. On one occasion, the great prophet Elijah got so discouraged that he even asked God to take away his life. (You can read of his struggle in 1 Kings 19.) There were probably many things that contributed to Elijah's depression—physical weariness, hunger, a sense of defeat because he felt he had not been successful, fear of the future, and even fear that his enemies would kill him. But the heart of the matter was that Elijah was concentrating on his circumstances rather than on God. God's answer was to meet his physical needs by giving him rest and food—but more than that God gave him a new vision of the glory and power and love of God. Elijah went on to do many great things for God.

God loves you, and He wants you to know that He is with you in every situation. Christ can take away your fears, and He can give you strength to live each day. The Bible promises, "Fear not, for I have redeemed you; I have called you by name; you are mine. When you pass through the waters, I will be with you; and when you pass through the rivers, they will not sweep over you" (Isaiah 43:1–2). This can be your experience as you walk with Christ each day.

I have just been released from a mental hospital where I was treated for severe depression. I am much better now but in the back of my mind there is always the fear that it will return. For the first time in my life I am thinking about my need of God, although one of my friends says religion is just a crutch and I should learn to stand on my own two feet.

It is not a sign of weakness to admit that you need God. In fact, I would suggest that your friend is the one who is actually weak, because he is unwilling or too proud to be honest with himself and admit that he also needs God. Don't let his remarks keep you from the most important decision you can make in life— your decision to follow Christ.

We all need God, whether we admit it or not. We need Him first of all for forgiveness, because only God can truly forgive us for all the sins we have ever committed. We also need Him because He alone knows what is best for our lives, and we need His guidance if we are to live as we should. We need Him as well for strength—strength to resist temptation, strength to do what is right, and strength for daily living. And we need God because He alone can give us true hope for the future, both in this life and for the life after death.

Yes, we need God—and the wonderful thing is that God loves us and wants us to come to Him. He loves you. He knows all about your problems and your fears, and He wants you to trust all of those into His hands. How do we know this is true? We know it because God sent His Son to this earth to die for our sins on the cross.

God has promised to make you His child if you will simply ask Him to. The Bible says, "To all who received him, to those who believed in his name, he gave the right to become children of God" (John 1:12). You can go to bed tonight knowing Christ is with you, and He will never leave you no matter what the future holds for you.

I have just been told by the doctor that I have a form of cancer. He claims that it can probably be cured, but sometimes I wonder if it is even worth trying. Why does God let things like this happen?

It is understandable that you feel depressed over this news and wonder if it is even worth the effort to try to combat it. But I pray you will not give in to your despair. Your doctor undoubtedly has good reason for saying you have a good chance of being cured (although you may want to get a second opinion on this also). There have been remarkable advances in the fight against cancer in recent years, and it would be wrong for you to turn your back on these possibilities. In addition, you should remember that there are others who love you and depend on you, and for their sake you should seek the right answer to this problem.

We do not always know all the reasons why God allows things like this to happen to us. But I want to tell you something that I have heard time after time from people who have faced similar difficulties—and which I have also experienced. It is this: God can use even the painful experiences in our lives to draw us closer to Himself and accomplish His purposes. The Bible reminds us, "No discipline seems pleasant at the time, but painful. Later on, however, it produces a harvest of righteousness and peace for those who have been trained by it" (Hebrews 12:11).

Therefore, whatever the eventual outcome of your illness may be, I pray that you will constantly be open to whatever

God wants to teach you. Perhaps, for example, God wants to teach you about the importance of putting Him first in your life. Perhaps He is teaching you to trust Him more and more in every situation. Perhaps He is teaching you that the things of eternity are more important than the things of time. Don't let bitterness or anger overcome you, but use this time to discover more of God's love and mercy in your life.

What does the Bible say about suicide? Would I be forgiven if I committed suicide?

Normally I do not answer anonymous letters, but I have made an exception in your case because I sense that you are a deeply troubled person who is on the verge of doing the most serious and final thing you can do—taking your own life. With all my heart I pray that you will not take that step, for I am convinced it would be wrong. Yes, God knows our hearts, and He can forgive our sins. But that must never, never be an excuse for doing what is wrong. And if you do not know Christ, I must tell you frankly that death would not end your problems. You would instead have an eternity ahead of you of sorrow and loneliness, separated forever from God and Heaven. In other words, I want to impress upon you the seriousness of the step I sense you are about to take.

But I especially want to impress you with another great truth, and that is that God loves you and wants to come into your life right now to take away your despair and give you hope and peace. Perhaps you think that is not possible—but it is, because God is more powerful than your problems, whatever they may be.

Listen to what Jesus says to you: "Come to me, all you who are weary and burdened, and I will give you rest. Take my yoke upon you and learn from me, for I am gentle and humble in heart, and you will find rest for your souls. For my yoke is easy and my burden is light" (Matthew 11:28–30). Countless people throughout the ages have discovered this is true—and you can discover it as well as you cast your burdens on Christ. Don't give in to depression and despair—God has a plan for your life, and the most important thing you can do is to discover Him and invite Christ into your heart by faith.

A friend told us you said in a column that God would not save a person who committed suicide, no matter what the circumstances were. Our son suffered from a terrible mental problem for years and eventually committed suicide, although I really believe he knew God. What is the basis of your position?

This is not my position. Either your friend misunderstood something in the column or—as sometimes happens because of space limitations—your newspaper omitted part of the column. I regret very much this misunderstanding.

I receive many letters every week from people who are thinking about suicide. I always try to be very careful in answering them, because suicide is a terribly serious matter and I would never want someone to use something I might say as an excuse for committing this terrible act. Life is given to us by God, and He alone has the right to take it away. Furthermore, even in the midst of very difficult circumstances God is with us when we know Christ, and He can help us gain victory over them. On one hand, therefore, I must stress the fact that suicide is wrong and not part of God's plan.

But there also are situations when a person may not understand what he is doing because of mental disability, as in the case of your son. God understands such situations—even when we don't. "As a father has compassion on his children, so the Lord has compassion on those who fear him; for he knows how we are formed, he remembers that we are dust" (Psalm 103:13–14). The Bible also promises "that neither death nor life . . . nor anything else in all creation, will be able to separate us from the love of God that is in Christ Jesus our Lord" (Romans 8:38–39).

Only one thing will keep us from Heaven, and that is our refusal to turn to Christ in faith and trust. We are never saved by our good works, because we can never be good enough to earn God's favor. God saves us by His grace alone as we trust Christ. We must never presume on God's grace or think that it means we can do anything we want without paying the consequences. But take comfort in God's grace as you remember your son—and seek to live for Christ every day.

Why is it that some of the most glamorous people in life also seem to be so miserable? I think of some of the movie stars, for example, who can't seem to find a happy marriage and even end up committing suicide.

The Bible tells us that we were made for God, and when we refuse to give Him His rightful place in our lives then things go wrong and our lives become distorted. I have discovered that often people who seemingly have everything in terms of fame and fortune believe that somehow they will eventually find happiness by pursuing those things even more. But it is a dead end road, for lasting happiness and peace can only come from God.

This is what King Solomon discovered. During his reign, Israel had peace and was very wealthy. Solomon could have anything money could buy, and in search for happiness he tried everything imaginable—wealth, sex, power, pleasure, alcohol, even religion (although it was only a dead and formal kind of religion for him). "I denied myself nothing my eyes desired; I refused my heart no pleasure!" (Ecclesiastes 2:10). But what was the result of Solomon's search? "Yet when I surveyed all that my hand had done and what I had toiled to achieve, everything was meaningless, a chasing after the wind" (Ecclesiastes 2:11). Finally he realized that lasting happiness and meaning in life could only be found in God.

These things should be warnings to us, to be sure that we do not seek to fill the emptiness in our lives through things that can never satisfy our hearts. Only God can do that—and He will if we will open our hearts to Jesus Christ. Jesus said, "I have come that they may have life, and have it to the full" (John 10:10). This has been the experience of Christians throughout the ages, and it can be your experience as well as you open your heart and invite Jesus Christ into your life.

Centuries ago, God, through the prophet Isaiah, declared, "Why spend . . . your labor on what does not satisfy? . . . Give ear and come to me; hear me, that your soul may live" (Isaiah 55:2, 3). This is His invitation today as well, inviting you to come to Christ and find the true meaning of life.

I hear a lot of talk these days about the so-called "mid-life crisis." Does the Bible say anything about this?

This term is, of course, just a few years old but I think there are probably some good examples of it in the Bible. As I understand it, those who speak about a "mid-life crisis" are referring to the fact that many people (especially, I believe, men) undergo a time of crisis in their middle-age years as they think about their goals and what they have (and have not) accomplished. For some people this "crisis" causes them to flee from their responsibilities or strive to be young again—often in foolish ways, such as a middle-aged man who suddenly leaves his wife and falls in "love" with a teen-aged girl.

I wonder if in some ways King David had something of a similar experience when he reached his middle years. You may recall that one time he was supposed to be in battle with his troops, but for some reason he had grown slack and stayed instead at the palace. There he saw a beautiful woman named Bathsheba. She was another man's wife, but David committed the sin of adultery with her. It was a dark time in the life of a man who otherwise had tried to obey God, and for some months David lived out of fellowship with God. (You can read about this in 2 Samuel 11.)

But eventually David faced his sin and realized the foolishness—and the evil—of what he had done. One of the most eloquent prayers of repentance in the whole Bible is found in Psalm 51. "Have mercy on me, O God, according to your unfailing love; . . . Wash away all my iniquity and cleanse me from my sin" (Psalm 51:1, 2).

If you sense that you are facing this kind of crisis—or any other kind—realize that the most important thing in life is to yield your life to Christ and then seek to do His will. If we know we are in the will of God, there need not be moments of self-doubt and crisis. As David said elsewhere, "You have made known to me the path of life; you will fill me with joy in your presence, with eternal pleasures at your right hand" (Psalm 16:11). You can know this also as you follow Christ as your Lord.

I guess I am going through sort of a mid-life crisis, because suddenly I have realized I am getting older and I have wasted so much time. I have always acted as if I would always be young and able to do anything I wanted, but now I know it isn't true. I don't know why I am writing you, but somehow I feel as if I need to rethink my life and where I am heading.

I am thankful you are facing these questions; one of the saddest things I know of is to see persons who come to the end of life and have never asked who they are or why they were here.

You are not here by chance; God put you here. He put you here for a purpose, and the most important thing you can do is discover that purpose and to commit yourself to it. What is God's purpose for you? First of all, God wants you to come to know Him personally by giving your life to Jesus Christ. Then He wants you to discover in your daily life what it means to live for Him and follow His will. The Bible says, "But seek first his kingdom and his righteousness" (Matthew 6:33).

What have you been living for? Money? Pleasure? Security? Happiness? Success? Whatever it has been, it can never give you lasting happiness or security. You were made for a relationship with God, and you will only find true meaning and purpose in Christ. So far you have made yourself the center of your life. Now make Christ the center of your life by asking Him to come into your heart as your Lord and Savior. Then you can say of God with the Psalmist, "You have made known to me the path of life" (Psalm 16:11).

I have read a lot recently about mid-life crisis, and I think it fits my husband exactly. He has always worked very hard and been successful, but now he says he is fed up with everything and wants a

new career and a new family. Our heart is broken, but he has left us
for his girl friend, who is much younger. Is there anything I can do?

I know a lot has been written in recent years about the so-called mid-life crisis—a time when some people become disillusioned with their lives and decide to strike out in radically different ways. Whatever the cause, decisions such as the one your husband has made inevitably bring heartache and unhappiness—not only to those around him, but eventually to the person himself.

Pray for your husband. As did the prodigal son in the story which Jesus told (Luke 15:11–32), your husband has deceived himself into thinking that he will find happiness by fleeing his responsibilities and disobeying God's moral law. Only God can awaken him to the tragedy and foolishness of what he is doing. Pray that God will break through the moral blindness which has gripped him, and convict him of his sin. Pray also that your husband will realize his need of repentance, and that he will turn to Christ for forgiveness.

Then in whatever ways are open to you let your husband know that you still love him and want to forgive him. The time may come when he (like the prodigal son) will sink so low that he will come to his senses and realize the only right thing to do is to return home. The father of the prodigal son welcomed him, and you should let your husband know you will welcome him if he will turn from his wrongdoing. Let him know also that you are willing to make adjustments if they are necessary—adopting a more relaxed lifestyle, for example, so he does not feel trapped by a constant push for success.

Finally, do all you can to help your children right now. It is a difficult time, but seek God's wisdom and strength to carry on and help your children mature. If Christ has never been the foundation of your family before this, turn to Him and make it your goal to help your children understand that God never fails us—even when our human fathers may fail.

I understand that the Bible tells us to forgive our enemies many
times. Although I have tried to forgive a certain person for a wrong
done deliberately, I simply cannot. I have no other enemies. Do you

*think God will judge me for having just this one person whom I
cannot forgive?*

Even the non-Christian has friends and loved ones, but he loves
them because they love him in return. Here is the distinctive-
ness of the Christian life. Jesus said: "Love your enemies, and
pray for those who persecute you" (Matthew 5:44). On another
occasion He said that we should forgive until seventy times
seven. God can and will give a forgiving spirit when we accept
His forgiveness through Jesus Christ. When you do, you will
realize that He has forgiven you so much that you will desire
to forgive any wrong. In the world, a policy of getting even
with the other fellow is generally accepted. We Christians,
on the other hand, should follow the policy of enduring wrong
for the sake of Christ and forgiving that men might through us
discover the grace of God in forgiving the sinner.

15 | *Why Do I Act the Way I Do?*

I don't understand why I act the way I do. I grew up with an alcoholic father, and I always hated it and swore I would never be like him. Well, now I find I can't control my drinking either, and secretly I fear ending up the same old way he did. Why am I this way?

Children of alcoholics often end up on the same road as their parents—in spite of the destruction they have seen.

There may be several reasons for this. Some recent research, for example, suggests some people are physically very susceptible to alcoholism, and that this tendency may even be inherited. But it also is clear that for many people alcohol becomes an easy "solution" to escape from their problems (although it is never a real or lasting solution). In other words, possibly you have been scarred and hurt emotionally by your background—and in spite of your better judgment, you had turned to alcohol to try to take away some of that hurt.

But whatever the reasons may be, the important thing is for you to face it and get the help you need. Don't assume you can deal with this on your own; alcoholism can destroy you. The Bible warns, "Who has woe? Who has sorrow? Who has strife? . . . Those who linger over wine . . . In the end it bites like a snake and poisons like a viper" (Proverbs 23:29, 30, 32). There are organizations in your community that can help you. Share your problem honestly with your pastor and/or doctor and let him help you get the help you need.

Above all, you are very important to God and He does not want you to allow yourself to be destroyed. He loves you, and He wants to help you. Commit your life to Christ and ask Him to guide you to the help you need.

My home life was chaotic when I was growing up—alcoholic father, mother who ran around a lot, eventual divorce, running away from home, foster homes, etc. My aunt always told me I was to blame for all the troubles my parents had because I was just a problem to them. Now that I am an adult I find those accusations still haunt me and I feel like I am worth nothing. What ideas do you have about overcoming these feelings?

Feelings like this which have their roots in long-lasting childhood experiences are not easily overcome. It may even be helpful for you to seek out a counselor (a trained psychologist or psychiatrist) who can help you work through these things and understand them better; your pastor can perhaps suggest someone if this is necessary.

However, the greatest thing you can do is discover the great truth of how God feels about you. You feel very negative about yourself, but have you ever thought about how God looks at you? Listen: He loves you, and you are very valuable to Him. This is a *fact*, no matter what your *feelings* may tell you. Our feelings, you see, can deceive us. They can actually trick us into believing something which is not true. There are reasons why your feelings are the way they are—but they still are not telling the truth, because God says you are very precious to Him.

Ask Christ to come into your life by a simple prayer of faith. Then read the Bible on a daily basis. Start with the Gospel of John or the little book of 1 John and note what is said repeatedly about God's love for us. The Bible says, "Perfect love drives out fear" (1 John 4:18)—and God's perfect love can drive out your fear that you are worthless, as you realize the wonderful truth of His love for you.

I am always getting excited about projects of various sorts, and throw myself into them with all my energy. But then I lose interest and it seems like I never finish anything I start out to do. I wonder why I can't seem to overcome this. I guess this isn't a spiritual problem, but maybe you have some ideas.

Every problem has a spiritual side to it and yours is no exception. Let me assure you also that God is concerned about the problems we face in life, and He wants to help us deal with them.

Have you ever really asked yourself why you back away from projects and never seem to complete them? I do not know the answer, and there may be several reasons—but I would encourage you to examine this. For example, some people never finish a task because down inside they are afraid of failure—and the easiest way to avoid failure is to avoid doing the project in the first place. But we should not let fear of failure or embarrassment keep us from doing things in life; God, after all, accepts us just as we are. I suspect you would begin to overcome this problem if you would stay with one project all the way (perhaps asking others to help you stick to it)—and discover you really can do it.

But let me point you to a far more important question: Have you let this attitude spill over into your spiritual life? Has there been a time in your life when you got excited about following Christ and doing God's will—and then you drifted away? Or have you ever faced your own need of God and given your life to Christ? Commit your life to Him, and then with His help "run with perseverance the race marked out for us. Let us fix our eyes on Jesus . . . so that you will not grow weary and lose heart" (Hebrews 12:1–3).

Both my brother and sister are very gifted. I am just ordinary. They get many chances to do work in our church while I only get a few. This makes me feel very discouraged, for I feel the Lord can't use me as He does them. How can I avoid getting so discouraged?

The Bible is full of ordinary people. As a matter of fact, God uses ordinary people far more often than He does the rich, the powerful, the famous, and the influential. Jesus chose ordinary people as His disciples. Moses had grave doubts about his abilities.

God uses the humble, not the proud, to achieve His objectives. You say that your brother and sister are very gifted, but so are you. When God gives the gift, it is valuable, no matter what it may be. God's greatest gift to man is salvation and it is the greatest gift we can give to others.

The Bible says that God has chosen the foolish (or ordinary) things of this world to confound the wise. You are very valuable to God because He made you just as you are. Ask God to show you His plan for your life. When you discover God's plan for your life and act on it, you will begin to see yourself as God already sees you: as an extraordinary person whom God loves and needs.

I have just completed a prison sentence of three years. Upon returning home, I find that I am not accepted in society anymore. I have no work, and almost no friends. Do you think I am wrong to be resentful toward people who will have little to do with me? I want to go straight, but it seems that people want to push me back down where I was.

Yours is one of the problems common to every person who has violated the law and been imprisoned. Your problem is not new. What you must realize is that you have given people a reason to distrust you, and now it is up to you to give society a reason to accept you. It won't be easy, and it is one of the aspects of your punishment. I would suggest two things for you to do.

The burden is upon you, first of all, to convince society of your intention to go straight. This will take time and will be painful for you, but it will be worth the effort.

Second, discover a power that will hold you true to the purpose you have set before you. You cannot go the road alone, for you too are a social creature. Remember that to begin with, God made you to have fellowship with others. Even though society cannot forget quickly your crime, God will forgive your sins the moment you take Jesus Christ as your Savior.

You have already gone halfway in repentance in being sorry for your sin. Why not go the other half of the way and turn to God who right now is seeking for your heart and for your faith? Then find a fellowship of Christians who will accept you. There are some, even though you do not think so now. If you do that, God will sustain you through the days of readjustment, and even more, He will keep you to the end of life in fellowship that is more precious than the best friend can provide.

I think I must be addicted to television soap operas. I know I spend too much time watching them, but I get hooked on them and just can't seem to break the habit. Do you think there's anything harmful in this?

I suspect that you know the answer to your own question, because I detect a sense of guilt in your letter and a feeling that you know you should be using your time in a more productive way. Yes, I think you need to re-examine the way you spend your time.

There are at least two reasons I say this. First, I suspect there is a good chance you are spending so much time watching television (from what you say) that you are neglecting other things that you ought to be doing. Time is a very precious thing—once a minute is lost, it is lost forever. The Bible tells us to "redeem the time" (Colossians 4:5 KJV). There is a legitimate place for relaxation and recreation. But we also have been given responsibilities by God—within our family, our job, etc.

Second, you need to ask yourself if your time can be used to better advantage or profit, and even if this sort of activity could be harmful to you. (We should ask this about anything that threatens to absorb our interest and I don't mean to single out soap operas any more than any other activity.) The Bible gives a general principle which should guide our thinking and our activities: "Whatever is true, whatever is noble, whatever is right, whatever is pure, whatever is lovely, whatever is admirable—if anything is excellent or praiseworthy—think about such things" (Philippians 4:8). By this standard I am afraid many of our activities (including, frankly, much that appears in the media today) do not measure up.

I have been urging you not to escape from your responsibilities. But I would include especially your spiritual responsibilities in this. Have you ever thought seriously about your own relationship with God? Are you spending time each day in prayer and Bible study, seeking to learn more about God's will for your life?

My husband has been a fine man in many ways, but our home is being wrecked because he is obsessed with gambling. He is always hoping his luck will change. He says he doesn't see anything morally wrong with it, but I wonder what your opinion is.

What your husband is doing is wrong for several reasons, and I hope he will have the courage to face this, turn from what he is doing, and get help. It may not be easy, I know; some people are so compulsive about gambling that it becomes almost like an addictive drug. But there are organizations that can help such people—and most of all God wants to help you and your husband deal with this and get your home back on a solid foundation.

Let me mention two reasons why your husband's compulsive gambling is wrong. First, it is wrong because of the motive behind it. Greed can easily take over someone who is deeply involved in gambling, and even if such a person wins he will often keep on gambling hoping to win even more—which usually doesn't happen. The Bible wisely says, "Whoever loves money never has money enough; whoever loves wealth is never satisfied with his income" (Ecclesiastes 5:10). One of the Ten Commandments declares, "You shall not covet" (Exodus 20:17). Why does the Bible warn us against covetousness and greed? Because God knows that when greed consumes us it pushes out of our lives things that should be there, and makes us do things that are wrong.

Second, it also is wrong because of its effects. Your letter indicates that your husband has incurred some serious debts because of his gambling. In addition, he is spending time and energy on his gambling habit and is neglecting his responsibilities as a husband and father. The Bible rightly says, "A greedy man brings trouble to his family" (Proverbs 15:27).

Pray for your husband, and seek to talk frankly—but not in anger with him. If he is honest he will realize he needs to

turn from his habit, and seek the help and strength that God
wants to give him.

*Do you think God is concerned about how we take care of our bod-
ies? I have never taken very good care of it and I'm seriously over-
weight, although I am still in my twenties.*

God is concerned about our bodies. He gave them to us, and it
is wrong for us to abuse them. But if you know Jesus Christ as
your Lord and Savior, there is a further reason to take care of
your body, and that is because God the Holy Spirit now lives
within you.

This is why the Bible says, "Do you not know that your
body is a temple of the Holy Spirit, who is in you, whom you
have received from God? You are not your own; you were
bought at a price. Therefore honor God with your body"
(1 Corinthians 6:19–20). Note that the Bible here teaches that
one reason Jesus Christ died for you on the cross was to make
you His own, including your body. You no longer "own" it—it
is God's. You therefore are to be a good steward or guardian of
it, and not abuse it or use it for purposes that dishonor God.
Instead, the way you treat your body should be a sign of how
you treat God. We can abuse our bodies in many ways—
overeating, drugs and alcohol, lack of proper exercise, etc. Of
course we also can become overly concerned about our bodies,
so that we spend all our time and money trying to impress
others with our beauty or strength. Either extreme—neglect, or
overindulgence—is wrong.

But this leads me to ask you a very direct question. Have
you ever seriously considered the fact that you need to offer
your whole life—not just your body, but everything else, including your mind and your future—to Jesus Christ? God is not
only concerned about your body, He is concerned about you.
He wants to come into your life as Lord. He loves you and
wants you to experience His love every day.

There may be many reasons why you have not taken care
of yourself as you should. Perhaps you do not really see yourself as a person who is worth something, for example. But God

says you are worth something! And He wants to take your life
and turn you into the person He created you to be.

*I am a married man, with a good wife, and seven healthy, happy
children. I work hard, and can barely make ends meet. But my neighbors who have no children get a new car every year, are able to go on
trips, and eat much better than we do. I must confess I am a little
envious of them. How can I keep from envying them?*

I wouldn't be surprised to find out that your neighbors envy you
more than you envy them. By almost every measure, you are a
rich man. Happily married, a good wife, seven happy, healthy
children, and able to work. You are one of the wealthiest persons
in town.

  The Bible says: "Better is a dinner of herbs where love is,
than a stalled ox and hatred therewith" (Proverbs 15:17 KJV).
If you could stand back and look at yourself objectively, you
would see that you have every reason to be happy.

  Perhaps you lack just one thing. The Bible says: "Better is
a little with the fear (reverence) of the Lord than great treasure
and trouble therewith" (Proverbs 15:16 KJV). Your display of
envy shows that you have a spiritual need. Slip to your knees
tonight and say: "Dear God, forgive me for being envious of my
neighbor who in reality has much less than I. Help me to reverence You and to live for You." See if this doesn't help you.

*All my friends think I am a very happy person, but on the inside I
know it is not so. I really feel empty inside, and I don't know what
to do about it, do you?*

Where do you suppose that empty place in your heart came
from? The Bible says that it came from God. You see, you were
created to have fellowship with God, and to have Him at the
center of your life. That is true for all of us. But when we leave
God out of our lives, it leaves a blank or empty space that
nothing can fully fill. No matter how hard we try or what
means we use—material possessions, money, pleasure, drugs,
or whatever—the emptiness is still there.

There is only one lasting solution to this problem. If the void or empty place in our hearts is there because we have left God out of our lives, the only solution is to let Him come back into our lives and assume His rightful place.

Is this possible? Yes, it certainly is, and I have seen it happen to countless people of every background. I have experienced it in my own life. Apart from Christ, the Bible tells us, we are "harassed and helpless, like sheep without a shepherd" (Matthew 9:36). But God loves us, and one reason He has allowed you to have this feeling of emptiness in your heart is that He loves you and wants you to seek Him. He wants to enter your life and take up residence there. Jesus says to you today, "Here I am! I stand at the door and knock. If anyone hears my voice and opens the door, I will come in and eat with him, and he with me" (Revelation 3:20). Christ stands at the door of your heart, asking to come in, and promising to enter your life and have fellowship with you if you will turn your life over to Him.

How can you do this? Imagine that someone offered you a lovely gift. This person has paid for it—all you had to do was reach out and take it. Christ has already paid the price for your salvation—the shedding of His blood on the cross. All you have to do is reach out by faith and accept it. Then you can know the peace of Christ in your heart.

I just don't understand what is wrong with me. I don't have any problems in my marriage and our children are all grown up and are successful. I have a lot of friends and more than enough money. However, somehow I feel completely empty inside. What is wrong?

I believe that your question could be echoed by many people in our society. We are the richest society that has ever lived. Yet we have discovered that it takes more than wealth or leisure or pleasure to satisfy the deepest longings of the human heart.

Why is this? The reason is that God created us for a purpose, but as long as we turn our backs on Him and decide to run our own lives without Him we will always be unfulfilled. Many centuries ago King Solomon of Israel accumulated great wealth—in fact, he was apparently the wealthiest man of his time. But his heart was empty, so he began to search for ways to fill it. He tried everything—from even greater wealth to pleasure to alcohol. But in the end, he realized that only God could fill the emptiness of his life. (You can read of his search in the Old Testament book of Ecclesiastes.)

Let Christ come into your life and give you meaning and purpose. Let Him fill the empty space you sense is there. Let Him become the center of your life, instead of all the substitutes you have tried to use to give happiness to you. You need Christ, and you need to discover the amazing truth that God loves you. Jesus said, "I have come that they may have life, and have it to the full" (John 10:10). Invite Christ to come into your life by faith right now—there is no reason to delay.

Then learn to walk with Him each day. He is as near as a prayer. He is as near as your Bible—which you should turn to each day to understand more of what God has done for you and what He wants you to do. "Why spend money on . . . what does not satisfy? . . . Give ear and come to me; hear me, that your soul may live" (Isaiah 55:2, 3). How good God has been to you in a day when many families are falling apart.

I have always been a nervous and high-strung person, but recently it has become worse and I am constantly worrying and anxious about the future. Do you suppose some people are just this way, or can I do anything about it?

People have different temperaments and personalities, and some individuals undoubtedly have a tendency toward excessive worrying. But God wants to help us at the exact places where we are weak, and He wants to help you overcome this problem.

The key is to realize that nothing—not a single thing—takes God by surprise, because He knows all about the future. And when we are in His hands, then we need not fear the future either, because we know He is with us every step of the way. "So do not fear, for I am with you; do not be dismayed, for I am your God. I will strengthen you and help you; I will uphold you with my righteous right hand" (Isaiah 41:10).

What should you do? First, commit your life to Jesus Christ by asking Him to come into your heart as your personal Lord and Savior. Then turn to Him each day, and in prayer commit every day and every problem into His hands. Let His Word, the Bible, also be part of your life every day, and learn to trust the promises God has given you in it. God knows your weaknesses and your fears, but He will strengthen you as you learn to trust Him and thank Him. "Rejoice in the Lord always . . . . Do not be anxious about anything, but in everything, by prayer and petition, with thanksgiving, present your requests to God. And the peace of God, which transcends all understanding, will guard your hearts and your minds in Christ Jesus" (Philippians 4:4, 6–7). Let this be your experience as you trust every detail of your future into His loving hands.

16 | *I Worry about the Future*

I am retired, and I am consumed with worry about the future. It seems like every time I open the newspaper they are talking about the terrible state of the economy, and I wonder if I'm going to have enough to live on in my old age. I know I shouldn't worry so much, but I can't seem to help it.

As long as you look only at the situation in the world today, it will be very hard for you, I think, to overcome your worries because it is true that there are many problems and the future is unknown to us. I'm sure that as a retired person you find much of what is happening in the world to be frightening.

But I want you to lift your eyes beyond your circumstances and learn instead to trust God and His goodness. You can't see the future, no matter how hard you try. It may bring problems—or it may not. (And worrying about it won't change anything, of course, although it is easy for us to forget that.) Jesus said, "Who of you by worrying can add a single hour to his life?" (Matthew 6:27). But note this very carefully: you don't know the future, but God does. And even more importantly, God is in control of the future. And because He loves us and is in control of the future, He can be trusted to take care of us and watch over us.

Let me suggest two phrases that should constantly be in your heart as you think about the future. They are "Give thanks" and "Trust God." First, learn to give thanks to God for what you have, and for the ways He has blessed you. Even when life may be difficult, we should thank God for all He does for us—which we do not deserve. We should be "always giving thanks to God the Father for everything, in the name of our Lord Jesus Christ"

(Ephesians 5:20). Most of all, we should thank God for what He has done for us in Jesus Christ. Have you ever done that, and have you accepted Jesus Christ into your heart by faith so that you know you will go to be with Him in Heaven? Your relationship to Christ is the most important thing you should be thinking about right now, and you can settle it once and for all by turning to Christ in faith and trust.

And when you come to Christ, then you realize you can trust God for your future—both now and eternally. Read what Jesus had to say about worry in Matthew 6:25–34, and look to Him to supply all your needs.

I am seventy-two years old. I have a depressed and hopeless feeling. I have no living relatives. Is there anything left in life for a man of my age? If so, how can I find it?

A very old man—much older than you—when he lay dying, said, 'I have found that all the sugar is at the bottom of the cup." Life can grow sweeter and more rewarding as we grow older if we possess the presence of Christ. Sunsets are always glorious. It is Christ who adds colors, glory, and beauty to man's sunsets. Try to find one person a day whom you can tell about your new joy in Christ.

I am a very old man now. I have been very wicked all my life. Just recently I found Jesus through one of your radio broadcasts. Is there any way I can redeem the years I have lost?

Sin makes an indelible impression on us in this life. You will never get over the regret of having lived for the devil all these years. But God can do the impossible. God can do more with a few days of your time if given completely to Him, than He can with a whole life characterized by a half-hearted service. The lukewarm Christian can accomplish nothing with a whole life in which to do it. If you have lived for sin and self these many years, your witness will have telling effect on all who have known you. They will see the change and will be deeply impressed by God's power in your life. Take every advantage to let everyone know the change that has been brought about in you through your faith in Christ. God can, through your yield-edness, accomplish much in a short time. Now is not the time for discouragement, but for a song of triumph and victory. Let everyone know of God's grace toward you.

I have passed the proverbial "three score years and ten," have been pensioned by my company, and in general seem quite useless. Actually, I feel very well and would like to be doing things, but nobody wants my help.

You can have some of your most useful and happy years before you. With no responsibilities in employment you can devote your time, strength, and wisdom gained from experience to help in very worthwhile projects in your church and community. Your busy pastor has many tasks that are really important in themselves to which he can assign you. There are shut-ins to visit and widows and orphans to advise, the discouraged to cheer, the young men to counsel. With an old head and a young heart you can be a source of real strength to the many who need your cheer and encouragement.

In your community you will find tasks that should be done, but are overlooked or neglected by busy people in the prime of life, and which you can do very satisfactorily. If you seem to be "on the shelf" make sure that you are on a shelf so low that your friends and neighbors can reach you easily and enlist you to help them do the things for which you are much better qualified than they are. Just do not sit in the corner and look inward; rather, be on the corner to respond to the challenge—and above all make sure you have made preparation for the inevitable by accepting Christ as your personal Lord and Savior. Life does not begin at forty but with God.

17 | *Do I Need a Psychiatrist?*

I have some emotional problems, and my family doctor says that I need to see a psychiatrist. A friend of mine, however, says that if I just have enough faith these problems will go away. What do you think?

I would be the first to say that faith in God is very, very important. It is essential for our eternal salvation, and it is crucial for our everyday lives as well. But at the same time I do not agree with your friend, because God may choose to use an able psychiatrist to help you with some of the problems you are facing.

You see, when you have faith in God, you are actually trusting a problem into His hands. You are saying, in effect, "Lord, I don't know how to deal with this problem, but I have faith that You do. I trust You to lead me and give me wisdom, so I will know what is right. I trust You to show me the right answer to this situation." Faith, in other words, does not necessarily mean that we sit back and fold our hands, assuming that God will work without ever using any human tools.

Do you remember the incident when Jesus healed a man who had been blind since birth? (You can read about it in Chapter 9 of John's Gospel.) Jesus could have simply pronounced the man healed. But instead He used some mud which He put on the man's eyes, and then told him to go and wash it off in a certain pool of water. I believe one reason Jesus did this was to show us that at times He uses earthly tools or instruments to bring healing.

Therefore you should not feel that you are wrong in seeking the help of a psychiatrist or trained psychologist if that will help you deal with some deep-seated emotional problems.

Seek one who will not discourage you in your faith in God. (Your pastor can perhaps suggest a Christian psychiatrist in your area.) And at the same time ask God to help you grow in your faith in Him. I am convinced that many emotional problems today are caused by spiritual concerns. Some people, for example, are beset with deep feelings of guilt that they cannot shake. Christ, however, is the only ultimate answer to guilt because He alone can offer us full forgiveness. God bless you as you seek help to overcome these problems.

I am a homosexual. I have tried to conquer it and have prayed to God time after time, but nothing changes. I desperately want to deal with it, but I don't know what to do. Please help me.

God wants to help you with this problem, and I am thankful you are facing it honestly and not excusing it (as the tendency is in some circles today). Homosexual behavior is wrong in God's eyes, but He still loves you and can guide you as you seek to deal honestly with your situation.

There are steps that are crucial for you to follow if you are ever to conquer this. First, if you have never asked Christ to come into your life I urge you to do so without delay. Christ took all your sins upon Himself when He died on the cross. You need the forgiveness only Christ can bring, and when you turn to Him He freely forgives you by His grace. Right now you are burdened with the knowledge you have sinned but Christ can lift that burden if you will trust Him as your Lord and Savior.

Then get help from others for your problem. Don't be afraid to seek help or to share your problem in confidence with someone you can trust who also can help you. There may be many complex reasons for your homosexual tendencies, and a skilled pastor can probably point you to a Christian psychologist or psychiatrist who has had experience in dealing with others who have been in your situation. Such a person can help you understand yourself and why you have become the person you are, and will also help you—both emotionally and spiritually—

to leave your old way of living and become the person Christ
wants you to be.

Finally, several people who have dealt with persons such
as yourself have stressed how important it is for you to remove
yourself from every type of temptation. This has a strong grip
on you, and that grip will only become stronger if you do not
separate yourself from those persons and surroundings that
have entrapped you in the past. God bless you as you turn your
life over to Christ and take practical steps to overcome this.

*Why do you so often suggest that religion is a cure-all, when mod-
ern psychiatry has done so much for mentally disturbed persons?*

Religion is not a cure-all, but the gospel of Christ certainly is
the only answer to the sin problem. If the problem is one that
is related to sin and its consequences, then Christ is the answer,
and not psychiatry. If the disturbance is purely a mental one,
then a competent psychiatrist might give satisfactory help. It
would call for a psychiatrist with real spiritual insight to be
able to tell the difference between the purely mental problem -
and the spiritual one. Let it be known that Christianity is not
opposed to everything modern but only such claims that are
not totally true and that do injustice to the claims of the gospel.
I wish every mentally disturbed person might be counseled by
one who knows the functioning of the human mind and knows
equally well the message of deliverance through Jesus Christ.

*I have difficulty sleeping at night without sleeping tablets. Is it
wrong to use artificial aids for sleep?*

Physicians say that millions of Americans must take sleeping
tablets in order to sleep. I heard of one man who set his alarm
clock for 2 A.M. to wake himself up, so he could take another pill!

Sleeplessness is caused by a number of things: tension,
worry, and the lack of proper work or exercise. The Bible suggests another reason for sleeplessness: "But the wicked are like
the tossing sea, which cannot rest, whose waves cast up mire

and dirt" (Isaiah 57:20). Though I would not go so far as to say
that believing Christians are never troubled with insomnia, I do
believe that much sleeplessness is caused by a troubled conscience. I used to have sleepless nights when thoughts of my
critics raced through my mind. But as I dropped on my knees
and asked God to fill my heart with His love, I have found
peace—and rest.

Try repeating this verse from Isaiah over and over in your
mind when you can't sleep: "Thou wilt keep him in perfect
peace, whose mind is stayed on thee" (26:3 KJV). Let thoughts of
God's love, holiness, and majesty fill your mind, and I believe it
will help you to find rest and relaxation.

*My mother committed suicide some time ago. I have since been ob-
sessed with the fear that I would do the same thing sometime. Can
you tell me how to overcome such a fear?*

Apart from any religious meaning, I believe you are suffering
from a kind of identification with your mother, which is a common thing. No doubt you cared for your mother and also believe
that you might have some of the same potential within yourself.
You must recognize the fact that there is no reason why you
should be compelled to do the same, unless it is a result of concentrating on it. You must divert your mind and begin to think
on something else.

Your problem is not only psychological but also spiritual.
If you have given yourself completely to Christ and are abso-
lutely surrendered to His control, there can be no thought of
suicide. The apostle Paul once said: "Don't worry about anything; instead, pray about everything; tell God your needs and
don't forget to thank him for his answers. If you do this, you
will experience God's peace, which is far more wonderful than
the human mind can understand. His peace will keep your
hearts quiet and at rest as you trust in Christ Jesus" (Philippians 4:6–7 TLB). The apostle again said: "Fix your thoughts on
what is right and pure and good . . ." (Philippians 4:8 TLB).
Christ can so completely change your nature and control your
mind that you can find complete relief and joy in serving Him.

I would suggest that you see your minister and have a frank discussion with him.

I cannot forget the abortion that was performed on me. Can you help me find peace of mind?

You did not give any details about your case. Assuming that the termination of your pregnancy was for selfish reasons, other than to save your own life, it is clear that you have sinned, as did those who had a part in it. God gives life, and we have no right to take it. But we are not to assume that this sin is unforgivable. Moses once killed a man, but found forgiveness, and went on to become one of history's great emancipators. Saul of Tarsus had participated in the execution of Stephen, but he had an encounter with Christ on the Damascus Road, and became the first and perhaps greatest Christian missionary. This does not excuse abortion, nor should women seek an abortion simply because God can forgive a truly repentant heart, but to despair over the magnitude of your sin will only make matters worse. My suggestion is that you come to Him who said: "Come unto me, all ye that labor and are heavy laden, and I will give you rest" (Matthew 11:28 KJV). No person, regardless of the extent of his sin, ever responded to this call without finding rest of soul. Don't delay any longer. God is ready, able, and willing to forgive you and give you His peace.

I worry constantly. At the present time I am almost on the point of a breakdown. I know this is not fitting for a Christian. All those with whom I have counseled tell me there is nothing to be concerned about, but I believe there is much to worry about. With a sick husband, a boy in the Army, an uncertain job, and a few other things, I can't help it. Do you have any suggestions?

You certainly seem to have much to worry about. Your problems are great and without God's help, you cannot bear them. You are entitled to worry unless you believe God. Faith and worry are mutually exclusive. I would not tell you that there is nothing to be concerned about. But what I would tell you is that there is Someone who loves you and cares for you. There is Someone who knows your problem, and still better, He can take your cares. Peter tells us: "Cast all your anxiety on him because he cares for you" (1 Peter 5:7). So, although you have much to worry about, let Jesus take that worry. If He can carry the load of your sin and the sin of the world, He can also bear your present burden, lift the load, and give you inner resources that will enable you to live victoriously.

Although I am a Christian and do trust the Lord, I find I am becoming very nervous and irritable—often about quite trifling things. I feel I have just about reached the breaking point and cannot cope any longer. What do you think is wrong with me?

More than one thing may be wrong, but it sounds as though you are physically rundown and have got into a state of nervous exhaustion. In that case you need to relax a bit more, to find time for some recreation, and if possible to get away for a few days' holiday.

Remember that as a Christian it is your duty to keep yourself as fit as possible, spiritually *and* physically. You cannot be the best for God if you drive yourself to the point where you are practically dropping with fatigue and something within you is about to snap.

When the apostles returned from their first preaching tour the Lord Jesus said to them, "Come ye yourselves apart . . . and rest awhile" (Mark 6:31 KJV). He recognized that they had bodies as well as souls. He knew their need of rest if they were to be of further service to Him.

There is something else I would ask you to remember. When Jesus called those apostles to come apart and rest awhile, He was inviting them to spend time in communion with Him. I wonder how that applies to you? Are you finding time each day for fellowship with the Lord?

Nothing so restores mental equilibrium as regular, daily prayer. Try the apostolic formula: "Do not be anxious about anything, but in everything by prayer and petition, with thanksgiving, present your requests to God. And the peace of God . . .

will guard your hearts and your minds in Christ Jesus" (Philippians 4:6–7).

I have a chronic intestinal trouble which the doctor says is caused by worry. He tells me to relax, but how can I when the success of my business and the employment of thousands of people depends upon me?

Your question indicates that you believe your work is important. If that is true, it is God's work. He has given it to you. And He will help you do it, if you ask Him.

Begin each day by saying the Lord's Prayer. When you come to the words, "Give us this day our daily bread," remember that Jesus told us to ask only for the needs of one day. Most of our worries come from being too concerned about the future. When Christ was in Galilee He gave Himself entirely to the work there. He didn't wear Himself out by worrying about what would happen to Him in Jerusalem when it was time for Him to go there. He knew that when future trials came, He could meet them with the Father's help.

In the life of Christ we find our example. Trust in God. Each morning ask Him to guide you in the decisions you must make that day. Every hour take time to send a minute prayer to Heaven. You may have felt like a deep-sea diver who is suffocating for want of air. Prayer is the lifeline that brings divine oxygen to your lungs.

Then when you go from your place of business, leave all thoughts of your work behind. Enjoy your family and friends. Take time to read the Bible daily. Take some recreation each week.

Jesus said: "Take no thought for the morrow: for the morrow shall take thought for the things of itself" (Matthew 6:34). Do this. Live one day at a time, trusting in God, and you'll find no need to worry.

18 | *Is There Life after Death?*

I would give anything to know—really know—that there was a God and that there was life after death. But I have almost given up, because it seems like everyone has a different opinion on this subject.

How do you suppose we could know beyond doubt that God existed and that there was indeed life after death? If you think about those two questions, I believe you will agree that we could know that God existed only if He revealed Himself to us. And we could only know for certain that there was life after death if someone clearly came back from the dead.

And this is exactly what has happened! We are not left to guess or grope around for the truth—because God has shown us the truth. The Bible tells us something that is almost beyond our comprehension: God Himself has come down and walked on the planet. He did this by becoming a man, and He did it not only so we could know that God existed, but so we could know Him and have a personal relationship with Him. You can know God right now by committing your life to Jesus Christ. God loves you, and just as surely as you could have known Jesus Christ almost two thousand years ago, you can still know Him because He is alive in Heaven and wants to come into your heart.

But we also know that there is life after death because Jesus Christ died and then rose again to life. Christ died on the cross as a sacrifice for our sins, and He rose again to show us we can be forgiven and can have eternal life with God in Heaven. Some day all those who know Christ will be raised again and given new and glorious bodies, and we will be with Christ forever.

You can know—really know—God, and you can know the

joy of eternal life right now by receiving the gift of God's Son into your life and committing your life to Him. 'For God so loved the world that he gave his one and only Son, that whoever believes in him shall not perish but have eternal life. For God did not send his Son into the world to condemn the world, but to save the world through him. Whoever believes in him is not condemned' (John 3:16–18).

What do you think about these stories of people who have supposedly died and then been revived on the operating table, and experienced the sensation of feeling like they were being welcomed by a divine being clothed in light? Don't these prove there is life after death?

Several years ago, I wrote a book on the subject of death and life after death, and in the course of my research I investigated a number of these alleged incidents (which are, incidentally, relatively rare). Various explanations have been given for them-from the influence of chemicals on the brain to demonic hallucinations. Whatever the cause, however, they are not a conclusive proof of life after death. There are certainly other cases (including that of my own mother) when a dying person may be given a glimpse of Heaven.

We do not need to look to such experiences for proof of life after death, however. For the Christian there is one supreme reason for knowing there is life after death, and that is the resurrection of Jesus Christ. Christ died on the cross for our salvation, and God raised Him from the dead to demonstrate beyond doubt that there is hope beyond the grave. 'Praise be to the God and Father of our Lord Jesus Christ! In his great mercy he has given us new birth into a living hope through the resurrection of Jesus Christ from the dead, and into an inheritance that can never perish, spoil or fade—kept in heaven for you' (1 Peter 1:3–4).

Do you have this hope today? If you were to die tonight, do you know—beyond doubt—that you would go to be with God in Heaven forever? You can have the certainty, if you will confess your sins to God and trust Christ alone for your salvation. Give your life into His hands without delay.

I have never admitted this to very many people, but I think about death a great deal and worry about it because I don't know what will happen when I die. Right now I look on death as just the end of the road with nothing beyond, but I would give anything to know there is hope for life after death.

One of the greatest tragedies in life today is that countless people refuse to think about the fact of death—although there is nothing so certain as the fact that one day every one of us will come to the end of our lives.

Death is not the end of the road—it is merely a gateway to eternal life beyond the grave. The Bible teaches that every one of us will continue some type of existence after death—either in Heaven or in hell. The most important decision you will ever make is the decision you make about eternity.

How do I know death is not the end? I know it because Jesus Christ came back from the grave. His resurrection demonstrated once for all that there *is* life after death, and it also demonstrated that He alone can save us and bring us to Heaven. You see, the one thing that will keep us out of Heaven is our sin. But God loves us, and Jesus Christ came to take upon Himself the punishment we deserve for our sins. Christ died in our place, and by faith and trust in Him we can know our sins are forgiven and we are going to go to be with Him in Heaven forever.

Commit your life to Christ and trust Him for your salvation. He is alive, and you can know Him personally by turning to Him in faith. Put your hope and trust in Him, for the Bible says that Christ "has appeared once for all at the end of the ages to do away with sin by the sacrifice of himself" (Hebrews 9:26).

Then let Christ be your guide and ruler every day. Christ wants to give you hope for the future—but He also wants to help you right now and change you into the person God created you to be. He wants you to learn what it means to walk with Him every day, and He also wants to use you to tell others about His glorious salvation. When you come to Christ, God gives you eternal life—which begins right now as you open your heart to Him.

The doctor has just told me I must have triple by-pass surgery on my heart and I am frankly frightened. I have never thought about death much, and I am not sure I can get up enough courage to go through with this operation, although I know I will probably die without it. Help me deal with my fears.

Your fear is not just of the operation, but of death. The most important thing I can tell you is that we do not need to fear death if we have Christ in our hearts and belong to Him. Yes, death is a reality, and you are right to be fearful of it because apart from Christ you would have no hope of eternal life in Heaven. You would only face eternity alone, separated from God forever in hell. But Jesus Christ came to give us eternal life, and you can have that hope in your heart if you turn to Christ.

You see, the problem we all face is the problem of sin. We have sinned against God, and the Bible says "the wages of sin is death" (Romans 6:23). Our greatest need is forgiveness, and God has made that possible by sending His Son to die on the cross for our sins. We deserved to die because of our sins, but Christ died in our place. When we trust Christ for our salvation, then death simply becomes a transition between this world and the next—like walking through a doorway from one room to another.

The most important decision you will ever make is your decision about Christ. Some day you will die—whether you like to think about it or not—and then it will be too late. Accept God's offer of salvation right now, by asking Jesus Christ to come into your heart by faith and trusting your life into His hands. Then you will know that "neither death nor life . . . neither the present nor the future . . . nor anything else in all creation, will be able to separate us from the love of God that is in Christ Jesus our Lord" (Romans 8:38–39).

A friend of mine recently lost her husband. Although she has been a fine Christian, she seems to have lost interest in everything. What help or counsel should I give her?

The husband-wife relationship is the closest of all earthly relationships, and it is not to be wondered at that the death of one will come as a blow to the other. It does not mean that the bereaved is without faith. The Bible teaches that on the occasion of death "we sorrow" (1 Thessalonians 4:13). Abraham, who is cited as an example of faith, wept and sorrowed at the death of his wife, Sarah (Genesis 23:2). But the Christian does not sorrow as do those who are without hope. He looks forward to the time of the resurrection and reunion. Point out these wonderful truths to your bereaved friend, and pray for her that the Lord will use His Word to afford her comfort in a time of deep sorrow and loss. Show her that the loss is her loved one's gain, and at worst is only temporary.

I am afraid to die. I have tried to get over this fear, but cannot. Is there anything one can do to overcome it?

The fear of death is something that all people have at some time. With many, this fear is greatly aggravated. You did not tell me if you were a believer in Christ or not, but that makes a great difference. Christ has removed forever the fear of death for those who believe in Him. He has brought life and immortality to light through the gospel. Man, by nature, fears death because death is always associated with judgment and with the unknown. We fear it because we do not know what lies ahead. But Christ has made the way for us through His own death. He provides eternal life and has promised His presence in all of life's experiences, and even in death. "Yea, though I walk through the valley of the shadow of death I will fear no evil," said the Psalmist. You, too, can lose that fear when you commit your whole self to Christ. Trust Him for salvation from sin, and He will remove the sting of death, which is sin.

Last night I dreamed I was dying and woke up in agony of fear. Today I know I am not ready to die. What can I do?

God may have permitted you to have this dream to make you realize that you have neglected the most important thing in this life and in the next. You can have peace in your heart and the assurance of salvation if you will humbly acknowledge yourself as a sinner in God's sight, ask His forgiveness and cleansing, and trust in Jesus Christ, God's Son, as your Savior from sin. Christ died on the Cross to do just this very thing for you. Let me urge you to get a Bible and read, or ask someone to help you read, the following verses: Romans 3:12, Romans 3:23, 2 Timothy 3:5, Romans 3:19, Ephesians 2:8, Luke 19:10, Romans 5:8, Hebrews 7:25, Romans 10:13, and Romans 10:9, 10.

These are not magic verses. They simply tell us about our need and how to find that need met in Jesus Christ. You do not have to do some wonderful thing to be saved. All you have to do is accept the wonderful thing Christ has done for you. After you have this assurance in your heart, tell other people about it. Also, show by your daily life that Christ has changed it for His own glory.

Recently, some friends and I were discussing whether we go immediately to Heaven when we die. Can you answer this question?

The Bible clearly teaches that when a believer in Christ dies, he goes to be with the Lord. "Absent from the body . . . present with the Lord" is what Paul said about it (2 Corinthians 5:8 KJV). Also, in one of His parables Jesus told of the rich man and Lazarus who were already at their destination. But the Bible also teaches that there is a day of resurrection and judgment which is yet future (2 Timothy 2:18). Here reference to a past resurrection is misleading and in error. It is the coming event when Jesus comes again. The Bible says: "For if we believe that Jesus died and rose again, even so them also which sleep in Jesus will God bring with him . . . . the dead in Christ shall rise first; then we which are alive and remain shall be caught up together with them . . . to meet the Lord in the air" (1 Thessalonians 4:14–17 KJV). The answer seems to be that there is an intermediate state when we are with the Lord, but have not yet received the glorious body of the resurrection.

I am almost overcome with grief because of my husband's death several months ago. I just don't see how I can ever get over this.

However, I think it would be easier to bear if I knew that my husband and I will recognize each other in Heaven. Does the Bible teach this?

Yes, we will recognize our loved ones in Heaven, and they will recognize us. Furthermore, the Bible indicates that we will know them in a far deeper and closer way than was ever possible on earth—and without the imperfections and sins that mar our human relationships on earth. "Now we see but a poor reflection; then we shall see face to face. Now I know in part; then I shall know fully, even as I am fully known" (1 Corinthians 13:12).

The fact that we will know our loved ones who have died and gone to Heaven before us is clear from several passages of Scripture. For example, in 1 Thessalonians 4 Paul tells us that we are not to grieve "like the rest of men, who have no hope" (v. 13). He then goes on to say that those who have died in Christ will some day return with Him when He comes again. "After that, we who are still alive and are left will be caught up with them in the clouds to meet the Lord in the air. And so we will be with the Lord forever" (1 Thessalonians 4:17). Here it is clear that we will be with all those who have died and gone to Heaven before us—including our loved ones.

I know this is a difficult time for you, and I pray that you will take courage from the many promises of God's Word—not just about the fact that you will see your husband again some day, but that when we know Christ we have the certain hope of Heaven. Rejoice that your husband knew Christ, and that now he is safely beyond the touch of pain and suffering and death.

But you also should be praying that God would help you right now not only to get over your grief, but to grow closer to Christ and to serve Him more each day. God still has a purpose in your being on this earth—to glorify Him in all you do. Seek above all else to do His will in your life.

Do you think there is anything in the Bible that would forbid me donating some of my bodily organs (such as my kidneys or my eyes) after my death?

No, I find nothing in the Bible that would forbid this, and in fact it could be a very loving act on your part because it might give the gift of sight or even life to someone else after you have gone. Some day, the Bible teaches, we who are in Christ will be given new and perfect bodies by God in eternity, and He is not dependent on the elements of our old bodies to accomplish this miracle.

I am thankful you are thinking about ways you can help others—but I want to use your question to challenge you also. It is good to want to help people in this way (as long as you or your immediate family have no objections), but have you given much thought to ways you should be helping others right now, while you are still alive? If you know Christ as your Lord and Savior, the greatest treasure you can give to another is not merely the gift of physical help, but pointing them to Jesus Christ. It is important to help people who are in physical need—but it is even more important to help those who have spiritual needs. Are you praying that God will use you in the lives of other people, to encourage them and make them see their own need of Jesus Christ?

Your question also reminds me of what Jesus Christ has done for us through His death on the cross. You want to give the gift of life to others through your death—and in a far greater way, that is what Christ did for us. He took upon Himself our sin and our guilt, and in their place He offers us forgiveness, new life, and eternal salvation. "But God demonstrates his own love for us in this: While we were still sinners, Christ died for us" (Romans 5:8).

Life is brief, and no matter who we are it will soon be over. If ever we are going to trust in Christ and live for Him it must be now. May God encourage you and challenge you to live for Him as you yield your life to Him.

Do you believe there is really any proof that there is life after death? If so, do you think it is possible for a person to know what life after death is like?

Yes, there is life after death, and in fact the experience of death is but a gateway to an eternity of conscious life after death.

I want you to think a moment about how we might come to know beyond doubt that there is life after death. I believe you will agree with me that the only ultimate proof would be if someone were to die and then come back to life again and tell us if there was life beyond the grave. To make the test valid, the person would have to really die—not just be on the border of death for a few minutes—and then have his restoration to life witnessed by a large number of people.

Has this ever happened? Yes! It has happened only once, when Jesus Christ died, was placed in the tomb for several days, and then came back to life. The Bible tells us that over 500 people were witnesses to His resurrection (1 Corinthians 15:6). The resurrection of Jesus Christ is one of the best-attested facts of history, and demonstrates that there is life beyond the grave.

But the resurrection of Christ is important for several other reasons also, and they are all important for your question. For example, the resurrection shows that Jesus Christ was in fact who He claimed to be—the eternal Son of God, come down from Heaven to die as a sacrifice for our sins. The resurrection of Jesus also shows that He has conquered sin and death, and that we need not fear the grave if we belong to Him.

I said that there is life after death, but there is one other thing I must stress. The Bible teaches that for some people life beyond the grave will be joyous, because they will be in Heaven with God. For others, however, life beyond the grave will be "darkness, where there will be weeping and gnashing of teeth" (Matthew 25:30). That is why it is so important for you to come to Christ right now and accept Him as Lord and Savior of your life. Then you can know beyond doubt that Christ is your Savior and there is a joyous eternity ahead of you.

My husband has terminal cancer with only a few months to live. He smoked for over fifty years and he is dying with lung cancer. Do you think churches should say more about smoking?

God is concerned about the way we treat our bodies, and you are right—the church should be concerned about everything (including smoking, overeating, alcohol and drug abuse, and other harmful practices) that dulls our senses or hurts our bodies. The Bible says, "Do you not know what that your body is a temple of the Holy Spirit, who is in you, whom you have received from God? You are not your own; you were bought at a price. Therefore honor God with your body" (1 Corinthians 6:19–20).

There is, of course, a lot of interest in our society in physical fitness, and much of that is good. People need to be made aware of the dangers of abusing their bodies, and of the benefits of taking care of them. At the same time, however, we must never forget that the Bible places special emphasis on another type of fitness—spiritual fitness. The Bible declares, "Physical training is of some value, but godliness has value for all things, holding promise for both the present life and the life to come" (1 Timothy 4:8).

I pray that the next few months will be special months for you and your husband. I pray especially that there will be times when you and your husband sense in a wonderful way the presence of God in your lives. Do you and your husband know beyond doubt that you have committed your lives to Christ, and that no matter what the future holds, you both will go to be with Christ in Heaven when you die? You can make sure, by yielding your lives without reserve, trusting Him alone for your salvation.

It is never easy (humanly speaking) for us to face death—either our own, or that of a loved one. But Christ came to take away the sting of death. May you both come to know that in a richer way during these months.

I know this may seem silly to you, but recently my dog had to be put to sleep and it has made me grieve deeply. Do you think I will see my pet in Heaven?

I do not believe Scripture gives us any direct answer about this, although many Bible scholars believe the evidence suggests there will be animals in Heaven. The difference will be that they will no longer fight and kill, because in the heavenly kingdom all will be peace. "The wolf will live with the lamb, the leopard will lie down with the goat . . . . They will neither harm nor destroy on all my holy mountain" (Isaiah 11:6, 9).

There is one thing you can be certain of, however. God loves us, and He knows what our needs are. He also wants us to be completely happy in Heaven—and we will be. Therefore, if God knows we will be happier because there will be animals with us in Heaven, then you can be assured He will do what is best for us. Remember that our happiness and joy in Heaven will be based especially on the fact that we will be with Christ, and we will worship Him and serve Him there. "No longer will there be any curse. The throne of God and of the Lamb will be in the city, and his servants will serve him" (Revelation 22:3).

I realize that you may be very sad over the loss of this pet, but I want to challenge you to use this time to think more carefully about what you can do in the future to serve God more fully. For example, all around you are people who have never thought much about Heaven or about their relationship to Christ. There also are people around you who are facing many problems and heartaches. Are you praying for them, and are you seeking to share Christ's love for them as God gives you opportunity? And are you growing spiritually yourself, learning to trust God more and more each day and learning more about Him through His Word, the Bible? The most important thing in life should be our relationship to Christ, and my prayer is that He will have first place in your life.

Do you believe God will give people a second chance after they die to believe in Him and go to Heaven?

The Bible does not teach this. In fact, it teaches the opposite. It stresses that the time to decide for Christ is now, because once we die it will be too late. As the author of the book of Hebrews in the New Testament declared, "Man is destined to die once, and after that to face judgment" (Hebrews 9:27). This verse also, incidentally, shows us clearly that there is no such thing as reincarnation—the idea that our souls return again and again to this earth.

The important thing for every one of us to realize is that God has done everything possible to bring salvation to us, and there is no reason for us to delay accepting His plan for our lives. God sent His only Son, Jesus Christ, into the world to die for our sins on the cross. This was something that no one else could ever do, because only Christ was without sin and could therefore be a perfect sacrifice for our sins. All we must do is turn our sins over to Christ, and trust Him for our salvation by faith. God's salvation is a wonderful gift to us that we can never earn. All we have to do is receive it.

I have often asked myself why many people who know what Christ has done for them still delay coming to Him for forgiveness. I suspect some people delay because secretly they hope that somehow there will be another chance for them after they die. That is one reason I have wanted to answer your question, because it would be tragic for them to miss out on God's greatest gift—salvation throughout all eternity in the joy of Heaven—because they mistakenly thought somehow they would have another chance. I am sure many people also delay turning to Christ because they think somehow that being a follower of Christ will be dull and unexciting, or because they want to continue in their sins as long as possible.

But none of these reasons is valid, and my challenge to you is to invite Christ into your life, if you have never done so, without delay. "I tell you, now is the time of God's favor, now is the day of salvation" (2 Corinthians 6:2).

I know you believe in life after death, and so do I. But I don't believe a loving God would send anyone to hell. In fact I don't think there is such a thing and I believe everyone will go to Heaven when they die. I find great comfort in this, because I know I am not perfect.

It is a very sobering thought to realize that hell is real and not everyone will go to Heaven. But the Word of God makes it clear that hell is just as real as Heaven.

Let me point out two things you may not have thought of. First, if there is no hell then there is no judgment for evil—and we therefore live in an unjust universe. Do you honestly believe the Hitlers of this world will never be judged for their crimes, but will be allowed to spend eternity with God in spite of the fact they fought against God and broke every moral law He gave us?

Second, if there is no hell then Christ is a liar—because

He repeatedly warned us about its reality. "The Son of Man will send out his angels, and they will weed out of his kingdom everything that causes sin and all who do evil. They will throw them into the fiery furnace, where there will be weeping and gnashing of teeth" (Matthew 13: 41–42). But if Christ did not tell the truth about this, how do you know you can trust what He said about anything—including His death for our eternal salvation? But Christ can be trusted because He is God—and God does not lie.

The good news, however, is that you do not have to face hell. Why? Because Jesus Christ took upon Himself the punishment you and I deserve when He died on the cross for our sins. Don't deceive yourself, but turn to Christ and trust Him for your salvation.

What is your opinion with regard to the soul after death? Does it lie in the grave until the resurrection or does it go straight to God?

It is unwise to speculate beyond those things clearly stated in the Bible. To the repentant thief on the cross, Jesus said: "Today shalt thou be with me in paradise." This would indicate that the soul of a Christian at death goes immediately to be with the Lord in glory. At the same time, that is not the final state of the believer for at the resurrection, the bodies and souls of believers will be reunited and will be given a glorified body which will live forever in God's presence. In the first book of Thessalonians we are told: "For the Lord himself shall descend from heaven with a shout, with the voice of the archangel, and with the trump of God; and the dead in Christ shall rise first: then we which are alive and remain shall be caught up together with them in the clouds, to meet the Lord in the air: and so shall we ever be with the Lord" (4:17). There are many mysteries that have been withheld from our knowledge. But this we can affirm: the person who puts his trust in Jesus Christ and what He has done for us is immediately changed from death to life; and he has been born again and physical death can never separate him from God. If you believe in Christ, you have eternal life now and death is but a transition into His presence.

*In the afterlife, will a man and woman who have been married
remain married? When a person dies, will he remain the same age
throughout eternity?*

The marriage contract terminates at death. 'Until death do us
part' is the clause we repeat when we are wed. Legally, and in
the sight of God, all marriages are dissolved when one or the
other of the partners enters eternity.

The Sadducees asked Jesus this same question and He
said: "The people of this age marry and are given in marriage.
But those who are considered worthy of taking part in that age
and in the resurrection from the dead will neither marry, nor
be given in marriage" (Luke 20:34–35).

Yet I am certain that in Heaven everything we need for
our complete happiness will be there. I am equally certain that
married couples will know and love each other in the afterlife—though the relationship will be no longer physical but
spiritual.

As to remaining the same age throughout eternity, Heaven
has no clocks nor calendars, and "time will be no more." The
thing with which we should be most concerned is preparing
for eternity, and though we may find the answer to every mystery, but fail to prepare to meet God, we will be in hopeless
straits in the world to come.

*After a person has died and gone to another life, does he know or
realize what he did while on this earth?*

While it is not given us to know all of the details about the
afterlife, we are given some insights into some aspects of it.

In the parable of the rich man and Lazarus, Christ indicated that the rich man could recall many of the events of earth.
Particularly did he remember the sins of omission. He remembered that he had ignored the need of the beggar Lazarus. He
remembered his five brothers and feared that they might also
end up in hell, and asked that a messenger might be sent to
earth to warn them.

There are evidences that we will remember many of
the events of life. In the light of eternity, we will see that the

things we thought so important were unimportant, and that the things we considered unimportant were really the things we should have attended to. Part of hell's torments will be the suffering of remorse, and of regretful memory.

For the saved, there will be the joys of having been faithful, and the thrill of unfolding knowledge throughout eternity. The Bible says: "Now we see but a poor reflection; but then we shall see face to face. Now I know in part. I shall then know fully, even as I am fully known" (1 Corinthians 13:12).

Part IV

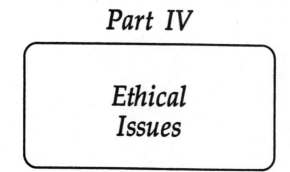

*Ethical
Issues*

19 | Why Doesn't God Do Something about the Evil in the World?

Why doesn't God do something about all the evil in the world? For example, today's paper tells about suffering in one part of Africa because of a famine, and how hundreds of thousands could die as a result. Why doesn't God wipe out all the evil, if He really cares about us?

We do not know all the reasons why God permits evil. We need to remember, however, that He is not the cause of evil in this world and we should therefore not blame Him for it. Remember that God did not create evil, as some believe. God created the world perfect. Man chose to defy God and go his own way, and it is man's fault that evil entered the world. Even so, God has provided the ultimate triumph of good over evil in Jesus Christ, who on the cross, defeated Satan and those who follow him. Christ is coming back and when He does, all evil will be ended forever and righteousness and justice will prevail.

Have you ever thought about what would happen if God suddenly eliminated all the evil in this world? Not one person would be left, because we are all guilty of sin. "If you, O Lord, kept a record of sins, O Lord, who could stand?" (Psalm 130:3). As the Bible says, "Because of the Lord's great love we are not consumed, for his compassions never fail" (Lamentations 3:22). Or again, have you thought about how many evils in this world are caused by human greed and lust? For example, isn't it ironic (and tragic) that the bestseller lists are filled with books on dieting—while millions starve in other parts of the world? Man—not God—must bear the responsibility.

Evil is a reality—but God's whole purpose is to eliminate it, and in fact that is why Christ came and died on the cross for our sins. "The reason the Son of God appeared was to destroy the devil's work" (1 John 3:8). Have you asked Christ to take away the sin in your life—and then to use you as His instrument to combat sin in the world?

I guess some people would consider me old-fashioned, but I am appalled at many of the things that are on television today—sex, violence, alcohol, drug abuse. Do you think there is anything we can do about this?

I suspect there are many people who feel as you do, because the tendency to ignore—or even laugh at—moral values in the media today is very strong. In part this is a reflection of the drift away from moral values in our society today. But this also encourages even greater levels of immorality within our society, and that trend will have tragic consequences if it is not reversed.

You need to remember that in our nation, television, radio, magazines, and other aspects of the media are all supported by advertising. Companies purchase advertising on a program because they believe people will be receptive to their message and eventually buy their products. But if advertisers become aware of the fact that many people are offended by the programs they are sponsoring, and are therefore not going to purchase the products they sell, then those advertisers will put pressure on the programmers to come up with programs that are acceptable.

Do you, therefore, have a way to let your voice be heard? Certainly! If a program offends you because of its language or subject matter, take down the names of the sponsors and write them directly. Tell them you do not believe they should be sponsoring that type of program. Write the television station also, and even the network. I have had several people in that industry tell me that only a few negative letters can have a strong impact. Don't be angry in your letters, but let your views be known clearly.

Whether or not such things do change, remember that those of us who claim to belong to Christ must not give in to the pressures in our society that would call us to forget God's standards. "What kind of people ought you to be? You ought to live holy and godly lives as you look forward to the day of God" (2 Peter 3:11–12).

Why do people seem to be so rude today? I grew up in a small town where people were courteous to each other and cared for each other, but I have moved to a large city and it seems that no one shows even a little bit of courtesy. I even find myself becoming indifferent to others. Does the Bible say anything about good manners, or do they vary from culture to culture?

Although many social customs differ from one culture to another, the Bible makes it clear that such things as courtesy and thoughtfulness should be part of our lives, no matter where we live. It is perhaps best summed up in the words of Jesus (which have come to be called "The Golden Rule"): "In everything, do to others what you would have them do to you, for this sums up the Law and the Prophets" (Matthew 7:12). Notice that this is a positive command; that is, we are not simply to refrain from doing evil to others, but we are to go out of our way to do what is good. Courtesy and kindness are part of this.

Why does courtesy seem to be declining in our society? One reason is that we have lost sight of the Bible's teachings about how we should live and act toward others. We also live in a society which has encouraged selfishness—the "me first" attitude—and that destroys common courtesy and kindness.

Yes, I wish there were more kindness in the world. But the real problem is a spiritual problem, because we have left God out of our lives.

Do you think it really pays to be good in today's world? It seems like the only way to get ahead is to live for yourself and bend the rules a bit.

I know that this often seems to be the case, but there are several things I want you to think about before you decide that this is the way you want to live.

It is not always true that this is the way to get ahead in the world. Some of the most successful people I know have been people who had strong moral principles and stuck to them regardless of the situation. Their reputation for honesty and hard work has won the respect of other people, and they have often found that people preferred to deal with them because they could be trusted. The Bible constantly exhorts us to be honest, because it is right in God's eyes and we are accountable to Him.

Think about the fact that those who "bend the rules a bit" often end up in great difficulty. It may be that they eventually do something illegal and are caught, bringing great heartache to their families and punishment to themselves. There is a strict biblical principle which declares that eventually our wrong deeds will create havoc in our lives. The Bible declares, "Do not be deceived: God cannot be mocked. A man reaps what he sows. The one who sows to please his sinful nature, from that nature will reap destruction" (Galatians 6:7–8).

That is why I want you seriously to consider the claims of Jesus Christ on your life. He calls you to follow Him. It is not always easy, and most people may not think it is worthwhile. But doing the will of God is the most important thing in life—and the most rewarding as well.

How do you account for the fact that in some places in the world people who claim to be Christians are constantly fighting and killing each other?

There have been far too many instances in history when people and groups who claimed to be Christian have acted in ways that were not in accordance with the teachings of Jesus.

The real problem is that the word "Christian" has lost much of its original meaning. Today it often does not refer to a true follower of Jesus Christ, but simply to someone (or to some movement or group) that only claims to be Christian or has a vague Christian heritage. We should remember the sober warning of Jesus: "A good tree cannot bear bad fruit, and a bad tree cannot bear good fruit . . . . Not everyone who says to me, 'Lord, Lord' will enter the kingdom of heaven, but only he who does the will of my Father who is in heaven" (Matthew 7:18, 21).

What is a Christian? The first occurrence of the word "Christian" in the Bible is in Acts 11:26, which says "The disciples were first called Christians at Antioch." The word meant "one who follows Christ," and you will note that the Bible applies the term to those who were disciples, or active followers, of Christ. Jesus said, "If you hold to my teaching, you are really my disciples" (John 8:31). In other words, a Christian is one who has committed himself to Jesus Christ as Savior and Lord, and is actively seeking to follow Him and His teachings in his everyday life.

Do not be distracted by people who may claim to be Christians but are not following Christ as they should. Instead, make it your goal to follow Christ yourself, and look to Him every day. He is worthy of your trust and our faith.

Does the Bible say anything about smoking marijuana? My boyfriend says it doesn't and it is therefore okay to smoke it, but I'm not sure.

The Bible strictly commands us not to do anything which would dull our minds or make us lose control of our moral judgment. This is clearly seen, for example, in the statements of the Bible against drunkenness. "Do not get drunk on wine, which leads to debauchery. Instead, be filled with the Spirit" (Ephesians 5:18).

Therefore, although the Bible does not mention marijuana by name (since it was apparently unknown to the biblical writers), the Bible makes it clear that any drug which can distort our judgment is wrong. (You should remember that alcohol is actually a drug.) The medical consequences of marijuana are still being studied, but there can be no doubt that it—along with other drugs, such as cocaine—influences the mind. I know there are some people who substitute their drug experiences for an experience of God, and this is tragic because it keeps them from knowing the joy and peace and forgiveness that God alone can bring to our hearts.

I hope you and your boyfriend will honestly reconsider your involvement in drugs—no matter how popular they may be with some of your friends. But more than that, my prayer is that you will both reconsider with an open mind your need of God. God created you, and He has a perfect plan for your lives. He wants you to come to know Him and follow Him. He wants you to learn what it means to love Him and to love others for His sake.

There is no greater joy in life than having Jesus Christ as your Lord and Savior, living in your heart and giving you hope for the future. No drug experience—or any other kind of experience—can really do this for you. Open your heart to Christ right now by faith and commit yourself to follow Him every day as you walk with Him in the light of His Word.

Why do you think we ought to be so concerned about things like world hunger? It seems to me we have a lot of people in our own country who need all the help we can give them.

Yes, we need to be concerned about people in our own country who face needs of various kinds and are unable to help themselves. But we also need to be concerned about the pressing needs of people in other parts of the world, millions of whom will die as a direct result of malnutrition and starvation.

God is concerned about the whole world, and He commands us to be concerned about the whole world also. This is true in evangelism; those of us who have come to know Jesus Christ have been commanded to "go and make disciples of all nations" (Matthew 28:19). But it is equally true for our concern about the physical needs of others as well, because God is concerned about the whole person—body, mind, and spirit. Man's greatest need is spiritual because the human race is lost and apart from God, but our love for others includes a concern and compassion for their physical needs as well.

Consider the example of Jesus, who healed the sick and fed the hungry during His ministry on earth, as well as preached the Gospel of salvation. Jesus warned His disciples that they would be judged for their failure to help those who were in need, wherever they might be found. "Depart from me, you who are cursed, into the eternal fire prepared for the devil and his angels. For I was hungry and you gave me nothing to eat, I was thirsty and you gave me nothing to drink . . . whatever you did not do for one of the least of these, you did not do for me" (Matthew 25:41–42, 45).

Ask God to give you love for others, even if they are very different from you. Ask Him to help you find practical ways to help them. This is part of our responsibility.

Do you think that the Bible teaches that the world is going to end in a nuclear war? If so, doesn't that mean that we may be nearing the end of time?

Some of the descriptions in the Bible which portray the end of history as we know it are very vivid, and some Bible scholars have pointed out that they could be describing the type of thing that would happen in an all-out nuclear war. No one can say, however, that that is exactly what the Bible is picturing for us.

It is not so important for us to try to figure out exactly what will happen at the end of time when Christ returns to establish His kingdom. More important is the fact that some day God will intervene and the world as we know it will come to an end. The Bible stresses that "No one knows about that day or hour, not even the angels in heaven, or the Son, but only the Father" (Matthew 24:36). Some day the sin and evil of this world will be completely conquered, and Christ will reign in righteousness. "But in keeping with his promise we are looking forward to a new heaven and a new earth, the home of right-eousness" (2 Peter 3:13).

Christ could come today, or His coming might be delayed for another thousand years. Certainly there are many signs that His coming may be near, and we need to take them seriously. But the real question is, are we ready for His coming? "Therefore keep watch, because you do not know on what day your Lord will come" (Matthew 24:42). The end of the world as we know it and the establishment of Christ's kingdom should not lead us to laziness or complacency—quite the opposite. We should instead be busy doing the Lord's work and living for Him. We should do all we can to tell others about Christ's salvation, for "Night is coming, when no one can work" (John 9:4).

Make it your goal, therefore, to live for Christ, no matter what the future may hold. God is not finished with His plans for this world, and we should seek to live for Him every day of our lives.

Should a Christian participate in defense measures of war involving the use of weapons, considering that this purpose is to kill other children of God?

The purpose of war is not to kill other children of God. If they are killed through the ravages of war, it is because they are members of a warring society and incidentally Christians. War is one of the consequences of living in a fallen world in which sinful men and women are unable to settle differences between each other by peaceful means.

I believe there are just wars, World War Two, for example, in which a tyrant sought to take over the world while at the same time eradicating an entire race of people. Only war put a stop to his bloodshed and enslavement of others. But war is certainly not the Christian way to settle either individual or global problems.

We must accept our responsibility as citizens. A man may protest against war and criticize his government for becoming involved in war, but as a citizen accepting the privileges and benefits of his government, he must also accept certain responsibilities. If we are in entire disagreement with our government, we can always elect to take our citizenship elsewhere. John the Baptist said one time when soldiers inquired of him concerning their duty: "Extort from no man by violence, neither accuse any one wrongfully; and be content with your wages." But he did not tell them that they must cease being soldiers.

A Christian would find it hard to be a loyal citizen in a nation that promoted warfare. We can thank God that we are part of a nation that first seeks to solve problems by peaceful means.

I read a lot in the newspapers about trying to control nuclear weapons and the arms race, and I know you have said that you think we should try to do something about the arms race. But do you really think there is any hope of eliminating war?

No, I do not believe that war will be completely eliminated from the earth until Jesus Christ returns to establish His Kingdom. At that time He will rule with complete justice and authority, and the ancient prophecy of Isaiah will be fulfilled: "He will judge between the nations and will settle disputes for many peoples. They will beat their swords into plowshares and their spears into pruning hooks. Nation will not take up sword against nation, nor will they train for war anymore" (Isaiah 2:4).

This does not mean we should be cynical about efforts for peace, because nations can from time to time come to agreements that give a temporary measure of peace. The catastrophic consequences of a possible nuclear war must also cause us to be alarmed, because in a nuclear holocaust hundreds of millions of people could die. If we suddenly discovered a hundred million people were going to die of starvation in some distant country I suspect we would do all we could to help them. I am not a pacifist nor do I believe in unilateral disarmament, but we should encourage the leaders of the world's great nations to work for peace and avoid a disaster.

War comes from the human heart, which Christ alone can change, and as long as there are sinful men on this earth there will be war. But God can restrain evil and we should be diligent in praying that He will guide our leaders. The Bible declares, "I urge, then, first of all, that requests, prayers, intercession and thanksgiving be made for everyone—for kings and all those in authority, that we may live peaceful and quiet lives in all godliness and holiness. This is good, and pleases God our Savior" (1 Timothy 2:1–3). This gives us a clear command which we should obey every day. At times we may feel like we can do very little to influence world events. But God is at work, and the most important thing we can do is pray for our world and its leaders.

Why don't you ever say anything about drunk driving? We recently lost our only daughter to a drunk driver, and the judge let the driver off with almost no penalty.

I have actually spoken out frequently against drunk driving, as well as other automobile-related safety matters—but perhaps not as frequently as I should. Drunk driving is clearly one of the most serious social problems we face in our nation. Probably well over half of the fatal car accidents in our nation are alcohol-related—a terrible toll of tens of thousands of lives each year.

Certainly you have put your finger on one of the problems we have in combating this critical issue. Undoubtedly there has been a tendency by our legal system to treat drunk driving as a minor offense instead of the serious matter it is. If someone walked into a crowded shopping mall waving a loaded pistol and threatening to shoot anyone who got in his way, I suspect the police and the law courts would treat it very seriously. If someone gets on an airplane and threatens to blow it up, it is treated as a very serious offense. But a drunk driver on the loose on the roads is every bit as dangerous, and we must support much stronger penalties for this offense. (Some countries in Europe have done this, and have much less a problem with drunk drivers.)

Drunk driving is only one part of the larger problem of alcoholism that plagues our nation today. Right now there may be someone reading this who knows that alcohol has taken possession of him, or that person may even have refused to face the fact that they have gotten hooked on alcohol (or some other drug). If that is your situation, my prayer for you is not only that you would never, never drive while drunk, but that you would face your need honestly. The first step to take—and the most important step in life for any of us—is to open your heart to Christ and ask Him to help you fight this problem. It may not be easy, but you need God's help and He wants to help you if you will turn to Him in faith and trust.

In a world that seems filled with terrorism, can't we rely on the fact that we are a good nation and that God won't allow evil men to overcome us?

I wish I could have such confidence, but unhappily it is not according to God's pattern nor His Word. Many good nations have been overrun by those who were wicked. That is because there are so many hidden elements involved in judgment. We see only the surface appearance. But you have also raised a question concerning goodness. Are we really a good people? If taking the lead among the nations for crime is goodness and if exalting the sensuous is goodness, then we are. But if it is otherwise, then we may be lagging in basic integrity and morality.

Even if we are better than some other nations, God might still chasten us under the hand of another nation to bring us back to a place of fearing and loving Him.

One of the prophets complained, "For the wicked surround the righteous, so justice goes forth perverted" (Habakkuk 1:4). But God corrected his error and told him that "I am working a work in your days, that you would not believe if told" (Habakkuk 1:5). In an age such as this one, the people of God were counseled to live by faith, and not to judge by appearance of the moment. That is what we must do in ours.

In college I have been studying a course in ethics. I find that quite often a higher standard of ethics is held by secular thinkers than I experience in my contact with religious people. Is there any explanation for this?

There is an explanation for this. You must understand that culture and training have a great influence upon conduct. In the study of ethics, you are dealing with the highest ideal of human conduct that man is capable of expressing. Such expressions of conduct are theoretical, and the Bible clearly tells us that "Indeed, when Gentiles, who do not have the law, do by nature things required by the law, they are a law for themselves, even though they do not have the law, since they show that the requirements of the law are written on their hearts . . ." (Romans 2:14, 15). Most people know in theory what is right. What secular ethics does not and cannot provide is the motivation for right action. There is a great difference between the theory a man holds of conduct and the conduct itself.

You must also remember that the Christian is subjected to many temptations that are not common to those who are not Christians. On the average, you will find that the ethical and moral level of true Christians is now and always has been the highest. Only Christianity provides both the ethical standards and the adequate motivation.

My husband and I would like to have children, but it seems to me that the world is in such terrible shape that we worry about what might happen to our children in the future. Do you think it is right to think this way?

If you were to pick up a book which surveyed the history of the world, I doubt if you could find a single time throughout human history when conditions were ideal or the future was not clouded with uncertainty and threats of war. Even when social and political circumstances have been reasonably good, the world has been ravaged by natural disasters and plagues.

That is not to dismiss the fact that the world is in bad shape right now. We do live in a time of great uncertainty, and if, on the one hand, modern medicine has removed many of the things which threatened life only a generation or two ago, on the other hand, modern technology has developed weapons of mass destruction that can wipe out entire civilizations in a few hours. And new diseases such as AIDS rise up to threaten our survival.

But God is in control of the future. "The Lord reigns, let the earth be glad" (Psalm 97:1). I think of the time of the prophet Jeremiah in the Old Testament. It was a terrible time in many ways, with the Jewish people being carried away into captivity in Babylon and facing a very uncertain future. I am sure many of them must have asked the same question you have asked, but Jeremiah told them, "Marry and have sons and daughters . . . . For I know the plans I have for you, plans to give you hope and a future" (Jeremiah 29:6, 11).

Jeremiah could say this because he knew that God was Lord over the future as well as the past and present. It does not mean everything will be easy for our children. But our responsibility is clear: if God gives children to us, we should do whatever we can to strengthen them spiritually so that they too can face the future with a confident hope in God.

| 20 | *How Can We Know What Is Right and Wrong?* |

How can we know what is right and what is wrong? There are so many conflicting ideas, and one becomes confused. Is there really any rule to go by?

"If any man's will is to do his will, he shall know whether the teaching is from God" (John 7:17 RSV). I think before one can know what is right and wrong, he must first align himself with God. Only then is he in a position to do right.

J. Wilbur Chapman once said: "The rule that governs my life is this: Anything that dims my vision of Christ, or takes away my taste for Bible study, or cramps my prayer life, or makes Christian work difficult, is wrong for me, and I must, as a Christian, turn away from it."

When I have a problem of deciding right from wrong I always give it three tests. First, I give it the common-sense test, and ask if it is reasonable. Then, I give it the prayer test. I ask God if it is good and edifying. Then, I give it the Scripture test. I see if the Bible has anything to say for or against it. Then, I may add a fourth: the conscience test. But the most important thing is to follow Jesus' suggestion: "If any man will do his will he shall *know* . . ." (John 7:17 KJV).

I have heard that you oppose abortion. I don't agree with this, since I think a woman ought to have a right to do whatever she wants to with her own body.

I know this is a very sensitive and emotional issue—I always get a great deal of mail whenever I deal with it. It has become a political issue today, but my concern is not political but moral and spiritual.

Yes, I oppose abortion (except in rare situations such as when the mother's life is clearly in danger and abortion becomes the lesser of two evils). The central question we have to face is this: is the little life within the womb just a piece of human tissue, or is it more than that—a human being—even when it is very young and could not sustain itself outside the womb? It is at this point that emotions tend to get in the way and people attempt to answer the question in a way that will agree with their own desires. But we need to look at this as reasonably as possible.

As a Christian my ultimate standard is the Bible, because I believe it to be God's Word which reveals absolute truth to us. I may have opinions about various things, but if God has spoken on a subject then I must submit my opinions to the rule of Scripture. Does the Bible, therefore, give any answer to the question of whether or not a fetus is a human being in God's eyes?

Yes, it does, giving us several illustrations to indicate that a fetus is a human being. God told Jeremiah, for example, "Before I formed you in the womb I knew you, before you were born I set you apart; I appointed you as a prophet to the nations" (Jeremiah 1:5). Or take the case of John the Baptist. When Mary, the mother of Jesus, became pregnant by the Holy Spirit she went immediately to visit her cousin Elizabeth, who was pregnant with John the Baptist. John's mother declared, "As soon as the sound of your greeting reached my ears, the baby in my womb leaped for joy" (Luke 1:44)—implying that the fetus was fully human.

I hope you will reconsider your stand—but I also hope you will study the Bible for yourself, not just on this issue but on your own need of Christ.

There are two further things I would like to say about this subject. First, the widespread acceptance of abortion is a symbol or sign of something deeper within our society that should also concern us greatly. This is the tendency today to decide moral issues or questions only on the basis of whether or not they are convenient or bring pleasure to a person. For example, many people today have discarded the Bible's clear teaching on sexual relations outside of marriage, simply because they are absorbed only in their own pleasures and desires. The tragedy, however, is that we never break God's laws without paying for it. The Bible declares, "Do not be deceived: God cannot be mocked. A man reaps what he sows. The one who sows to please his sinful nature, from that nature will reap destruction" (Galatians 6:7–8). That can be true of nations as well. "It is a dreadful thing to fall into the hands of the living God" (Hebrews 10:31).

But the other thing I would like to say is that God loves us, and He is willing to forgive us of our sins. He has made it possible by sending His only Son to die on the cross as a sacrifice for our sins. If you, or a person you know, has been guilty of this serious sin, know that God still loves and wants to forgive all who come to Him in sincere repentance and faith in Christ.

I had four abortions before I got married, and now I have discovered I am unable to have children at all. Do you think God is punishing me for the things I did in the past?

Several doctors have told me that abortion can be a difficult (and even dangerous) surgical procedure which can have permanently damaging effects on the woman. It is not just a simple procedure that can be carried out without consequences—quite apart from the moral issues involved.

I cannot say whether or not God is using this directly as punishment in your life, although the Bible clearly teaches that when we turn our backs on God and choose to disregard His moral laws there are inevitable consequences. Furthermore it is not God who is to blame for the consequences, but the person who has broken His law. Let me use an illustration from physical laws. Suppose that you decided you would jump out of a second-story window. No matter how much you might wish it, the law of gravity is not going to be suspended when you jump. In a sense, the law of gravity is responsible for the bones you would probably break—but actually you are responsible, because you disregarded the law of gravity. Just as there are physical laws which we cannot break without harming ourselves, so there are spiritual laws as well.

But the important question at this stage is, where do you go from here? God loves you, and you need Him. You need His forgiveness for what you have done in the past. Also you need His guidance and help in your life every day. So far in your life you have neglected Him, and all it has brought you is heartache and trouble. Now I pray that you will face honestly your need of Him, and you will invite Christ into your heart by faith.

Then seek God's will for your future. God wants you to be the best wife you can possibly be with His strength. He has a plan for your life, if you will turn to Him and seek to follow Jesus Christ.

I know people like you are always talking out against abortion, but I think you are looking at things the wrong way. After all, as a woman I have rights, including the right to do with my body anything I want to do with it, and no one is going to tell me differently.

There are certainly many things I could say to you about this issue, and why I do not agree with your position because of the Bible's teaching. But in all honesty I suspect that you have heard all of the arguments before, and (as your last comment says) you aren't really open to them. Therefore I will deal frankly with the deeper issue you are facing—but may never have realized.

The real issue with you is not just abortion and whether or not you have a right to terminate the life of a child who is growing within you. The real issue is whether or not you will insist on running your own life according to your own standards, or whether you will instead let God run your life. You have made your declaration of independence, as it were—independence from anyone else's ideas of how you should live, and most of all independence from God. By doing so, you are saying that you know better than God does what is best for you. You also are saying that you do not need God.

But this is wrong. God created you, and furthermore He loves you. And because He loves you, He knows what is best for you and wants you to be fulfilled as a person by doing His will. Right now you are a slave—a slave to yourself and your own limitations, whether you like to admit it or not. But Christ wants to free you. He wants to help you discover the excitement and joy of knowing why you are here and where you are going in God's plan.

Don't be afraid of God, and don't be afraid of opening your heart to His Son, Jesus Christ, as your Savior and Lord. You need Christ, and you will never find the joy and inner peace you are seeking apart from Him. He was willing to die for you on the cross because of His great love for you. The way you are going right now is a deadend road—but Christ's way is "the road that leads to life" (Matthew 7:14).

For some time I have been stealing small amounts of money from the company that employs me. Now that I have come to know Christ, I feel that I must do something about this. I'm afraid to tell my employer lest I lose my position, yet I cannot live with my conscience troubling me as it now does. What would you suggest?

I think you will find that your employer will respect you for making an honest confession. Even though your life up until this time has been one of deception, yet the confession will convince him more than ever that something has taken place in your life. It is even possible that he will come to regard you as one of the most dependable workers he has. There is something even more important than clearing your own conscience, however. It is the thing you should do in order to give you the best possible opportunity to tell what God can do in the life of one who turns to Him. Having done what is pleasing to God, you can always leave the results to Him. We will pray that you will have courage to do what you know is the right thing.

I have always been a very proud person, but recently I have had a lot of financial reverses. Now I have lost my job and it looks as if I may have to go on some type of public welfare in order to survive. Do you think there is anything morally wrong with doing this?

Our society has a system of social welfare or assistance which is meant for people who are in genuine need. Yes, I know there are probably those who abuse it or use it as an excuse to avoid working—but the abuses of the few should not make you think that there is something wrong with the system as a whole. If you sincerely need the kind of help that our nation's welfare system is meant to bring to people, then you should not let your pride stand in the way. The ancient society of Israel had definite ways to assist those who were poor, and that is true of virtually any modern society today. The Bible says, "The righteous care about justice for the poor, but the wicked have no such concern" (Proverbs 29:7).

There are two other things I would like to mention concerning your question. First, although I know we live in difficult times economically, I hope you will continue to seek employment. Over the past several years the job market has been continually improving.

The other thing has to do with your reference to your pride. Elsewhere in your letter you indicate that you have never really had very much to do with the church or with God. I wonder if perhaps your pride has been a major reason for this—believing that you did not really need God because you were able to run your life quite satisfactorily without Him.

But you need God. You need Him right now in the midst of the problems you are facing, and you need Him for the future—both for the rest of your life and for eternity. Sometimes the hardest thing for someone like you to admit is that you need God—and sometimes God allows things to happen to us that show us we are not nearly as able to run things as we thought we were.

That is why this difficult time you are facing could be the best time of your life, if you were to face your need of Christ and turn to Him in repentance and faith. Don't let your pride keep you from the greatest gift in the universe—the gift of salvation which God offers you in Christ.

I have always loved rock music a great deal, but recently I began to listen to the words of some of the songs on my records. Do you think it is wrong to listen to that kind of music?

You need to remember that your mind is molded in many different ways—often in ways we are not aware of at the time. I am convinced that many things—the films we watch, the television we see, the music we listen to, the books we read—have a great effect on us.

Furthermore, you need to realize that if you belong to Jesus Christ you are called to live a life of purity and holiness. God wants your mind to be shaped by Him so that your thoughts and goals reflect Christ. That is why the Bible often places a high value on our minds and stresses the importance of what goes into them. The Bible tells us that we are not to live as unbelievers do "in the futility of their thinking . . . . You were taught, with regard to your former way of life, to put off your old self, which is being corrupted by its deceitful desires; to be made new in the attitude of your minds" (Ephesians 4:17, 22–23).

It is important, therefore, for you to pay attention to the words of the music you mention. Much modern music has strong sexual overtones in the words (and some people feel even in the rhythm). Some music today speaks favorably about drug experiences, or suggests that certain patterns of life are best—patterns which are wrong to a Christian who is seeking to please God. When this is the case with your music, then it is time to turn from it.

But beyond this is a deeper question—the question of what your goal is in life. Are you seeking to live for Christ, wanting to please Him in all you do? My prayer for you is that you will commit yourself to Him and put Him first in your life. Then you will want everything you do to honor Him.

What is your definition of greed? I admit I like nice things and comfortable living, and I think about money a lot because I know I have a responsibility to my family, but that isn't necessarily wrong, is it?

Greed is an unreasonable or all-absorbing desire to acquire things or wealth. It can take all kinds of forms (including a grasping desire for money, possessions, luxury, food, power, or any number of other things).

One test of greed is that it is never satisfied. The prophet Isaiah said of the greedy of his own day, "They are dogs with mighty appetites; they never have enough" (Isaiah 56:11). Another test is that the greedy person has little or no regard for the needs of others, and may think nothing of hurting others or taking advantage of others in order to get more. His life is dominated by selfishness.

Greed is repeatedly condemned in the Bible. One of the Ten Commandments declares, "You shall not covet your neighbor's house . . . or anything that belongs to your neighbor" (Exodus 20:17). Why is this true? One reason is that a greedy person is only concerned about himself—and is therefore not concerned with God and His will. One of the writers of Proverbs prayed, "Give me neither poverty nor riches, but give me only my daily bread. Otherwise, I may have too much and disown you and say, 'Who is the Lord?'" (Proverbs 30:8–9).

It is not wrong to want to work and earn a decent living; in fact, God has given work to us. But this legitimate desire can very easily cross the line into greed—especially in our materialistic society. We need to be on guard against greed, therefore. But above all we need to make sure our lives are centered in Christ and not things. Have you committed your life to Him?

I am a clerk in a small-town bank. I have reason to believe that the cashier is dishonest. I am afraid to report him lest I lose my position, yet I believe it should be checked on. What is my responsibility in a case like this?

Your report would never need to be made known. The bank examiners would appreciate any information and it would be kept in strictest confidence. You have a higher responsibility than to a dishonest employer. You are a servant of the community and you have a responsibility to them. To remain silent would be to participate in the crime just as much as we sin when we give assent to the misdeeds of others. The Christian has a great obligation to be ethical and honest in all things, even sometimes at personal hazard. It is in the difficult situation that the qualities of a Christian are seen. They may go without notice in normal conditions, but when the crisis comes, then the distinctive qualities of the Christian are clearly seen.

I have a job in an office which is so large and in which there is so little supervision that some of the women do practically nothing all day long. They say they are "riding the gravy train" and get mad when I say they are stealing. What is right?

Accepting pay for which a corresponding service is not rendered is dishonest. From what you write, I think that you are correct in saying these girls are stealing. But I am not sure you have approached the problem in a helpful way. If you are a Christian, your first obligation is to see that you yourself give a full day's work for your wages. Then, as opportunity presents itself, you can wisely bring up the discussion of what is right and what is wrong. If such a discussion is started in a proper spirit, some of these women may be led to be more faithful in their work.

If all tactful methods fail, it would not be unethical to suggest to the head of the office force that some system of supervision be set up to ensure more effective work by all. One of the Ten Commandments is "Thou shalt not steal." There are many ways of taking that which is not our own. Many of us have been guilty of failing to do all that we could to earn what we are paid. Make this problem a matter of prayer. See if there are not other Christian women in the office and ask them to join in praying about it. Above all, do not assume a holier-than-thou attitude. Be sure you are living as a Christian, not only in relation to your office work but also in other ways.

I am a partner in a small manufacturing concern. Due to business reverses we have been forced into bankruptcy. When the people of my church learned that I had filed bankruptcy, they insisted upon dropping me from the membership. Was my action so wrong that I can no longer have the fellowship with Christians?

That depends entirely upon the reasons and upon the motives of bankruptcy. Even people in the world of business recognize that there is a legitimate cause for bankruptcy when it is intended to avert law suits and litigation, in order to give you opportunity to make good on debts that have been honestly incurred. People unfamiliar with the procedure of business are not able to detect what your motives are. You will, however, have to give an answer to the Lord.

Our prayer for you will be that your reason was to glorify Christ by being honest in all your relations and this was merely a method to accomplish that in the shortest possible time. Meanwhile, do not condemn the people of your church for their action. They simply did not understand your reasons and acted most likely according to the best light they had.

Is it always right to tell the truth, especially when you know it will hurt someone? If I tell the truth about my business affairs, it will ruin chances for the happiness of my family.

I would rather answer you by stating the matter in quite another way. It is always wrong to be dishonest. Dishonesty is never justified. God will never approve, and even your own conscience will rise up to condemn you sooner or later. I have not known of a single instance when a man has been ruined or his family injured because of his basic honesty. It may not always be either wise or expedient to publicly announce all your personal affairs, but to conceal the truth from persons involved is never the right course of action.

If you had been sure of the matter you would never have raised the question. Romans 14:23 says: "But the man who doubts is condemned if he eats, because his eating is not from faith; and everything which does not come of faith is sin." Do nothing until all the doubts are removed. This is a fairly safe procedure in all matters.

I am associated in business with a man who is active in his church on Sunday but who cheats his customers during the week. This has disgusted me with Christianity.

Some of your customers may possibly pay you with a ten-dollar bill which proves to be a counterfeit. Will you stop accepting ten-dollar bills because of a counterfeit? If your business associate is a hypocrite, it is he who is wrong, not Christianity. One can but wonder how you are working out the proceeds of the cheating you mention. If you are profiting by it, you are just as guilty as he. To be perfectly frank, one must wonder if your so-called disgust with Christianity is not really an excuse for not being a Christian. You know that all of us need Christ. He alone can change our hearts and give us the grace and strength to live as Christians should live. You evidently have high ideals in your own life. You are probably right in your disgust with your associate. Let me urge you to give your heart to Christ so that you can set the right example before him. If you do this, both of you will honor the name of the Christ you profess.

Since becoming a Christian I have the problem of being in business with a man who is not one, and who does not conduct our business on Christian principles. My life's investment is in the business, so I can't very well leave without tremendous loss. What shall I do to make him change?

Your problem is a complex one for it also involves the matter of your Christian stewardship. You want to live your life and conduct your affairs as a Christian, and at the same time you must be custodian of your earnings and regard them as a stewardship. Many prosperous men make the mistake that is warned against in the Bible saying: "My power and the might of my hand hath gotten me this wealth." We have the right to say only that it is the Lord who "giveth thee power to get wealth" (Deuteronomy 8:17, 18 KJV).

But your partner has a conscience even if he is not a Christian. He will recognize the merit and rightness of the "Christian way" even though he may not accept the redemption provided in Christ for sinners. Get him to conduct the business on Christian principles as a trial and then depend upon God to change his heart.

I am studying the psychology of religion in college. My professor tells me that conversion is nothing more than a psychological phenomenon experienced by most religions. Right now I am plenty worried about things I learned in my home church, for they seem to be slipping away from me. Do you think my conversion was real?

Certainly your conversion was real, if when you were converted you came from darkness to the light of the gospel. If you received Jesus Christ as your Lord and Savior, then and there you became a new creature. I wouldn't take anything for granted, not even a religious experience. You see, your professor is right when he says conversions are experienced as a part of most religions. But don't allow that to disturb you, for although all men may have some kind of religious experience, only the ones who receive Jesus Christ in a moment of repentance and faith are born again.

The fact that others have similar religious emotions and conversions merely shows that God so made man that he is capable of being converted. How tragic it is when a man is converted falsely! This is what I would suggest. To overcome your fears and intellectual dilemma, just give as much time to the study of what God has to say about it as your professor does. Don't argue with him, but test everything he says in the light of God's Word. You need not fear then, for the Bible can stand the onslaught of any enemy.

I am a freshman in college and am greatly confused because we are being told that science has disproved much of the Bible and that I will have to "re-think" my faith if I expect to have any faith.

When you are told that science has disproved the Bible, ask specifically where such is the case. True science and a true understanding of the Bible are never at variance. Furthermore, at many points where it was thought a few years ago that science was disproving the Scripture, records have since been cleared up and the Bible is now admittedly correct. Of course, if one is definitely antagonistic to the Christian faith and the Scriptures, he is prone to back his position by supposed inaccuracies in the Bible. But the best answer to such people is to insist on a statement on their part of just what the inaccuracies are. In most cases they are not forthcoming. In others, if you do not have an explanation yourself you will be wise to ask your pastor or some biblical scholar who can give you the answer. In truly scientific circles today there is much less antagonism toward the Christian faith and to the Bible than was true a few years ago. This is due to the fact that scientific discoveries (not theories) are found more and more to fit into the record God has given us in His

Word. Before you "re-think" your faith it may be wise to examine the critics of the Bible. In the end your faith will be even stronger.

In my college class in advanced astronomy, the question has been raised whether the explosion theory of the origin of the universe permits the possibility of divine creation. What do you think?

I do not feel competent to speak on the various theories held by scientists with reference to the origin of the universe. But this one thing I am very sure of—any theory which leaves the Sovereign God out of His own universe is inadequate. For the creature to ignore the Creator is utter folly. To think that this universe, so vast that even now its limits are unknown, is the product of self-contained and self-directed matter seems hardly worthy of consideration.

In our own world there are evidences on every hand that in all of nature there is a perfection and a controlling and directing hand which must be infinite and divine. Had we never seen a watch before, and happened to find one, we would likely believe in some being capable of thought and design who made that watch. How much more do we have evidence on every hand of God and of His creative power and wisdom! Psalm 19 tells us that the heavens and the earth show forth the glory of God. In the first chapter of Paul's letter to the Romans we read:"For the invisible things of him from the creation of the world are clearly seen, being understood by the things that are made" (v. 20). Any theory of the universe that does not take into account the God and Creator of the universe is not worthy of serious consideration.

Since coming to the university, I find that unless I join a sorority I am just left out of the social life here. Still I can't approve the program sponsored by those I know about. Is compromise the only answer in this world, or do I have to be on the outside?

Many times the Christian feels at odds with the world, and if we are to depend upon the words of the Savior, it will continue to be that way. Jesus once said: "Behold, I send you forth as sheep among wolves." Although it may not appear that unconverted people are fitting that description, it certainly shows that there is no good way to effect a reconciliation unless they are reconciled to God first. In answer to your question about compromise, it will have to be said that when you do, only you are the loser. The very ones whose social pressure caused you to compromise will despise you for it. They probably respect your convictions and many of them wish they had the moral stamina to stand alone. May the Lord give you added courage to be a witness for Him, even in a hard place.

Don't be a prude, or snobbish, but let your life "glow" for Christ. We are lamps shining in the darkenss. Be attractive and winsome, but do not compromise your convictions for the sake of popularity.

21 *What about the Christian and Politics?*

Do you think the church ought to get involved in political issues? That seems to be all our preacher ever talks about.

The church of Jesus Christ has been given a distinctive and unique task in our world by God, and that is to proclaim the gospel of Jesus Christ. When we fail to do that, we are not doing what God wants us to do. We are under orders: "Therefore go and make disciples of all nations, baptizing them in the name of the Father and of the Son and of the Holy Spirit, and teaching them to obey everything I have commanded you" (Matthew 28:19–20). Those orders have never been changed.

This is why—generally speaking—I do not feel the church as an organization should become involved in political matters. There are times, however, when political issues also have moral and spiritual dimensions and when this is the case we have a responsibility to speak for the truth. I believe things like abortion are morally wrong, for example, and we have a responsibility to take a stand. At the same time, this must not be our primary task. This is not an easy question, but the greatest need of our hour is for Christians and the church to proclaim the gospel. Only Christ can change the human heart, and this is the basic cause of our problems today. On the other hand, if an individual Christian feels the call to become active in politics, I am all for such activity.

Pray for your preacher, and don't be afraid of letting him know of your concern. Be thankful for the sensitivity he demonstrates about some of the moral and spiritual problems that infect our world—but encourage him also to teach and preach the full message of the Bible. After a ministry of several years in

Ephesus the apostle Paul could say, "I have declared to both Jews and Greeks that they must turn to God in repentance and have faith in our Lord Jesus . . . . I have not hesitated to proclaim to you the whole will of God" (Acts 20:21, 27). Proclaiming "the whole will of God" should be the goal—and the joy—of every church and every preacher.

Don't you think that Christians should stay out of politics? Doesn't the Bible warn us "not to be entangled again with the yoke of bondage"?

I certainly do not think that Christians should be disinterested in the affairs of our government. Christ said: "Give to Caesar what is Caesar's and to God, God's" (Mark 12:17).

Nothing would please the racketeers, gangsters, and the underworld more than for all church people to stay away from the polls and to be uninformed about what is happening in Washington and in their own states and cities.

I would urge every Christian to vote and to show a keen interest in the politics of his community. I would even encourage him, if he felt so called, to take an active part in politics and to crusade for clean, honest, and upright handling of community affairs through good government.

The cliché, "Politics is dirty," is plainly untrue. I know men and women who are in government who have high principles, fine motives, and unquestioned integrity. They have dedicated themselves to a life of public service because they sincerely want to serve their fellowmen. While it is true that politics seems to attract some people of questionable principle, that fact makes it all the more imperative that good people everywhere cast their vote for the best candidates.

Recently I heard a preacher, while referring to politics during a sermon, make the statement that corrupt conditions in politics is the reason he has never registered or voted. Don't you think that Christians should vote?

Personally, I don't think people who are not even interested enough in what is going on in our country to register or vote are qualified to speak authoritatively on government. I know a great number of fine, upstanding Christian statesmen. Perhaps there are some who are unethical and ulterior in their motives. That gives even more reason why every Christian should vote. The ballot is part of our great American heritage and freedom. It is our only means of keeping government clean and proper. I think that it is not only the right, but the duty of every American to use his voting franchise, prayerfully and thoughtfully.

The old Soviet Union is an example of a country which was indifferent to corrupt politics, and when the Communists ruled, they destroyed the partisan system and, subsequently, the right of free franchise. Let us hope that the indifference of our people toward the importance of voting will not lead to a similar situation here in the years to come.

I find that there is still much racial prejudice in our country. What can we Christians do about it?

I think Christ was quite definite as to the position that every true Christian should take. He said: "Thou shalt love thy neighbor as thyself." We must approach our racial problems with love, tolerance, and a spirit of give and take, no matter what the conditions. There is no excuse for any Christian to participate in acts of violence against a person because of race. Proverbs 10:12 says: "Hatred stirs up dissension, but love covers over all wrongs." Again the apostle John says in 1 John 2:9: "Anyone who claims to be in the light but hates his brother is still in the darkness." A true Christian will have love, tenderness, compassion, and understanding when he approaches this problem that threatens to divide the country.

In Acts 4 we see the disciples selling all and putting their money in a common treasury, and all sharing alike. What is the difference between this and the Communistic belief?

There is a great difference. The "having all things common" of the early Christians was based entirely on love. There was no force or coercion. There were no police to enforce the will of authorities. In fact there were no authorities; it was entirely a matter of the heart.

At the time in Jerusalem there was much poverty and the disciples were just fresh from being filled with the Holy Spirit. They felt an inner compulsion to share with others; they were full of the new gospel, "Love thy neighbor as thyself," and it spilled over into their social life.

If we spent more time with the Lord and were filled with the Holy Spirit, we too would be compelled to share both our goods and our faith with others. We would not only give of our means, but of our goods, our time, and our talents that others might discover the joy we know.

Part V

Biblical Questions

22 | *Prove the Existence of God!*

I dare you to prove the existence of God. I want to be a scientist when I go to college, and I won't believe anything unless it can be proved. I don't see what room there is for religious belief in a scientific age like ours. Religion to me is just an outdated superstition.

Just a few days ago I came across a lengthy article which dealt with the religious views of a number of scientists. They came from various institutions (including Princeton and Stanford), and many of them are working on the frontiers of scientific research in such areas as physics and genetics.

They are, in other words, some of the finest scientific minds in our country—and without exception they were giving witness to their personal faith in God and their commitment to Jesus Christ. Far from being an "outdated superstition," Christianity is for them the very foundation of their lives and their understanding of the universe. One common thread in their thinking is that their research has pointed them to God. The world is so complex, they have realized, that the only logical explanation is that God created it. They also have realized that science has limits. For example, science can describe the world, but it cannot say where it came from or why we are here.

Let me challenge you therefore not to have a closed mind. Have you, for example, ever read the New Testament for yourself, seeking to discover what it really says? You see, the Bible says we can know God, because He has made Himself known to us. "No one has ever seen God, but God the only Son, who is at the Father's side, has made him known" (John 1:18). The most important discovery you will ever make is that God loves you and you can know Him personally by committing your life to Jesus Christ.

Did Jesus ever claim to be God? I have heard that He never did, but that the idea of Jesus being divine was thought up by His disciples later on. I would be interested to hear how you would answer this.

You cannot read the New Testament without realizing that Jesus claimed—frequently and clearly—that He was the divine Son of God, sent from Heaven to save us from our sins. It is also clear from the Gospel accounts that His disciples did not believe His claims at first, but only gradually came to understand and accept them (particularly after the resurrection, which proved beyond doubt that He was who He claimed to be).

His claim to be God is seen in many passages of Scripture. To His disciples He declared, 'I and the Father are one . . . Anyone who has seen me has seen the Father" (John 10:30; 14:9). When Thomas (a disciple who doubted that Jesus had been raised from the dead) met Christ after the resurrection, he exclaimed, 'My Lord and my God!"—and Jesus accepted his praise (John 20:28). Even the enemies of Jesus knew of His claim to divinity. On one occasion, for example, they picked up stones to try to kill Him "for blasphemy, because you, a mere man, claim to be God" (John 10:33).

Anyone could claim to be divine, of course, but did Jesus do anything to back up His claim? Yes! His miracles, which were witnessed by thousands, were an evidence of His unique nature. His resurrection verified His claim. But why is this important? It is important because only a divine Savior could truly save us from our sins. If Christ were just a great religious teacher, He would have no power to bring us forgiveness. But because He was God's only Son, He could die as a perfect and final sacrifice for our sins. Have you accepted the gift of forgiveness He offers you?

How can you say that there is such a thing as hell, if God is really a God of love?

Let me say at the beginning that God does not want us to go to hell; instead, He wants us to live with Him eternally in Heaven. The Bible says, "He is patient with you, not wanting anyone to perish, but everyone to come to repentance" (2 Peter 3:9). At the same time, the Bible also makes it very clear that hell is a reality, and it would be foolish for you to turn your back on that fact.

How can God, who loves us, also allow hell to exist? That is not an easy question to answer, but perhaps the right place to begin is to realize that God is not only a God of love, but a God of justice as well. He is holy and perfect, and He is also completely just in all He does. The Bible says, "The Lord is righteous in all his ways and loving toward all he has made" (Psalm 145:17). Let me put it this way: God has made this world in such a way that some things are right, and some things are wrong. It is always wrong to murder someone, for example, or to steal from someone.

But imagine what kind of world it would be if God did not ever judge evil. Imagine if the Hitlers of this world, who oppress and kill others, never had to give account for their sins or be judged. But that is not the way it is! "For God will bring every deed into judgment, including every hidden thing, whether it is good or evil" (Ecclesiastes 12:14).

You have, in other words, two great truths: God judges sin because He is righteous; God also loves us. And yet if we are honest we must admit that we have sinned against God and we only deserve to be judged. We have not followed His will, and have turned our backs on Him. But now I want you to see a very important truth: God in His love has made it possible for us to escape His judgment—because Christ was sent from God to take upon Himself the judgment that we deserved. God loves you, and that is why "he gave his one and only Son, that whoever believes in him shall not perish but have eternal life" (John 3:16).

Do you think that the gospel of the first century as stated in the Bible is relevant for our present time?

The Bible says that the grass withers and the flowers fade, but the Word of our God stands forever. It also says that Jesus Christ is the same yesterday, today, and forever. Ideas, books, and people come and go, but the Bible and the truth it contains is for all time. That is why the Bible is a living Book and can be trusted for its advice and direction and knowledge of God at the end of the twentieth century just as much as it could be trusted by first-century Christians. God has given us a message that is not only for past times and this time, but for all time.

I know you place a lot of emphasis on the Bible. But does it really have anything to say about our practical, modern-day problems, since it was written so long ago?

Yes, I place a great deal of emphasis of the Bible—and one reason I do so is precisely because it is so practical and deals with problems we all face in our everyday lives.

Why is this the case? It is true because first of all it is God's Word to us. It is not a book of human ideas and advice—it is God's Word, given to us by Him to teach us how to live. "All Scripture is God-breathed and is useful for teaching, rebuking, correcting and training in righteousness, so that the man of God may be thoroughly equipped for every good work" (2 Timothy 3:16–17). God knows what we are like—far better than we know ourselves—and He knows what we need if we are to live as we should.

It also is true because man does not change. Yes, we live in a world which is much different from that of the biblical writers. But man is the same. Our greatest need is to be reconciled to God, who created us, and in the Bible we discover the wonderful truth that this is possible through faith in Jesus Christ. We also need to know how to live. We need to know what is right and wrong, and we need to know how to love others and get along with others. The Bible shows us the way. "Your word is a lamp to my feet and a light for my path" (Psalm 119:105).

I invite you to discover the Bible for yourself. (A good place to start would be with the Book of Proverbs in the Old

Testament and the Gospel of John in the New Testament.) Read it every day, and ask God to show you its truth for your life. If you do, you will not only discover that it will guide you in your daily living, but you will discover the wonderful truth that God—the Bible's author—loves you and wants you to be His child through faith in Jesus Christ.

I suppose this may sound like a dumb question to you, but where are the Ten Commandments found? Does God still expect us to follow them? It seems like I never hear any sermons on them.

Don't apologize for asking what you think is a "dumb question"! Tragically, many people never get around to asking the really important questions of life (such as "how can we be saved?") because they are afraid someone will laugh at them. But it is far better to know God's truth than to be ignorant of it.

The Ten Commandments are found in two places in the Bible. The first is in the Old Testament Book of Exodus, chapter 20, verses 1–17; the second is in the Book of Deuteronomy, chapter 5, verses 6–21. In both places it is stressed that the Ten Commandments are given to us by God, and they tell us what God expects of us. If you look carefully at them you will notice that the first four commandments especially concern our relationship to God, telling us that we are to love God and serve Him above all else. The second set of commandments (the last six) tell us how we are to act in our relationships with other people.

The Ten Commandments are just as valid today as they were when God gave them to Moses. They reflect the moral character of God, and they also provide the foundation of right living with others. God's character does not change, and neither does His moral will for us. You will find that the New Testament has much to say about these commandments.

But there is one central truth you also need to remember. The Ten Commandments reveal God's standard for us—but if we are honest, we know that none of us are able to keep them completely. None of us have ever loved God completely and perfectly. None of us have ever avoided completely the sin of coveting what was someone else's possession. In other words, we can never be saved by keeping the Ten Commandments, because none of us can keep them perfectly. But Christ did! And by faith in Him we can be forgiven of our sins and know the joy of following Him every day.

I have been in college now for a few weeks, and it seems like I am questioning everything I have ever believed. I even am beginning to wonder if God is real, or if He is just a product of our imagination or wishes. Can you help me?

It is not uncommon for someone like yourself to go away to college and suddenly find that things you have believed are questioned by others who appear smarter than you.

But there are answers to the questions you may be having—good, solid answers. Many highly intelligent men and women have been (and are) faithful followers of Christ. Your pastor or a Christian worker on campus can direct you to books that deal with these questions.

Then seek the encouragement and strength of other Christians. On your campus there are undoubtedly many sincere Christians, and you should pray that God will guide you to them. (Several interdenominational groups work especially on college campuses, such as Intervarsity, Navigators, or Campus Crusade.) You will find others who have worked through the same questions you are facing, and you will be strengthened by the regular fellowship of other believers.

In addition, you need to spend time alone with God each day. There is no substitute for a personal walk with God through systematic Bible reading and prayer. In this way you can get to know God better and be able to face the temptations and doubts Satan wants to throw at you. You also will be able to help others who are struggling with questions about God. "Always be prepared to give an answer to everyone who asks you to give the reason for the hope that you have" (1 Peter 3:15). And if you have never really given your life to Jesus Christ, this is a time to learn more about Him and His claim on your life.

I agree that Christianity has some good ideas, but I think that we ought to look at all the religions of the world and get the best from each of them. What do you find wrong with that idea? What does the Bible say?

I suspect many people would agree with your ideas—although few actually would begin to search seriously through the major religions of the world. If they did, they might come to realize more fully how contradictory some of them are and how impossible it is to take the various ideas they have and draw them together into an intelligent system

There are two problems I want to point out concerning your plan. First, how will you judge or know whether the ideas you are taking from each religion are really true? Unless you have some kind of standard, you are as likely to take ideas which are false as you are to take ideas that are true.

There is a still more important fact to be noted, however. There are many religions in the world, and they have developed because various people have had various ideas about God. But Christianity makes a unique claim. Christians claim that we do not need to grope after God or guess what He is like. We can know what He is like—and in fact we can know God personally. Why is this possible? It is possible because God Himself has come down to us in human form in the person of His Son, Jesus Christ. Do you want to know what God is like? Then look at Christ. "No one has ever seen God, but God the only Son, who is at the Father's side, has made him known" (John 1:18). If this is true—and it is—then you need not search the religions of the world for truth, because Christ is "the way and the truth and the life" (John 14:6).

God is not an object to be studied and analyzed, like a butterfly or a chemical solution. He is our Father, who created us and loves us. Commit your life to Jesus Christ, and you will not only know the truth about God but you will come to know God personally.

23 How Should We Read the Bible?

I am ninety years old and in the last fifty years I have read the New Testament through over two hundred times. I find something new in it every time I read it. I wish you would encourage people to read the Bible more.

Thank you for the testimony about the importance of the Bible. Yes, I find something new in the Bible every time I read it also, and that can be the experience of everyone who comes to it wanting to discover more of God's truth.

Your words point out several things about Bible reading that I think are important to stress—things you have learned by personal experience across the years. You give us a good idea about how we should read the Bible.

How should we come to the Bible? First, we should come expectantly. The Bible is not just another book—it is the Word of God, given to us by God to help us and instruct us. The Psalmist declared, "Your word is a lamp to my feet and a light for my path" (Psalm 119:105). Therefore, when we come to the Bible we should come expectantly—expecting God to teach us and show us new truths about Himself and His will for our lives. That is one reason why we should always pray when we open the Bible and ask the Holy Spirit (who inspired the writers of the Bible) to illumine or make clear its meaning for our lives. It means we also should read it carefully, not just hurrying through a passage or reading it without understanding.

Second, we should read the Bible systematically. I am thrilled by your testimony of reading the New Testament more than two hundred times during the last fifty years—an average of once every three months! I'm sure there were many times you were very busy and could have found other uses for your time, but you discovered the value of systematic and disciplined reading.

Finally, we should read the Bible obediently—ready to obey the truth that God has for us. God gave the Bible to us "for teaching, rebuking, correcting and training in righteousness" (2 Timothy 3:16), and the Bible can change our lives as we read it and obey its teachings every day.

I'm beginning to read the Bible for myself. Are there any particular study methods I should observe?

Very definitely there are. To begin with, you must read the Bible with a desire to know and to accept any truth you discover. You can be critical but you must be fair and open-minded. Then, you must read systematically, and not just at random. The Bible will yield the richest blessing in the long run to those who study systematically. Begin regular reading of the Bible from beginning to end in your morning Bible-reading time, and concentrate on a specific book in your evening time. I would suggest the Gospel of John and then the Book of Romans.

In addition, you must study prayerfully, relying upon God to enlighten your mind and enable you to understand what you read. Pray frequently as you read and you will discover a fellowship with God that is both intimate and satisfying. Finally, make use of dependable helps but do not rely upon them. Many helps are actually a hindrance. Make sure you are learning the Bible and not the views of some individual. You may be in perfect agreement but there is a blessing in knowing you got it from God.

I would like to have a better understanding of the Christian religion, but never seem to get much out of the Bible when I read it. Can you tell me of some book or commentary that will answer the question in a more simple way?

No book ever takes the place of the Bible. It is its own best commentary. I would urge you to go on studying the text of the Bible itself. Only when you find it in the Bible are you sure it is Scriptural truth. As a help, I would make a few simple suggestions.

Be open-minded. If you begin with a prejudice, you will be blind, or else you will read into the Bible what is not really there.

Act upon the basis of what you discover. The Bible is a guidebook, leading men to God in a personal faith. Like a map or guidebook, it will show you the way, but you must take it one step at a time.

Ask God to enlighten your mind. In other words, read it prayerfully The sound of the words will not help, for you must understand what you read. God provides enlightenment for those who wish it.

Finally, *continue your study.* Be patient, for the knowledge of God comes gradually and slowly. The fact that God is infinite makes the study of His word a lifetime occupation. The Bible is to your soul what bread is to your body. You need it daily. One good meal does not suffice for a lifetime.

I have recently begun to read the New Testament. Now I am told that the church existed before the New Testament, and therefore is in possession of more authority than the Bible itself. Can you explain this problem to me so that I can study with restored confidence?

The church was in existence before the New Testament was written. That does not place it in authority above it, for you will notice that the writers always appeal to the existing Old Testament as authority. Also, you will notice that God approved the genuineness of the work and the dependability of the writer, by miraculous demonstration and by general consent of the body of believers in every place. The books we call canonical were able by the weight of their contents to separate themselves from all spurious and pseudo books. The evidence is in the books themselves, not alone because of the power of their combined message. The vitality the Bible exhibits in every generation causes this work to commend itself to you as being superior to continuing organizations or conflicting voices in any age. Its power to transform lives is its best apologetic.

My friend says the Bible doesn't say anything about drugs. Is that true? I used to feel guilty when I first started experimenting with them, but now I know drugs can help me and make me much more creative. I know some drugs can harm you, but if you know what you are doing they help you.

It is not true that the Bible is silent about such things. The Bible condemns the use of any substance which alters or distorts our thinking (including alcohol, which was the most common drug in ancient times). It may interest you to know that the Greek word used in the New Testament to designate a sorcerer or a person who practiced occult magic is "pharmakeus," or one who mixed drugs and used them to induce spells. (We get modern words like "pharmacy" from this ancient Greek word.) Such practices are included in the list of "acts of the sinful nature" in Galatians 5:19–21 that God will judge.

Your letter concerns me greatly, however, because it is clear you have allowed yourslf to be deceived and enslaved by drugs. One of the characteristics of some drugs (such as cocaine) is that they make a person feel strong and alert—when in fact the opposite is the case. Don't allow yourself to be deceived. You are on a deadend road, in spite of what you tell yourself, and my prayer is that you will realize it and turn back before it is too late.

The Bible says, "Be self-controlled and alert. Your enemy the devil prowls around like a roaring lion looking for someone to devour. Resist him" (1 Peter 5:8–9). How can you resist the temptation to escape from life through drugs? First, admit your helplessness and turn to Christ for forgiveness and strength. Then surround yourself with His Word and with His people who can help you fight this problem.

If the Bible is the Word of God, as you constantly say, why are there so many off-color stories in it?

Because there are so many sinners in the world. The Bible is not an idealistic fairy story. Rather it is a record of God's dealing with mankind and of many individual men and women. There is nothing which indicates the inspiration of the Scriptures more than the factual and faithful record of men and their failures. For instance, one of the greatest men in the Bible is King David. And yet, the Bible tells us he was guilty of both adultery and murder. But it also tells us of his repentance and turning back to God. All of these records are for our warning and instruction. They show us how sinful man needs God and His redemptive work in Christ and they tell us of many who accepted this love and were transformed. There is one thing about the stories in the Bible where sinful acts are mentioned: they do not glorify sin, nor do they make people want to go out and copy them. The Bible always shows sin up for what it really is, an offense against God and something to be repented of and turned from. Try studying the Bible with that attitude and you will find out for yourself.

Some people say we should not take a critical attitude toward the Bible. How can one be intellectually honest and not do so? Are we to swallow the whole thing without examining it?

The answer to your question centers in part on the meaning of the word "critical." In the ordinary usage of the word this means to be fault-finding or censorious. There are, of course, other meanings of the word. However, in the study of the Bible the word means to evaluate, analyze, and also to study the historic, cultural, and linguistic backgrounds of the times during which the Bible was written. Such a critical study of the Bible has produced a tremendous volume of information, has clarified the meaning of many passages, and has made it possible for us to understand far more clearly the messages God would give us.

On the other hand there is a form of biblical criticism which starts with certain preconceived ideas and which seeks to interpret the Bible in the light of these presuppositions. For instance, if one rejects the miraculous and the supernatural, one will reject these elements of the whole written revelation from God. One can approach the Bible with a cold rationalistic attitude or one can do so with reverence and the desire to hear God speak. I have a friend, a physician, who says there is a difference between the attitude of a scientist dissecting a dead body in a dissecting hall and that of a surgeon who operates on a living person in the operating room. The Bible should be approached with the assurance that here we have God-breathed literature and that it is our privilege and joy to find out what He has to say. Paul tells Timothy: "All Scripture is God-breathed and is useful for teaching, rebuking, correcting and training in righteousness, so that the man of God may be thoroughly equipped for every good work" (2 Timothy 3:16–17). That is the attitude with which we should approach the Bible.

Almost all of my family and acquaintances are Christians. They keep telling me to read the Bible and find out how to live the Christian life. Honestly, I get bored when I sit down to read it and when I try to pray I keep thinking of a thousand other things. Is there something wrong with me?

I don't think there is anything wrong with you that is not typical of most young people. Having grown up in a religious atmosphere, you are right now passing through a period of revolt. You want to be on your own and make your own decisions without your family's influence.

There is another fact you should know. One of the devil's methods is to attack everyone, old and young, in this matter. He knows that the Word of God is powerful, and he will try to keep you from it. That means you are involved in a spiritual warfare.

If you would stop for a moment and think as a mature person, you would realize that your parents are trying to get you to do what is for your good. Don't rebel, but give God the opportunity to change your life and help you over the problems of youth, for they are many. Solomon once said: "Remember your creator in the days of your youth" (Ecclesiastes 12:1), and this is what you should do to find the greatest joy.

I find it helpful to read my Bible on the train on my way to work each morning. Some of my friends tell me I ought not to do this, as it is flaunting my religion in the face of others and probably makes them feel uncomfortable. What do you advise?

If I were you I would not worry too much about what other people say or think in a matter of this kind. If you bother unduly about the opinions of others you will never do anything at all!

By all means read your Bible on the train if you find this helpful. While those around you are filling their minds with the bad news about man in their daily papers steep yourself in the good news about God in His precious Word!

Of course, I will admit that a crowded railway car is not the best place for reading the Bible, for it is not easy to concentrate in such circumstances; and real Bible study requires concentration. Nevertheless, it is well to use every moment of the day to the best advantage, and no doubt a great deal of time is wasted on such journeys that could be employed in a much better way.

I do not quite understand why the fact of your reading the Bible in public should make others feel uncomfortable—unless they are non-Christians or backsliders. And in that case they have no right to be comfortable! They need to be aroused out of their comfortable indifference and reminded of the claims of God's Word; and it may be that your example will serve to remind them of the Book they have neglected.

24 Does the Bible Say Anything about Life on Other Planets?

I am fascinated by space travel and things like that, and if there is intelligent life on other planets maybe we could learn things from them—like how to have world peace, for instance.

No, the Bible is silent about the possibility of life on other planets. At the same time the Bible does not explicitly say there is no life on other planets; it is simply silent on the question.

While it is interesting to speculate about such questions, let me point out that God has already given us a blueprint for peace. Have you ever asked yourself why we do not have peace in the world—in spite of the fact the yearning for peace is universal? The problem is not that we lack knowledge. The problem is the human heart, which by nature is self-centered. The Bible says, "What causes fights and quarrels among you? Don't they come from your desires that battle within you? You want something but don't get it. You kill and covet, but you cannot have what you want. You quarrel and fight" (James 4:1–2).

Our greatest need is for the human heart to be changed. But how can that happen? Education is not enough. Peace treaties or more just economic or political systems are not enough. No, the only answer is God, for He alone can change our hearts. In fact that is one reason Jesus Christ came—to reconcile us to God so we could have peace with Him, and then to reconcile us to each other. "We love because he first loved us" (1 John 4:19). Have you come to know God's peace in your own heart, by turning to Christ and asking Him to come into your life? Don't put your hope in speculations about life on other planets, but put your hope in Christ alone.

I am a student of the physical sciences. Some of my associates are inclined to believe that there is life on other planets. If there are people who inhabit these planets, what does that do to our faith in the gospel? Can it be that God is primarily interested in this planet?

From my studies in the Scriptures I can find nothing that would change our essential faith in the gospel if we did discover life on other planets. Our Bible is clearly designed for this particular planet with its particular problem of man's sin. When we observe this fact we are on safe ground. It is not a part of the Bible's message to inform us of what God has done elsewhere. Its message is concerned with earth dwellers, their origin, the reason for their existence, the cause of their misery, and the plan of redemption for a fallen race. I am sure that if there are dwellers on other planets, they are either not involved in the sin problem, or else God has made satisfactory provision for them. The God of the Universe is the God of our Lord Jesus Christ. He is entirely able to support all of creation and is able to govern it in righteousness.

Are the disasters of space vehicles God's warning to us about space exploration? Are we interfering with the planets in any way, such as the power of the sun, or the disarrangement of the earth or moon? If so, can the Lord stop these adventures into space?

Though I am a minister and not a scientist, I have no qualms about space exploration upsetting the order of the universe. It would be just as logical to get upset at children casting stones into the ocean, fearing that their childish actions might upset the rhythm of the tides. God's universe is so vast and limitless that man's probing into space is less expansive than a minute pinprick in the outer skin of an onion. Our solar system is just one of billions in God's colossal creation. No, I don't think you need to fear that our space vehicles are endangering the universe.

Perhaps all this is to beckon our attention to the greatness and majesty of God. The Bible says: "When I consider thy heavens, the work of thy fingers, the moon and the stars, which thou hast ordained: What is man, that thou art mindful of him? . . . O Lord, how excellent is thy name in all the earth" (Psalm 8:3–4, 9 KJV).

25 | *Is Jesus Coming Back?*

On what grounds do you base your statement that Jesus Christ is coming back? Did not Christ say, "Lo, I am with you always, even unto the end of the world"?

We look for the return of the Lord because He said many times that He would come—and because it is one of the most frequently mentioned subjects in the Bible. Christ is with us today through His Holy Spirit, and He will be with Christians and with the church down to the end of the age. When He ascended up into heaven, the disciples were told by two angels standing by that He would return again as they were now seeing Him go (see Acts 1:11).

This climactic event of history is yet in the future. It will be sudden and final—the culmination of the ages. It will take the unbelieving world by surprise, and people will try to hide from His holy presence. At the return of Christ the resurrection of believers will take place. They will be gathered together to be with the Lord forever. We can only speculate about the exact details of His return. The important thing is that He is coming again and that we yet have time to trust in Him as our Savior and Lord. The Bible says all people must face Him at that time—as either Savior or Judge: "When the Son of Man comes in his glory . . . he will sit on his throne in heavenly glory" (Matthew 25:31).

Do you believe that Jesus Christ is going to make a visible, physical return to this earth?

Yes, I believe this with all my heart, not because of the opinions
of others, but based solely on what the Bible plainly teaches. In
the Old Testament there are prophecies which can only be fulfilled by our Lord's return. In the New Testament we find more
than three hundred references to the Second Coming. For instance, Christ Himself said again and again that He is coming
back: "I am going . . . to prepare a place for you. And if I go
. . . . I will come back and take you to be with me that you
also may be where I am" (John 14:2–3). He also said: "They will
see the Son of Man coming on the clouds of the sky, with
power and great glory" (Matthew 24:30).

In 1 Thessalonians 4:16 Paul said: "For the Lord himself
will come down from heaven, with a loud command, with the
voice of the archangel and with the trumpet call of God . . . ."

His coming will be visible: ". . . he is coming with the
clouds, and every eye will see him. . ." (Revelation 1:7). When
our Lord ascended up into heaven, two men suddenly stood by
the disciples and asked, "Men of Galilee . . . why do you stand
here looking into the sky? This same Jesus, who has been taken
from you into heaven, will come back in the same way you have
seen him go into heaven" (Acts 1:11). In Revelation 1:8 Jesus
said: "I am the Alpha and the Omega . . . . who is, and who
was, and who is to come, the Almighty." The fact that Christ is
going to return is both a glorious hope and a stern warning:
". . . now is the time of God's favor, now is the day of salvation" (2 Corinthians 6:2).

*I have heard people talk about someone or something called the
antichrist, which I believe is mentioned in the Bible. Who or what
is this? Or is it just a term used to describe anyone who tries to do
things against the Christian message?*

The term "antichrist" is found several times in the Bible, and
refers to a person who will come in the days just before Christ
returns to establish His Kingdom. "You have heard that the antichrist is coming" (1 John 2:18).

This person is not Satan, but will use every evil device of
Satan to oppose the work of God. The apostle Paul uses the term
"the man of lawlessness" or "the lawless one" to speak of this

individual (2 Thessalonians 2:3, 8). He will be the embodiment of evil, and will have great power to deceive those who choose to follow him. "The coming of the lawless one will be in accordance with the work of Satan displayed in all kinds of counterfeit miracles, signs and wonders, and in every sort of evil that deceives those who are perishing" (2 Thessalonians 2:9–10). The time will come, therefore, when someone who is totally opposed to Christ will achieve great influence. However, in the end, he will be defeated by Christ.

At the same time the Bible warns us there are many in the world who have the same spirit as the antichrist and oppose the work of God. "Even now many antichrists have come" (1 John 2:18). This means we need to be discerning and not be misled by those who oppose God's truth. How can we avoid being led astray into falsehood? The most important thing is to yield our lives to Jesus Christ, and then to know more and more the truth God has given us in His Word, the Bible.

Do you really believe that this world will come to an end?

Yes, I believe that this world, as we know it, will come to an end. When, I do not know, but all history is pointing toward a climactic event when everything now seen will be purified by fire. This is not fanciful imagination but the clear and repeated testimony of the Bible. In both the Old and New Testaments we have this climax foretold. Our Lord Himself said such would take place. A study of this universe, in which this world is but an infinitesimal speck, shows that any one of a number of factors could bring about this physical cataclysm.

The Bible says: "But the day of the Lord will come like a thief. The heavens will disappear with a roar; the elements will be destroyed by fire, and the earth and everything in it will be laid bare" (2 Peter 3:10). This same Bible says: "Believe in the Lord Jesus Christ and you will be saved—you and your household" (Acts 16:31).

Your Personal
Commitment

A friend of mine once asked me, "Billy, if I become a true believer in Christ, will all of my problems go away?"

My answer was, "No. but you can have the power to deal with them."

We live in a fallen world. It is not the world that God designed, which was perfect, without pain, without suffering and without death. When our first parents, Adam and Eve, decided they knew better than God what was best for them, sin, with all of its terrible consequences for the human race, entered the world.

That is why I believe most problems have a spiritual answer. We often want our own way, not God's way. We often seek to please ourselves first, instead of God. What is interesting is that when we seek to please God first, very often we discover that we end up far more pleased than we did when we put ourselves first.

In order to begin to find solutions to our problems we must first change our attitude. How do we do that? By exchanging our old, selfish nature for God's selfless nature.

And how do we do that?

The Bible tells us that each of us is born with a propensity to sin. We know that we behave the way we do because of that nature. Have you noticed that children do not have to be taught to be selfish or jealous? It comes to them naturally and that is because as David, the great king of Israel said, "I was born in sin. . . ."

In order to begin to really solve our problems, we need a *new* nature. How do we acquire a new nature? By giving up our old one and accepting God's new nature through Jesus Christ.

The apostle Paul wrote, "If any man be in Christ, he is a

new creation. Old things are passed away; behold, all things have become new."

There is no adequate human analogy to this spiritual truth. All I know is that I have seen it work tens of thousands of times and in the same way with everyone who has accepted the promise that God has made.

When you accept Christ as your Savior and make Him your Lord, He gives you the Holy Spirit. The Holy Spirit is given to guide and lead you so that as you read the Bible and desire to serve God instead of yourself, you develop a new attitude, a new perspective on your life and the problems you face.

It does not happen overnight. Your problems will not instantly disappear in most cases. But your problem of not having a relationship with God will immediately disappear and He will give you the power to deal with your problems and to sustain you in them and see you through them that is not available anywhere else.

God loves you with a perfect love no human being can fully understand. Human love is conditional. God's love is unconditional. It is so unconditional that the Bible says even while we were yet sinners, God sent His Son, Jesus Christ, to die in our place, to pay the sin debt that we owed to God. How many people do you know who would be willing to pay all of *your* debts, particularly when you were rebelling against them and had no desire to be their friend?

God has paid the greatest debt you will ever incur and once you understand the incredible sacrifice He has made just for you, you will feel compelled to turn to God and to accept Jesus Christ into your heart.

Will you accept what God has done for you today? It is so simple. Just pray a prayer something like this: "Dear God, I confess to You that I am a sinner and have tried to do everything my own way. Please forgive me. I now invite Jesus Christ into my heart and life and ask Him to save me from my sins. Please help me to get to know You and please give me the power to deal with the problems in my life. In Jesus' name, Amen."

If you prayed that prayer, or one like it, and sincerely meant it from your heart, God has done what He promised He would do. He has come into your heart and life, perhaps for the first time, or to renew your spirit.

I urge you to immediately locate a church near you where the Bible is taught as the Word of God and to begin attending every Sunday. You should also become involved in a Bible study so that you might discover the wonderful riches God has to pour out on your life.

It is important that you have your own personal quiet time with God every day, reading from His Word and praying to Him. Like a good diet and proper exercise helps the body, a good spiritual diet requires "digesting" the Word of God and "exercising" your spiritual muscles through prayer.

I hope you will write me about your decision. The address is: Billy Graham, 1 Billy Graham Parkway, Charlotte, NC 28210. I would like to send you some literature that will help get you started in your new walk with Christ, who is the *real* answer to every problem that confronts us.

Scripture Index

Subject Index

Because of the way this book is structured, the Part and Chapter titles describe the content quite thoroughly. However, if you are looking for specific subjects within these categories, this index should prove helpful.

STEPS TO PEACE WITH GOD

1. **RECOGNIZE GOD'S PLAN—PEACE AND LIFE**

   The message you have read in this book stresses
   that God loves you and wants you to
   experience His peace and life.

   The BIBLE says . . . *"For God loved the
   world so much that He gave His only Son,
   so that everyone who believes in Him may
   not die but have eternal life." John 3:16*

2. **REALIZE OUR PROBLEM—SEPARATION**

   People choose to disobey God and go
   their own way. This results in separation
   from God.

   The BIBLE says . . . *"Everyone has sinned
   and is far away from God's saving presence."
   Romans 3:23*

3. **RESPOND TO GOD'S REMEDY—CROSS OF CHRIST**

   God sent His Son to bridge the gap. Christ
   did this by paying the penalty of our sins
   when He died on the cross and rose from
   the grave.

   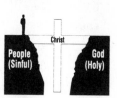

   The BIBLE says . . . *"But God has shown
   us how much He loves us—it was while we
   were still sinners that Christ died for us!"
   Romans 5:8*

4. **RECEIVE GOD'S SON—LORD AND SAVIOR**

   You cross the bridge into God's family
   when you ask Christ to come into your life.

   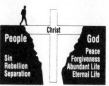

   The BIBLE says . . . *"Some, however, did
   receive Him and believed in Him; so He
   gave them the right to become God's
   children." John 1:12*

THE INVITATION IS TO:
REPENT (turn from your sins) and by faith RECEIVE Jesus Christ into
your heart and life and follow Him in obedience as your Lord and Savior.

PRAYER OF COMMITMENT
"Lord Jesus, I know I am a sinner. I believe You died for my sins.
Right now, I turn from my sins and open the door of my heart and life.
I receive You as my personal Lord and Savior. Thank You for saving
me now. Amen."

If you want further help in the decision you have made, write to:
Billy Graham Evangelistic Association
1 Billy Graham Parkway
Charlotte, NC 28210

A Message From the Billy Graham Evangelistic Association

If you are committing your life to Christ, please let us know! We would like to send you Bible study materials to help you grow in your faith.

The Billy Graham Evangelistic Association exists to support and extend the evangelistic calling and ministries of Billy Graham and Franklin Graham by proclaiming the Gospel of the Lord Jesus Christ to all we can by every effective means available to us and by equipping others to do the same.

Our desire is to introduce as many people as we can to the person of Jesus Christ, so that they might experience His love and forgiveness.

Your prayers are the most important way to support us in this ministry. We are grateful for the dedicated prayer support we receive. We are also grateful for those who support us with contributions.

Giving can be a rewarding experience for you and for us at the Billy Graham Evangelistic Association. Your gift gives you the satisfaction of supporting an organization that is actively involved in evangelism. Also, it is encouraging to us because part of our ministry is devoted to helping people like you discover and enjoy the stewardship of giving wisely and effectively.

Billy Graham Evangelistic Association
1 Billy Graham Parkway
Charlotte, North Carolina 28201
www.billygraham.org

Toll-free (U.S.): 1-877-2GRAHAM
(1-877-247-2426)

Billy Graham Evangelistic Association of Canada
20 Hopewell Way NE
Calgary, Alberta T3J 5H5
www.billygraham.ca

Toll-free (Canada): 1-888-393-0003